ISTANBUL APPEARANCES

Gender, Culture, and Politics in the Middle East
miriam cooke, Simona Sharoni, and Suad Joseph, *Series Editors*

For a full list of titles in this series, visit
https://press.syr.edu/supressbook-series
/gender-culture-and-politics-in-the-middle-east/.

Istanbul Appearances

Beauty and the Making
of Middle-Class Femininities
in Urban Turkey

Claudia Liebelt

Syracuse University Press

For a listing of books published and distributed by Syracuse University Press,
visit https://press.syr.edu.

ISBN: 978-0-8156-3790-5 (hardcover)
          978-0-8156-1156-1 (paperback)
          978-0-8156-5587-9 (e-book)

Library of Congress Cataloging-in-Publication Data

Names: Liebelt, Claudia, author.

Title: Istanbul appearances : beauty and the making of middle-class femininities
      in urban Turkey / Claudia Liebelt.

Description: First Edition. | Syracuse, New York : Syracuse University Press, [2023] |
      Series: Gender, culture, and politics in the Middle East | Includes bibliographical
      references and index.

Identifiers: LCCN 2022037793 (print) | LCCN 2022037794 (ebook) |
      ISBN 9780815637905 (Hardcover : alk. paper) | ISBN 9780815611561 (Paperback :
      alk. paper) | ISBN 9780815655879 (eBook)

Subjects: LCSH: Beauty, Personal—Turkey—Istanbul. | Human body—Social aspects. |
      Feminine beauty (Aesthetics)—Turkey—Istanbul. | Beauty shops—Turkey—Istanbul.

Classification: LCC GT499 .L54 2023 (print) | LCC GT499 (ebook) |
      DDC 391.6094961/8—dc23/eng/20230112

LC record available at https://lccn.loc.gov/2022037793

LC ebook record available at https://lccn.loc.gov/2022037794

Contents

Illustrations

Abbreviations

AKP	Justice and Development Party (*Adalet ve Kalkınma Partisi*)
ANAP	Motherland Party (*Anavatan Partisi*)
CST	cosmetic surgery tourism
Diyanet	Turkish Directorate of Religious Affairs (*Diyanet İşleri Başkanlığı*)
İGDESO	Istanbul Trade and Artisanal Chamber of Beauty Experts and Beauty Salon Employees (*İstanbul Güzellik Uzmanları Güzellik Salonu İşletmecileri Esnaf ve Sanatkarlar Odası*)
İKKMO	Trade and Artisanal Chamber of Istanbul Hairdressers for Women and Manicurists (*İstanbul Kadın Kuaförleri Manikürcüler Esnaf ve Sanatkarlar Odası*)
IPL	Intense Pulsed Light (depilation technique)
ISAPS	International Society of Aesthetic and Plastic Surgeons
İSMEK	Istanbul Metropolitan Centre for Lifelong Learning (*İstanbul Büyükşehir Belediyesi Sanat ve Meslek Eğitimi Kursları*)
RP	Welfare Party (*Refah Partisi*)
SGK	Social Insurance Foundation (*Sosyal Güvenlik Kurumu*)
THY	Turkish Airlines (*Türk Hava Yolları*)
TOKİ	Public Housing Development Administration (*Toplu Konut İdaresi Başkanlığı*)
TPRECD	Turkish Society of Plastic Reconstructive and Aesthetic Surgeons (*Türk Plastik Rekonstrüktif ve Estetik Cerrahi Derneği*)

Acknowledgments

The idea for this book was conceived a long time ago, originally sparked during research in the Philippines, and began taking shape during a return visit to Istanbul, where the huge number of newly opened beauty salons and clinics caught my eye. It finally came into existence thanks to the intellectual and infrastructural support of a large number of persons. The research for this book was supported by the German Research Foundation (No. LI 2357/1-1) during the years 2013–2018 and by the Chair for Social Anthropology at the University of Bayreuth. I am grateful to the German Research Foundation, as well as to my colleagues at the University of Bayreuth, who agreed to a sabbatical semester that enabled me (almost) to complete the writing.

My deepest gratitude goes to my research participants, who welcomed me into their beauty salons and treatment rooms, their homes and their lives. I particularly thank Eda Atacan Küçükağa, Seher Öğünç, Joanne Yıldırım, and Süleyman and Kemal Beşli for allowing me into their salons with great hospitality and for the many joyful hours I spent there. Ülkü and Serdar Çağlayan allowed me access to their clinic and provided much support and hospitality throughout my stays in Istanbul. With her warmth and generosity of mind and spirit, Feride Çelik Aykal became an invaluable guide in the urban world of beauty.

I thank Erdmute Alber, Paula Schrode, and Sabine Strasser, who mentored me through this project with steady guidance and intellectual rigour. Erdmute Alber provided me with an excellent institutional environment during the entire process and over the years has become a mentor in the full sense of the term. I would also like to thank Michael Steffen and Mirjam Oschwald for helping with the final editing and for their meticulous work on the list of references and the index. Burcu Şener, İlke Şener, Merve Keskin, Biray Anıl Birer, Ariya Toprak, and Metin Kılıçay have translated and transcribed interviews. With his rigorous and immensely quick language editing, Robert Parkin made the book more readable.

During research in Istanbul, I was affiliated with the Department of Sociology of Boğaziçi University. My colleagues there gave me enormous intellectual support and generously shared their ideas with me, especially Ayfer Bartu-Candan and Bülent Küçük. I am also grateful to Ayşe Akalın, Didem Danış, and Asena Günal, scholars in divergent fields, who offered companionship and unwavering support for this project during research, listening to worries from my field and sharing their own beauty salon stories with me, some even taking me along. My special thanks go to the colleagues who read and commented on drafts and discussed problems: Cati Coe, Nadia Fadil, Charles Hirschkind, Marcia Inhorn, Esra Özyürek, Melike Şahinol, Sertaç Sehlikoğlu, Virginie Silhouette-Dercourt, Pnina Werbner, and Aslı Zengin. I would also like to acknowledge the great collegial support of the members of the Anthropological Writing Workshop run by Erdmute Alber at the University of Bayreuth, including Anna Madeleine Ayeh, Abou Moumouni Issifou Boro, Tabea Häberlein, Lena Kroeker, Jeannett Martin, Sabrina Maurus, Carsten Mildner, Severin Penger, Taylor Anne Riley, Joh Sarre, Manfred Stoppok, and Maike Voigt. I am grateful to them not only for reading and commenting on parts of this book in various stages of its completion, but also for providing such a pleasant environment in which to work on and think through my research. The "beauty gang" at the Iwalewahaus, University of Bayreuth, especially Sarah Böllinger, Nadine Siegert, and Katharina Fink, contributed much intellectual inspiration, and I highly cherish our invaluable conversations and celebrations in the spirit of "Iwalewa" (Yoruba for "Character is Beauty").

I was able to do research and write this book with a young child only because of the childcare provided by Asiye Atlı, Kebire Yücesan, and Sevda İnan. My family in Turkey and Germany provided much love, support, and encouragement to me in undertaking this project. From my mother I learned a great deal about the pleasures, pains, and pressures of beauty, as well as about female strength and compassion. Ulaş Şener supported me in emotional, intellectual, and practical ways beyond description. He and our daughter Meira have lived with me through the years that it took to conduct the research and write this book, adding great joy to and providing ample distractions from the vicissitudes of academic life. They helped me time and again to see beauty in unexpected places, things, and moments in our shared everyday life.

Finally, the research for this book would have been radically different without the unwavering support of my research assistant Selen Artan-Bayhan, herself an excellent scholar. Selen was with me during most of the research encounters described in this book. Her local knowledge, sensitivity, and great sense of humor not only made possible many of these encounters, but also made the research itself an utterly enjoyable process. Her discerning questions and the long conversations we had during our joint rides on various means of transportation to and from research sites in Istanbul helped me enormously to reflect on the ways the research was going and to think up new ideas. For this invaluable companionship I thank her deeply.

Parts of chapter 2 are a revised version of an article published in the *Journal of Middle East Women's Studies* (Duke University Press 2016). Parts of chapter 5 are a modified version of an essay that appeared in an edited volume on *Beauty and the Norm* (Palgrave Macmillan 2019). Parts of chapter 7 are a modified version of an essay that appeared in *Secular Bodies, Affects and Emotion* (Bloomsbury 2019).

Istanbul Appearances

Istanbul Appearances

An Introduction

> Our civilization is one based on what is beautiful, good, true, and beneficial. When Our Lord created *insan* [human, Man], he was predefined as the most honourable and therefore the most beautiful. In one Hadith, our Beloved Prophet advises us to be beautiful always. Likewise, our honoured Master [Jalāl ad-Dīn Muhammad Rūmī, a 13th century Islamic scholar and poet] says: "The one who contemplates in a beautiful way sees beautifully; the one who sees beautifully, thinks beautifully; and the one who thinks beautifully receives pleasure from life."[1]

Turkey now ranks among the top ten countries worldwide with the highest number of cosmetic surgeons per capita and of cosmetic procedures (ISAPS 2019), and its cultural and economic capital Istanbul has become a regional center for the beauty and fashion industries. Speaking the words above to an audience of approximately 2,500 almost entirely female beauty entrepreneurs during a rally broadcast live on national television in late March 2017, Turkish President Recep Tayyip Erdoğan drew on several authoritative Muslim sources to invoke the idea of a shared "civilization" based on beauty. He referred to beauty as a moral and aesthetic, even sacred, value because what is beautiful is also good, true, beneficial, and honorable. Superficially, the speech accompanied the official signing of a

---

1. Recep Tayyip Erdoğan. 2017. "For a Beautiful Turkey, of course, YES" [Güzel Bir Türkiye İçin Tabii ki Evet], March 29, 2017; https://www.tccb.gov.tr/haberler/410/73534/ (March 18, 2021)

regulation extending the rights of beauty therapists, including the right to operate laser hair removal equipment. On a deeper level, it afforded an immense economic and political value to beauty in spite of its seemingly timeless removal from the global beauty industry that has grown enormously in the past two decades, not only in Turkey, but in almost every part of the world (Jones 2010).

Coming shortly before a referendum on constitutional reform in Turkey which some observers claimed was the most significant political development since the founding of the Turkish republic in 1923, the event briefly moved the national beauty sector into the spotlight of national and international attention. Entitled "For a Beautiful Turkey, of course, YES," it was commonly interpreted as an attempt to enlist support for the conservative government's "yes" camp in favor of constitutional reform. One observer claimed that the event also offered a "great photo opportunity" with the president being surrounded by hundreds of "young and charming women . . . waving 'yes' flags and cheering for [him]" (Tremblay 2017). In the social media, the "beauty decree," as it came to be called, triggered countless scandalized and sardonic comments that relied on a common understanding of beauty and beauty work as superfluous, politically irrelevant, and under any circumstances an inappropriate topic for an emergency decree and an hour-long live audience at the presidential palace at a time of political crisis.

In contrast, this book argues that the politics of beauty are intricately bound up with the politics of race, class, gender, and sexuality in contemporary Turkey and as such are located at the discursive core of social and political reproduction. In an atmosphere of social polarization and the frequent rhetoric of a growing social division between the secular and the Islamic after the consolidation of power and the increasingly authoritarian rule of the conservative, pro-Islamic Justice and Development Party (*Adalet ve Kalkınma Partisi*, AKP), which comes from an Islamist background but is "conservative-democrat" in its self-designation, there are strong and sometimes contrasting norms of feminine appearance that all place a particular emphasis on self-discipline and on an ethos of female citizens "taking care of themselves." It demonstrates that it is in the numerous beauty salons and clinics, where most of the research for this book took place, that the heteronormative ideals and images of gendered bodies become real, incarnated not simply by patriarchy or consumer capitalism, but in a complex array of affective desires of who and what is considered not only beautiful, but also good, true, beneficial, and honorable—in short, proper.

Drawing on critical beauty studies and feminist approaches that recognize women's practices in making themselves beautiful and attractive within a heteronormative society as a form of "work," *Istanbul Appearances* analyzes a place-specific dynamic of the politics of beauty, sexuality, and gender in urban Turkey. It shows that, while the global market and media clearly inform everyday beauty practices, there are clearly differences in beauty's meanings, preferences, and models of femininity within cities, in this case Istanbul. Amid Istanbul's inclusion into an increasingly global economy of beauty, the consumption of particular beauty services and products has become a marker of urban belonging. Drawing on approaches that conceptualize citizenship as constituted by gendered and racialized performances and images of belonging rather than formal status alone, elsewhere I have proposed the notion of "aesthetic citizenship" (Liebelt 2019) as a tool of analyzing the negotiation of belonging through corporeal self-making in a particular urban consumer culture. This local belonging in a cosmopolitan world of beauty is negotiated by manipulating supposedly biological properties and qualities of the body that are nevertheless seen as malleable through acts of beautification. These are understood as both expressing and producing embodied differences and social distinction. They function affectively in that they are tied to desires and visceral judgements with regard to what is beautiful, proper, or sexy, as well as what is tasteless, unmannered, or vulgar.

This book focuses on self-identified urban middle-class women; that is, on those who can typically afford to attend beauty salons and consume different kinds of aesthetic body modifications on the one hand, and those who are not yet part of the small elite that tends to avoid beauty salons and public clinics, preferring to be treated in more exclusive spaces, such as private homes or clinics. Thus, my approach to middle-class formation is mostly based on field research, relying on women's self-classification as being "in the middle" or "middle-class" (*orta sınıf*). Nevertheless, it also draws on conceptual work on class formation and middle-class reproduction in Turkey's recent past.

Not least, *Istanbul Appearances* seeks to contribute to an emerging anthropological literature on the global beauty boom that provides material on its repercussions in different places around the world. While it is firmly placed within a feminist framework, it adopts an anthropological approach that seeks to complicate the "negative hermeneutics" (Felski 2006, 273) of many feminist studies on beauty, which often focus on the oppressive, painful, and harmful aspects that beauty work involves for women. Rather, an anthropological approach analyzing women's desires and practices of beautification, as well as of the sites that produce and require feminine beauty, makes possible an understanding of beauty as a deeply affective gendered norm embedded in particular social universes. From such a perspective, the main research focus is not on individual women's motivations for engaging in beautification and undergoing aesthetic surgery, but on the political and moral economy of appearances and its affective politics with regard to social norms, desires, and subjectivities in a particular urban landscape.

Like other norms, beauty norms significantly shape and support our bodies long before they come into material existence. This study is based on a notion of the body that stresses its affective potential and questions the dichotomy between the body and the mind, as well as between the social and the biological that has long been maintained and reproduced within Cartesian thinking. This aligns with cultural conceptualizations of the body and embodied beauty in the non-Western world, including in Turkey, where Cartesian body dualism—itself a cultural trope—is less firmly rooted (see also chapter 3). Drawing on concepts of the body within new materialist scholarship (cf. Alaimo 2010; Barad 2003; Grosz 1987, 1994; Massumi 2014), *Istanbul Appearances* thus foregrounds the materiality of the gendered body as something that is "less an entity than a relation, [one that] cannot be fully dissociated from the infrastructural and environmental conditions of its living" (Butler 2016, 19). From such a perspective, the materiality of the body is linked to the materiality of the world. Indeed, it is "*of* the world," as Karen Barad (2003, 828) puts it, affecting it and being affected by it, moving it and being moved by it, modifying it and being modified by it. Such a perspective recognizes no "natural" or "given" body, in contrast to one that has been artificially modified, altered, or enhanced to conform to dominant ideals. To "have" a body, Bruno Latour writes in an essay on the training of expert noses in French perfumery, "is to learn to be affected" (2004, 205). In training olfactory perception, the perfumer subject becomes "articulate" not only in terms of language, but also in ways of bodily doing. Like odors, multisensorial beauty may trigger strong bodily affects, including erotic desire, and function as a motor for gendered becoming. A body recognized as beautiful, as I will show, likewise relies on skills and training, on continuous attention to and investment in beauty. Hence the body—or rather bodily matter, to underline the idea of its relationality—can only be understood as malleable and in a state of becoming rather than being, dependent on relationships that are always already embedded in larger biopolitical regimes.

From this perspective, it is clear that beauty norms cannot be changed easily or at will, nor can any other gendered and racialized norms for that matter. Categories of difference, such as gender, race, class, age, sexuality, and (dis)ability, define and prescribe bodies. Indeed, this book speaks of the deep-seated, affective, and corporeal aspects of normative beauty that inform Turkish women's (as well as men's) aesthetic desires and practices on a daily basis. It shows that these norms are tied to subjectivities in an abiding manner that is difficult to change or challenge, even collectively. While contemporary beauty regimes affect all genders, they do so in different ways, with particular beauty norms and practices being linked to models of heterosexual femininity and masculinity in a quasi-existential way. Drawing on the large body of feminist literature on beauty, this book focuses on bodies gendered as female rather than male, while also including the latter's perspective, given that gender norms are always negotiated intersectionally, including across the divisions drawn between the genders. In Turkey, desire (*arzu*) is configured differently for those who are gendered male and female respectively, with female desire commonly seen in need of social control and discipline (cf. Sehlikoglu 2021, 6).

This introduction provides an underpinning for the following chapters of the book in theoretical, historical, and methodological terms. It first outlines the debates on beauty and femininity to which I seek to contribute, also giving an account of the current situation of beauty studies in anthropology and feminist research. It then introduces the historical context of the research, namely the socioeconomic and political changes in Istanbul's recent past in respect of their relevance to the topic of this study. Finally, it outlines the research methodology, process, and methods used and closes with outlines of the remaining chapters.

Gendered Becomings and the Making of Middle-Class Femininities

> [O]ur bodies are trained, shaped and impressed with the stamp of prevailing historical forms of selfhood, desire, masculinity, femininity. (Bordo 1993, 165f)

As famously stated by Simone de Beauvoir (1973, 301) and conceptualized by many feminist scholars since, "One is not born, but rather becomes, a woman." Such an understanding, in Judith Butler's reading (1986), relies on the distinction between "sex" as the factic and anatomically distinct female body on the one hand and "gender" as the variable and cultural "modes of that body's acculturation" (Butler 1986, 35) on the other, implying that being female and being a woman "are two very different sorts of being" (Butler 1986, 35). While the latter insight is recognized widely and may be considered one of the founding premises of gender studies, the conceptualization of sex as something materially given and stable has been analyzed as a cultural construct predominantly by Butler herself, as well as by a number of early feminist anthropologists, including Shelly Errington (1990) and Emily Martin (1991).

As Butler's work shows (1990, 1993), gender is made in a process that is never completed or finished, but that requires the constant performance and reiteration of gendered norms. For those who wish to be recognized as "women," norms of outer appearance and standards of "feminine" beauty play a crucial role in accomplishing this task. Much has been written on beauty as an external symbol of femininity that is intricately linked to female identity and the self, typically from a critical feminist perspective. In one of the foundational feminist works on beauty, Sandra Lee Bartky (1990) analyzes the existentiality of the link between women's bodily appearance and femininity that the feminist critique of beauty norms calls into question "any political project that aims to dismantle the machinery that turns a female body into a feminine one may well be apprehended by a woman as something that threatens her with desexualization, if not outright annihilation" (Bartky 1990, 105).

It is, however, important to note that "[b]eing, becoming, practising and doing femininity" (Skeggs 1997, 98) can mean very different things to women, depending on their social and racial categorization, as well as their age and nationality. As Beverly Skeggs argues in her ethnography of white British working-class women, femininity is the process through which the category "woman" is "occupied, resisted, experienced and produced through processes of differentiation" (Skeggs 1997, 98). Thus, Skeggs elaborates how the category of femininity emerged as an ideal in the eighteenth century and was tied to the habitus of the upper class "lady" (Skeggs 1997, 99). In the nineteenth century, white middle-class femininity, coded as respectable in terms of conduct and appearance, became an ideal that all women were encouraged to invest in "to gain access to limited status and moral superiority" (Skeggs 1997, 99). For the British working-class women that Skeggs studied in the 1980s, the ongoing ideal of a "respectable" middle-class femininity was difficult to attain, not only due to the high costs involved in investing in its visible markers, but also because the corporeal capital necessary for the attainment of middle-class femininity is often a class privilege (Skeggs 1997, 102). The younger women Skeggs studied nevertheless put great effort into the collective performance of femininity, investing in a feminine appearance especially when going out on Friday and Saturday nights. Skeggs notes that, even though they may have "passed" in appearance on these occasions, their public conduct, which included moving around in groups of female friends, drinking and laughing out loud, was commonly read as non-bourgeois and therefore as unfeminine. Moreover, the women saw a feminine appearance as being of little value and even as embarrassing in some contexts, and investments in it typically decreased once they had children and made "greater investments elsewhere" (Skeggs 1997, 103). For working-class women, Skeggs concludes, "femininity is not an aspiration, but something which is struggled with to gain some value and to ameliorate invalidation" (Skeggs 1997, 108).

The fact that the making of femininity may involve "struggles" also becomes clear when looking at the process from the perspective of trans women. For trans women, passing as a woman mainly means being recognized as such in the course of everyday life. Accordingly, a growing number of trans women opt for facial feminization surgery, with some even preferring it to genital surgery (Plemons 2017). In their ethnography of the procedure, Eric Plemons reads facial feminization surgery as "the material result" (Plemons 2017, 10) of a shift in the conceptualization of sex/gender norms, away from a model of binary distinctions and genital-centric definitions of sex toward a performative model that rests on the recognition of and willingness to invest in femininity/masculinity. In Venezuela, a political economy that places beauty at its very center, this willingness is commonly shared by trans women and beauty pageants. In *Queen for a Day*, Marcia Ochoa (2014) investigates the construal and performance of what she calls a particularly Venezuelan type of "spectacular femininity." Drawing on Harold Garfinkel's notion of "accomplishment" of femininity (1967, quoted from Ochoa 2014, 5) and Judith Butler's conceptualization of gender performance as a speech act (1993), she shows that, by investing in beauty and performing spectacular femininity through their bodies, both groups participate in transnationally mass-mediated spectacles that transcend their precarious existence in the "perverted" democracy of Venezuela. Spectacular femininity provides both beauty pageants and transformistas "legibility, affirmation, income, and other elements necessary for survival" (Ochoa 2014, 8).

In the context of Islamic gender-segregation and conservative gender regimes, women's striving for feminine selves means yet something else. In one of the rare works on contemporary femininity in the Middle East, French sociologist Amélie Le Renard (2014) analyzes young Saudi women's practices with regard to gendered expectations in Saudi Arabia, namely of what women should do, how they should act, and what kind of places (both literally and figuratively) they should occupy. Talking to women in diverse semipublic spaces such as the female campus of King Saud University, a charitable organization, religious meetings, and shopping malls in urban Riyadh, she found different models of femininity, including more liberal, Islamic, and even subversive ones. However, Le Renard notes that all younger women "must conform to a model of consumer femininity founded on the display of consumer products purchased in shopping malls" (Le Renard 2014, 26). This includes the shifting of cultural norms such as showiness, from showing off one's gold jewelry toward displaying luxury brands, including designer fashion, handbags, or mobile phones, as demonstrative signs of wealth and modernity (Le Renard 2014, 131–46). Women's characterizations of each other as "feminine," "respectable," "deviant," "masculinized," or "dirty" depended not solely on their family reputations and class positioning, but also on their participation in global fashion and self-presentation. In the public, all-female context of the shopping mall, doing one's hair and putting on makeup, for example, was an "explicit and conscious obligation," and not being knowledgeable or even interested in it violated the unwritten rules of femininity (Le Renard 2014, 131).

Le Renard's study forms part of what Sertaç Sehlikoglu (2018, 82) sees as a shift in the recent anthropological literature on gender and women's agency in the Middle East, namely from the study of piety and ethical self-making in the wake of Saba Mahmood's *Politics of Piety* (2004) toward the decisive role of "joy, desire, and fun" in the emergence of feminine subjectivity. Whereas in the 1990s and early 2000s mostly secular feminist scholars grappled with the apparent paradox of women's participation in the Islamic Revival that characterized politics across the region, more recently researchers interested in gender politics in the Middle East have begun studying fashion, youth cultures, the arts, or sports. In doing so, they have challenged the usual binaries of tradition vs. modernity, Islam vs. the West, secularism vs. religion. The "new feminist task," Sehlikoglu (2018, 85) writes, is the exploration of Muslim women's subjectivities through seemingly nonreligious everyday practices. *Istanbul Appearances* contributes to this task by showing how female subjectivities in a Muslim-majority context are not only multiple and shifting, but actively struggled with, desired, and "made" in the drama of corporeal gendered becoming and contemporary consumer society.

The examples above show that there is no noncultural, ahistorical, or nonpoliticized ideal of femininity which can be applied to all persons rendered female, whether Muslim or not. As elsewhere, there are different, competing ideals of femininity in contemporary Turkey, which are tied to different practices, identities, situated contexts, representations, and desires of what it means to be properly Muslim and feminine in a particular time and place. Concretely speaking, after decades of debate following the banning of the headscarf in the public sector during the 1980s and 1990s in Turkey,[2] women's bodies have recently become a battleground again between imaginations of modernity and tradition, between self-defined secular and conscious Muslims, and between those claiming the city as theirs and those perceived as urban newcomers and provincial Others. It is the urban and secular-fashionable middle-class feminine body that has long been the unmarked category in Turkey, against which other women have been measured and found wanting.

This normative ideal has to be seen within the context of Turkey's nation-building process as a young republic seeking to replace and modernize a supposedly "degenerate" Ottoman elite, one that nevertheless already regarded itself as part of European cosmopolitan society based on civilizational principles and the desire for modernity (Aydin 2007). Women's bodies have historically played a decisive role in defining the nation. As Nükhet Sirman (2005) has pointed out, they were crucial in the reformulation of citizenship in the early Republican period, when women were invited "to remake themselves in the image of republican femininity," an image "disseminated throughout the first half of the twentieth century through numerous mass media such as cheap romances, weekly women's magazines, films and even more literary journals" (Sirman 2005, 163).

In her analysis of beauty contests in early republican Turkey, A. Holly Shissler (2004) shows the pivotal role of the public presentation of feminine bodily beauty in Republicans' attempts to project images of a modern and civilized nation. The public presentation of uncovered yet "honorable" (in Turkish, *namuslu*) women in state-sponsored beauty contests redefined patriarchal concepts of honor and shame in order to "secularize Islam" and "normalize the female body" (Shissler 2004, 117). The outcome was an imaginary ideal of the secular Republican woman and exemplary

---

2. In recent years the ban on wearing the headscarf in public institutions, issued during military rule in the early 1980s, has progressively been lifted, first on university campuses (2010), later in state institutions (2013) and high schools (2014), and finally in the police and armed forces (2017).

female citizen that one pious interlocutor in Jenny White's ethnography of the pious new middle class described as "blond and modern, also honorable (*namuslu*), clean, sexually honorable (*iffetli*) . . . [and wearing] her skirt below the knees" (quoted from White 2013, 141). In recent decades, this hegemonic ideal has been challenged by the emphasis on hyperfemininity, sexual attractiveness, and youth in global, neoliberal consumer capitalism on the one hand (Elias et al. 2016) and socioeconomic and political changes toward more pious norms of femininity in Turkey on the other. Thus, as analyzed by Deniz Kandiyoti (2011, np), the idea that gendered identities are "distinct and divinely ordained natures" of "men" and "women," expressed in the Muslim concept of *fitrat* (literally disposition or nature), has recently gained ground and has repeatedly been voiced by members of the AKP regime, including President Erdoğan. Similar to what has been said of places as different as Saudi Arabia, the United States, or Venezuela, the making of contemporary femininities in urban Turkey prominently includes one's investment in outward appearances and particular practices of consumption.

Thinking about the making of contemporary femininities from a sensual and corporeal perspective means going beyond a conceptualization of the gendered body as culturally constructed to emphasize the relationality of bodily matter instead. *Istanbul Appearances* is embedded in neo-material thinking in that it looks not only at the normative models of femininity in present-day Turkey, but also at the affective desires, the mediated and digital infrastructures, and the intimate encounters in various beauty salons and clinics in a complex urban space. Before moving on to provide more background on the contemporary socioeconomic and political constellations of beauty in Istanbul, in what follows I outline the emergence of a market of commercial body-centered services that has dramatically changed the availability of middle-class femininity for its residents.

Istanbul within a Global Market of Beauty

As the classical anthropological literature shows, while human beings, whether gendered as male or female, have always invested in their physical appearance, the emergence of a global market in beauty products and images is a fairly recent historical phenomenon. According to the beauty business historian Geoffrey Jones (2010), it can be traced back to the commercialization of perfumery in late eighteenth-century France (Jones 2010, 17) and became a slowly growing industry in Western societies in the late nineteenth century, relying on colonialism "making available new raw materials" (Jones 2010, 22). Whereas in Europe, North America, and Japan the beauty and cosmetics industry became an increasingly significant market segment after the Second World War, centered around Paris and New York as its first global hubs, it was not until the late 1980s that a truly global market for beauty began emerging (Jones 2010, 300–318), including in the Middle East. Ever since, the beauty industry has continued to grow, with megabrands such as L'Oreal or Procter & Gamble establishing themselves worldwide and new regional markets emerging in the so-called BRIC states—Brazil, Russia, India, China (Jones 2010, 300–318)—as well as in Turkey.

Within Turkey, Istanbul has been the unrivaled center of an emerging beauty industry since the mid-1980s, with a rich landscape of beauty that includes private beauty schools, salons and clinics, beauty fairs, and makeover reality television series produced in the city. Unisex or women's hair and beauty salons, which first opened in the 1920s in the modern city center, namely the European quarter of Pera, today's Beyoğlu, are now found all over the city, even in the most staunchly conservative Muslim neighborhoods and on the city's outskirts (see chapter 1). In 2014, over seven thousand hair and beauty salons were listed by the Istanbul Chamber for Women Hairdressers and Manicurists alone.[3] When in 1961 the Turkish Chamber for Plastic and Reconstructive Surgeons was founded by the only three plastic and aesthetic surgeons practicing in Turkey at the time, they had to recruit other physicians, among them a dentist, to meet the state requirement to have seven founding members.[4] In contrast, in 2019 Turkey came ninth on the list of countries with the highest number of plastic reconstructive and aesthetic surgeons worldwide (ISAPS 2019).

3. Interview with Oktay Erkal, president of the Istanbul Chamber of Women Hairdressers, Manicurists and Artisans (İKKMO), April 9, 2014.

4. Interview with Prof. Dr. Ismail Kuran, July 10, 2014.

It ranked even higher, at number seven, when the total number of cosmetic procedures was taken into account (ISAPS 2019).

Istanbul has also become a regional center for cosmetic surgery patients among other "medical tourists" from the wider Middle East, Central Asia, and Western Europe. Medical tourism is now a source of national pride for Turkey, with the ministries of Health, Economy, Culture and Tourism, EU Affairs, and Development organizing global health tourism fairs and quoting reports according to which Turkey is ranked number five among the most popular cosmetic surgical tourism destinations worldwide, after the United States, Germany, Thailand, and India.[5] Not least, the beauty market seems to be unhindered by the economic and political crises that have erupted in Turkey since 2012; in 2016, the Turkish daily *Cumhuriyet* (2016) quoted figures provided by the journalist Ayşenur Yazıcı, author of several books on the topic, that the Turkish beauty market had grown by six percent in the past two years. As *Istanbul Appearances* shows, the growing market for body-centered services and beauty has profound effects on urban residents' body images, desires, and practices of beauty.

In the scholarly literature, the significance of the global beauty market has been hotly debated in relation to the commercialization and normalization of the human body it rests on, as well as with regard to the Westernization of global standards of beauty analyzed by some scholars. Indeed, the global beauty and fashion industries seem to disseminate mass-mediated images of men and women whose bodies have startling similarities, despite their differences in shade and attire. They are often described as dominated by Western or Caucasian beauty norms promulgated by the mass media and the global beauty industry (see, for example, Jha 2016). From this perspective, beauty practices such as the bleaching of skin, the straightening of hair, or surgery such as the so-called "correction of the negroid nose" (cf. Edmonds 2010, 145) or "double eyelid surgery" in Asia and among Asian Americans are attempts to mimic Western or Caucasian beauty ideals as global hegemonic norms. By engaging in such

5. See https://gb.worldhealthsumex.com (accessed September 14, 2022).

beauty practices, Kathleen Lennon (2014) has argued, the consumption of beauty services and aesthetic body modification may be understood as a process of "normalization" on a global scale:

> By regimes of dieting, makeup, exercise, dress, and cosmetic surgery, women, and increasingly men, try to sculpt their bodies into shapes which reflect the dominant societal norms. Such disciplinary practices attach not only to the production of appropriately gendered bodies, but to other aspects of bodily identity subject to social normalization. Hair straightening, blue tinted contact lenses, surgical reconstruction of noses and lips, are practices in which the material shapes of our bodies are disciplined to correspond to a social ideal, reflecting the privileged position which certain kinds of, usually, white, always able, bodies occupy. (Lennon 2014, np)

From this perspective, globally hegemonic beauty norms and images of thinness or whiteness, for example, are based on a concept of the normal "as a principle of coercion" (Foucault 1995, 184) rather than direct force. Drawing on Michel Foucault's work on the disciplinary and "normalizing" power of social institutions such as hospitals, schools, prisons, barracks etc. (1990, 1995), the increasing consumption of body-centered services is here understood as a desire for the creation of docile, that is, aesthetically pleasing and normatively gendered bodies that relies on the self-monitoring of one's appearance.

Nevertheless, as Jones remarks (2010, 3), beauty markets remain highly fragmented, such that for global beauty entrepreneurs it is the "persistence of local differences, not the homogenization of global preferences, [that] is most striking." An emerging anthropological literature on beauty practices and images worldwide likewise demonstrates that, in their quest for beauty, modernity, or enhancement, bodies are embedded in particular yet collective fantasies that are not determined by Western or "global" images. Instead, this literature documents how different styles of bodily appearance and their alteration are tied to particular, historically produced and socially situated affective imaginations of modernity and urbanity.

For example, in her ethnography of Taiwanese bridal photography, Bonnie Adrian (2003) interprets the photographic staging of the bride as a "Western baby doll" as a creative response to a transnational visual imagery, which in this context is dominated by American representations of female beauty. Alexander Edmonds (2007, 2010) studies the localized form of a beauty industry in Brazil that developed in the encounter "between global media and medicine and a distinctive logic of aesthetics and race in Brazil," speaking of it as a form of "indigenization" (Edmonds 2007, 374). In an edited volume on *Global Beauty, Local Bodies*, Afshan Jafar and Erynn Masi de Casanova (2013) use the term "beauty cultures" to explain related practices and sets of ideas about bodily attractiveness that may stretch across national borders and coexist with other beauty cultures in the same terrain. Arguing against assumptions of the homogenization or Westernization of beauty practices and ideals globally, the volume promotes a transnational perspective on "local" bodies, arguing that bodily practices are permeated by local and global bodily ideals simultaneously (Jafar and Casanova 2013, xx–xxii).

While such an approach seems promising for the study of beauty in varied regional contexts, the dichotomizing conceptualization of anthropologists' field sites as informed by "local" beauty cultures as opposed to mass-mediated "global" beauty images and ideals risks reproducing stereotypes of the global South as being somewhat removed from globalized modernity. Conscious of such risks, Laura Miller (2006) describes Japan's body aesthetics as unique and universal at the same time. Drawing on Appadurai's (1990) notion of global flows and "scapes," she explains how they function in a "global arena" of transnational body aesthetics and practices. Whereas Japanese women's beauty practices are unique in many respects, their overall concerns, she argues, "are no different from the defects women all over the world are taught through global advertising and imagery to hide or correct" (Miller 2006, 5). Likewise drawing on Appadurai, Holliday et al. (2015) speak of "beautyscapes" in analyzing the "assemblages" that emerge in "a particular form of coming-together" (Holliday et al. 2015, 299) between surgeons, patients, and their companions, different types of training and surgery sites, technologies, media, and body images, as well as cash flows in cosmetic surgery tourism in South Korea, Thailand, Tunisia, and elsewhere.

As I argue elsewhere (Liebelt 2018), techniques for measuring or weighing the body, lightening or tanning the skin, processing hair, and altering eyelids, breasts, or noses may indeed travel transnationally, within particular beautyscapes, as Holliday et al. state. However, in order to understand their relationship to particular normative practices and regimes of representation, it is crucial to analyze their multiple and changing meanings within a political and moral economy of beauty that is based on social and racial inequalities. Such an analysis is offered by Shirley Tate (2016) in her nuanced reading of the politics of skin bleaching, alias shade shifting, in the Black Atlantic. Tate shows that beauty practices may be understood as active critiques of global inequalities even when they are clearly embedded in them. She rejects interpretations of skin bleaching as "colonial" forms of mimicry, arguing for a decolonial perspective on whiteness and bleaching instead. She observes that, whether intended or not, beauty practices such as bleaching contribute to the *making visible* of global inequalities, in this case white supremacy and other pigmentocracies.

In contrast to the moral-normative reading of skin bleaching as racial faking, she shows how Black celebrities may "embrace 'fakeness' as part of a beauty regime which they can afford" (Tate 2016, 36). As a form of conspicuous consumption, skin bleaching may be read as a critique because it unsettles "global racial certainties in which the racial capital of lightness can be bought rather than merely born" (Tate 2016, 29f). Not least, Tate observes that the same kinds of practices are commonly interpreted in very different terms depending on who engages in them, with the (lighter-skinned) middle classes supposedly engaging in playful forms of "stylization" or "toning" based on self-affirmation and choice, and the population of the Black ghetto or inner-city districts presumably engaging in health-damaging skin "bleaching" or "whitening" based on self-hate and body shame. *Istanbul Appearances* likewise seeks to offer an analysis of a particular urban beauty economy and its political underpinnings, as a space where, in some ways similar to what Edmonds described of Rio de Janeiro, "anxieties surrounding new markets of work and sex mingle with fantasies of social mobility, glamour, and modernity" (2007, 366). These anxieties, as well as the resources to "treat" them, are spread differently across different groups of the urban middle classes, with some claiming to belong to an urban world of beauty, as opposed to those they exclude from it as its provincial, traditional and/or pious newcomers.

Urban Transformations in Neoliberal Times

Like elsewhere, the beginning of the commercial beauty boom in Istanbul dates back to the early 1980s, when the national economy was restructured in accordance with global neoliberal policies (Buğra and Savaşkan 2014). Neoliberalism, the geographer David Harvey (2005) has argued, is based on "accumulation by dispossession," namely through the privatization, redistribution, and commodification of public assets; the financialization of the economy, made possible by government deregulation; and the management and manipulation of crises. From an anthropological perspective, Loic Wacquant (2012, 66) likewise analyzes neoliberalism as more than an economic regime: he calls it a "political project of state-crafting"; that is, a project driven by the state with grave consequences for the market and citizenship. This understanding has much to offer to the analysis of the Turkish case, where neoliberal restructuring was put forward first by the government of the Motherland Party (*Anavatan Partisi*, ANAP), which followed the military coup d'état in 1980 and was led by Turgut Özal, and later by the conservative *Adalet ve Kalkınma Partisi* (Justice and Development Party, AKP), which has dominated the political system in Turkey since its first electoral success in 2002. According to Balkan et al. (2015, 1), Turkey's neoliberal revolution was achieved through "undemocratic political means" and, to a large extent, relied on the redistribution of state assets in the hands of an emerging (Islamic) bourgeoisie closely linked to the ruling political power.

These political and economic transformations had immense consequences for Turkish society, and social scientists seem to agree that the past few decades have seen radical social shifts. In the process, the social hierarchy of the society of the early republic, namely between a culturally and politically hegemonic urban secular, or rather, laic sector (*laik kesim*, in Turkish) and a more conservative (*muhafazakâr*) or traditional (*geleneksel*) Islamic sector (*İslami kesim*) in the Anatolian periphery, was eroded. Whereas Keynesian liberalism in the 1950s in Turkey—described by some as embedded in a model of national developmentalism that emerged in the early Republican era (Balkan et al. 2015)—strengthened the secular bourgeoisie, the neoliberal restructuring that followed the 1980 military coup led to its devaluation. In recent decades, the Turkish core middle class, that Rutz and Balkan (2009, 17) called the "salariat" of industrial and public administrative employees, was overtaken by a new middle class consisting of the professionals and managers of the neoliberal era (Balkan and Öncü 2015, 179). The discrepancies in accessing the financialized economy, including the skyrocketing of real estate prices and the high costs of an increasingly privatized health and education sector, created an "unprecedented fragmentation and polarization within the middle classes" (Kandiyoti 2002, 7). Not least, the early twenty-first century saw the rise of a new middle class within the Islamic sector, backed by the ruling AKP, which threatened the older secular elite not only in socioeconomic terms, but also in respect of their culturally hegemonic status.

These transformations are especially tangible in Istanbul, which turned into a global financial city at around the same time and in the second half of the twentieth century experienced rapid growth as the outcome of urbanization and migration from eastern Turkey. In Istanbul, a process of the deindustrialization of the city-center's urban economy paralleled the growth of a personal service sector, which developed its own, increasingly female professional middle class (Keyder 2005). Balkan and Öncü (2015, 179) describe how, until the mid-1990s, "the working class employed in both public and private industrial enterprises, along with an ocean of small shopkeepers representing the traditional petty bourgeoisie," dominated Istanbul's class structure "both numerically and culturally." In contrast, two decades later, they note how a newly emergent middle-class employed in the growing service sector "appears to dominate the social and cultural life of Istanbul" (Balkan and Öncü 2015, 179). As this book goes on to show, consumption practices, among them the consumption of beauty products and services, play a major role in the formation and reproduction of this urban middle class, as well as in the process of within-class differentiation.

These processes are in no way peculiar to Turkey, as is attested by the growing scholarly literature on the emergence of new (global) middle classes in the global South (Heiman et al. 2012, Kroeker et al. 2018). This literature shows that, while statistics often register a numerical increase in the middle classes, social inequalities are increasing in many of the rapidly transforming societies of the global South, where, as a result of neoliberal restructuring, new global elites are emerging and an increasing number of those in the so-called middle are suffering from a sense of socioeconomic insecurity. Paradoxically, and in spite of the interest in the (global) middle classes, class has been dismissed as both a theoretical concept and an identity. In their analysis of neoliberal "millennial" capitalism, Comaroff and Comaroff (2001) note how the concept of class "comes to be understood, in both popular and scholarly discourse, as yet another personal trait or lifestyle choice. Which is why it, like citizenship, is measured increasingly by the capacity to transact and consume" (Comaroff and Comaroff 2001, 15–16).

Indeed, the dominant subjectivity put forward by neoliberal capitalism, they argue, is one "made with objects" (Comaroff and Comaroff 2001, 4). As one of its core aspects, it offers up "vast, almost instantaneous riches to those who master its spectral technologies . . . simultaneously . . . threaten[ing] the very existence of those who do not" (Comaroff and Comaroff 2001, 8). From this perspective, the consumption of beauty products and services and their outcome, namely manufactured beauty, can be understood as one of such "locally modulated signs" of contemporary capitalism. In that they produce appearances that function affectively and speak of a particular class position or of the desire to belong to a higher social position, investments in beauty can indeed be seen as a "spectral technology," evoked rather than explained by John and Jean Comaroff as a defining feature of contemporary capitalism.

This understanding relates to the earlier notion of "distinction" and the multiple forms of "capital" from Bourdieu's theory of practice. In his well-known empirical study *Distinction*, Bourdieu (1984) develops a theory of taste in French society as a particular aesthetic and embodied disposition that is socialized early on during childhood and serves as a class-based distinction from other, typically lower-status social groups. Preferences for different kinds of food, styles, or forms of bodily deportment are determined by the access people have to multiple forms of capital. Bourdieu (1986) distinguishes between three forms of capital, namely economic capital, "immediately and directly convertible into money" (Bourdieu 1986, 51), and social and cultural capital, as institutionalized, for example, in the person's social networks or educational qualifications, which under certain circumstances are convertible into economic capital. Moreover, cultural capital can appear as an embodied form of "long-lasting dispositions of the mind and body" (Bourdieu 1986, 47), sometimes termed "physical capital."

Drawing on Bourdieu, Featherstone (1991, 90) has linked the growing investment in the body as a "project" with the expansion of what he calls a "new petit bourgeois habitus" in neoliberal times, closely linked to the expansion of the service sector. He claims that, "whereas the bourgeois has a sense of ease and confidence in his body, the petit bourgeois is uneasy with his body, constantly self-consciously checking, watching and correcting himself" (Featherstone 1991, 90). This understanding has been criticized for excluding the particular experiences of women, with Paula Black (2004, 163) stating that "for women, the body 'always, already' acts as a vital form of capital." The ethnographic perspective on Turkey shows that the consumption of particular beauty products and services has indeed been a defining criterion for urban middle-class women for many decades. What the neoliberal restructuring of the urban economy changed, then, was not the importance attributed to investments in bodily beauty by "bourgeois" women, but the availability and to some extent the increasingly mandatory nature of body-centered services for women of a lower social status.

In writing about Brazil, where the expansion of plastic surgery is actively supported by the state and anchored in the public health-care system, Alvaro Jarrín (2017) describes a form of "plastic governmentality" in which poor patients—those who cannot afford to undergo cosmetic surgery in the private sector—"must be willing to become experimental subjects [in teaching hospitals] to have access to beauty" (Jarrín 2017, 61). The class-transcending cosmetic desires that they describe for contemporary

Brazil are informed by an aesthetic hierarchy that is rooted in the eugenic thought of the nineteenth century "which pronounces certain bodies more beautiful and therefore more valuable than others" (Jarrín 2017, 30). Hence, they describe Brazil as ultimately based on an affective economy that condenses the inequalities of race, class, and gender and functions "not as a choice but as a mandate that Brazilian citizens must obey if they want to hope for a better future" (Jarrín 2017, 157). The "cosmetic citizen" thus created undergoes typically risky surgeries by inexperienced surgeons "to take on the burden of the risks of medicalization in order to access the promise of citizenship through surgery" (Jarrín 2017, 158). Citizenship in Turkey, I suggest, is likewise rooted in particular aesthetic hierarchies and tied to the widespread consumption of beauty products and services. These, however, do not automatically result in women's elevated social status, but rather in new forms of (upper) middle-class distinction, as well as anxieties over urban mixing. Thus, in contrast to Brazil, where cosmetic citizenship relies on the promise of inclusion through state-sponsored surgery, in urban Turkey aesthetic inclusion or "citizenship" relies on a wider perception of beauty as a particular middle-class "way of life," one that typically downplays the role of invasive procedures as occasional upgrades embedded in an all-encompassing discipline of urban women investing in their looks.

With respect to competitive urban marriage and labor markets, beautiful looks and investments in beauty have indeed been understood as a form of capital for women—that is, in Bourdieu's definition (1986, 241) of accumulated labor in the form of living or reified labor. Such an understanding has been proposed by scholars who explored the role of beauty in women accumulating "erotic capital" (Hakim 2011), the need for "aesthetic capital" in neoliberal times (Elias et al. 2016), "affective capital" in Brazil (Jarrín 2017), or the "beauty capital" described by Wen Hua (2013, 80) as a great concern for young Chinese women undergoing aesthetic surgery because it "can give them an edge in the job market." This book likewise analyzes beauty and investments in it as a form of work that may be employed for economic needs in some contexts. However, a beautiful appearance is not a static possession, but something that needs continually to be worked at. As such, it is tied to affective fantasies of social mobility, urban glamour, and modernity that cannot be explained fully by the rather mechanistic model of converting beauty or physical capital into economic capital. Not least, beauty practices are embedded in social relations and may be read differently depending on who engages in them.

To sum up, the neoliberal restructuring of recent decades had an immense impact on Istanbul's social constitution by creating riches that led to the emergence of new factions of the upper middle class while also creating the devaluation of older ones, "a new poor among the salaried classes" (Ozyegin 2015, 13). Not least, it produced particular female middle-class subjectivities that are tied to the consumption of beauty and other body-centered services in a transforming urban landscape. Thus, in Istanbul, the new middle class created its own commodity aesthetics, which includes a plethora of services directed at women amid a wider landscape of consumption. By studying beauty in relation to the making of middle-class femininities in Istanbul, I seek neither to measure nor displace "class" as an analytical concept, but rather to show how the various meanings, practices, and aesthetics of feminine beauty are tied to the formation of new gendered subjectivities and the reproduction of existing ones among those who define themselves as middle class. Most importantly, the consumption of beauty products and services acts as a form of bodily distinction both within the urban middle class and from what is perceived not to be properly modern, urban, and middle class. Finally, as an affective relation, beauty and beautification involve sensual aspects that exceed their economic value and cannot be explained fully by looking at the political economy of beauty alone.

An Anthropological Approach within a Feminist Framework

As mentioned above, the relationship between beauty and femininity has long been a prominent topic of feminist theorizing and debate, one that is informative for the critical study of beauty and bodily appearance, not least because it offers valuable methodological insights. Early feminist studies on beauty focused mostly on its role in the patriarchal subjugation of the female body in Western societies. For example, in the early 1990s, Naomi Wolf's *The Beauty Myth* (2002 [1991]) argued that, while US American women have gained influence as an outcome of the feminist struggles in the 1960s and 1970s, in the 1980s professional success and social, economic, and political power were increasingly tied to good looks and a standardized female appearance. According to Wolf, the mass media and beauty industry both produced and profited from women's insecurities. Women, who compared their own (imperfect) bodies with the "perfect" ones they saw in advertisements or the media, were increasingly unsatisfied and consumed beauty products or services in order to reach unattainable beauty ideals and images. From this perspective, vastly different beauty practices such as cosmetic surgery, eating disorders, or makeup constitute oppressive and often painful forms of patriarchal control over the female body, as Sheila Jeffreys (2005) puts it in her own volume on beauty, *Harmful Cultural Practices in the West*.

An important criticism of Wolf's study was its simplifying understanding of the impact of media images on women's body images. Relying on a methodology of "reading" the feminine body in relation to the pop-cultural images of advertisements, Susan Bordo (1993) showed that media images are representations embedded in wider normative regimes. While beauty practices are chosen seemingly freely by women, they are actually embedded in normative regimes of representation that clearly extend beyond individual control. Drawing on Michel Foucault, Bordo argues that beauty practices such as excessive dieting are "powerful normalizing mechanisms" (1993, 186) that rely on the self-monitoring and self-disciplining of "docile bodies" in compliance with these norms. More recently, and with the emergence of new media technologies such as "image cosmetics" or the visualization of expected surgery outcomes, the relationship between media images and women's beauty practices has been theorized further, beyond an understanding of images as representations. For example, the concept of "media-bodies" (Jones 2013, 2017) proposes that, within "ultra-mediatized contemporary landscapes," the boundaries between "bodies, images, and technologies like aesthetic surgery commingle to the degree that, for example, alterations made using Photoshop compared to those using scalpels are [becoming] indistinguishable to most viewers" (2017, 29f).

Most importantly, Wolf's publication triggered a heated debate and indeed a long-term gulf between feminist approaches that focused on women's creativity and agency in choosing particular beauty practices on the one hand, and approaches that emphasized the dominating and oppressive aspects of beauty for women on the other. Among Wolf's most vociferous critics was Kathy Davis, who claimed that "feminists have tended to view such women [that is, those who engage in aesthetic body modification] as the duped and manipulated victims of the feminine beauty culture" (2003, 80). Within such a framework, she argues, "it is difficult to attribute agency or 'choice' to women's desire for surgical 'enhancement'" (Davis 2003, 80). In her own work on beauty, Davis theorizes cosmetic surgery as a form of identity work that "may be, first and foremost, about . . . taking one's life in one's own hands" (1991, 23). As has been stated repeatedly since, a rejoinder between these positions and a more nuanced reading of beauty practices is necessary, not least because, while they are all embedded in structural inequalities, some beauty practices certainly carry more potential for creativity and self-realization than others.

Perhaps due to the fact that much feminist research on beauty has focused on invasive, medicalized practices such as cosmetic surgery, rather than on more directly observable and routine everyday practices such as hair coloring or nail polishing, it often relied on an approach that Suzanne Fraser (2003, 3), in slightly exaggerated manner, summarizes as "collecting interviews" on "why women do it." Along these lines, Rita Felski (2006), in her well-known review article on the feminist study of beauty, criticizes a focus on sociological methods and methodologies "that can only conceive of aesthetic experience in instrumental and functionalist terms" (Felski 2006, 277). She goes on to suggest: "Surely the pleasure of visiting a beauty salon is not entirely unrelated to the sensuous rhythms of a massage, the scarlet glint of a perfectly painted nail, the heady aroma of perfumes and richly scented lotions. Such experiences are shaped by the pressures of gender and race and class and sexuality, but they are also *aesthetic* experiences; to neglect the visual and the tactile, to overlook the seductive interplay of color and pattern and form, is to risk losing sight of why beauty matters at all" (Felski 2006, 277).

The effect of this neglect, explains Felski, is a largely "negative hermeneutics" of beauty, which focuses on women's oppressive, painful, and harmful experiences of beautification. Indeed, as Rebecca Popenoe (2004, 187–97) remarks, the desire and sexuality often inherent in beauty practices are surprisingly absent from many studies on the topic.

Aesthetic experiences, I argue, may indeed be seen as crucial for an understanding of beauty that draws on women's experiences and the meaning-making of beautification. This suggests research methods that go beyond interviewing to include participant observation as an embodied and reflective process of knowledge production. Moreover, it requires an analysis of the social embeddedness of beauty, which also looks at the sites where beauty is manufactured in a social encounter that includes a vast array of sensorial experiences, among them vision, smell, and touch. Accordingly, this study relies on participant observation in various sites where urban middle-class femininities are "made," transcending the common divide between services offered in beauty and hair salons on the one hand and in doctors' offices and clinics on the other. With beauty services such as weight management, the permanent removal of body hair, or the removal of skin blemishes being offered in both beauty salons and clinics, a growing number of increasingly popular, so-called "petite" surgeries being performed outside hospitals and some salons offering services that are legally restricted to the medical sector, the boundary between these two spheres is difficult to draw. Thus, the fact that "distinctions between cosmetic, hygienic, erotic and health practices are . . . often blurred," observed by Edmonds and Sanabria (2014, 203) with reference to Brazil, holds equally true for Istanbul.

While doctors' offices and clinics have only rarely been studied ethnographically for their role in producing feminine beauty—Edmonds' (2007, 2010) and Jarrín's (2017) work on Brazil are notable exceptions here—a number of ethnographic studies have focused on beauty salons for women (cf. Black 2004, Furman 1997, Ossman 2002). In contrast to male-dominated spaces such as the coffeehouse or the (Black) barbershop, which have often been theorized as crucial for the forging of a public sphere or political subjectivities (Habermas 1989, 36; Harris-Lacewell 2004; Özkoçak 2007), female beauty salons have been conceptualized rather as intimate social spaces that are seen as an extension of the domestic sphere, feminine care, and sharing. In this study, I go beyond their analysis as intimate to show their relevance for the making of public, even political middle-class subjectivities within a particular urban economy.

In yet another important review of feminist studies of beauty, Maxine Leeds Craig (2006) argued that much of it has been limited not only by its use of "individualist frameworks," but also by a neglect of the local ramifications of race and class. Discussing the works of Sandra Lee Bartky (1988) and Iris Marion Young (1980) in particular, Craig shows that these started out from the position of a generalized woman "that [is] racially unmarked, implicitly heterosexual [and] of unspecified class" (2006, 162). As Craig notes, "[t]he feelings of inadequacy produced by the presence of beauty standards in women's lives are, arguably, among the most personal manifestations of gender inequality in our lives" (2006, 162). This perspective suggests a notion of beauty as contested, paving the way for an anthropological approach that looks at the particular meanings, practices of, and challenges to hegemonic beauty norms in light of the "multiple standards of beauty in circulation" (2006, 160).

Following up on this, I argue that an anthropological study of beauty should begin by acknowledging power inequalities and the categories of difference they rely on and reproduce within any given scholarly field. Accordingly, this study is informed by what could be called an ethnographic intersectional approach, the most salient and widely discussed categories of difference in my research setting being age, class, and gender, and with "class" having strong topographical underpinnings in the urban context where the research took place. While ethnicity, nationality, and regional identity clearly matter in the context of Istanbul, for example, when the consumers or practitioners of beauty talk about a particularly "Turkish" beauty or make disparaging remarks about looks described as *varoş* (lower-class, hillbilly, literally "suburban"), these categorizations are often implicit, rather than explicitly stated, reiterating hegemonic ideas of Turkish nationality and citizenship.

These, Ergin (2008) argues, tend to subsume racial assumptions as somewhat "aberrational" with regard to national and/or ethnic identity. Arguing for the "conceptual autonomy" of race in his analysis of the Turkish case, he shows that race in Turkey "figures in a large body of *cultural* hierarchies, classifying 'low' and 'high,' producing 'them' and 'us,' and distinguishing 'sensible' from 'nonsense'" (Ergin 2008, 830, emphasis added). Secondly, he analyzes what he calls a "chromatic twist" in the development of Turkish citizenship, which in early Republican times fueled an immense interest in race science, ultimately seeking to answer the question "Is the Turk a White Man," originally quoted by the *New York Times* in 1909 in an article that discusses the positioning of Turkish citizens in the US American immigration regime (quoted from Ergin 2008, 827). As this book will show, there is an ongoing chromatic and racialized fascination with physiognomic characteristics in contemporary Turkey that is most commonly reflected in the popular distinction between so-called "White" and "Black" Turks (cf. Demiralp 2012). During research, such identities were only rarely made explicit but surfaced in relation to class distinction, family histories of migration and/or discrimination, and patterns of residence in the city, and also in the way looks were attributed to different kinds of people.

To sum up, an anthropological approach to beauty does not stop at an analysis of women's accounts of why they engage in beautification but looks at the social and historical embeddedness and sensorial registers involved in the making of femininities. It does so by relating experiences of beauty and beautification to speakers' structural positions, as well as by looking at the locations and techniques of the making of beautiful female bodies. This makes possible an understanding of beauty as an affective process embedded in a particular political and moral economy in present-day Istanbul.

Research Methods and Process

This study draws on fifteen months of field research in Istanbul, including an uninterrupted period of fieldwork between summer 2013 and 2014 and five additional, short field trips since 2011. A total of 110 ethnographic guideline interviews, mostly scheduled and recorded, have been conducted with customers and patients of hair and beauty salons and clinics (n=66), beauty salon owners (n=9) and workers (n=18), aesthetic surgeons and other physicians practicing in the field (n=7), as well as other experts (n=10), among them tattoo artists, activists in various feminist and social organizations, a fashion photographer, and an Islamic scholar who rules on the permissibility of beauty treatments. Moreover, the project employs media analysis, including the systematic analysis of the newspaper archives of four leading dailies, a study of discussions on two online forums on the topic (*kadınlar kulübü* and *fetva meclisi*) and so-called "makeover" shows on private television. In 2013 and 2014, I visited the annual Istanbul Beauty and Care Fair,[6] also distributing questionnaires on beauty practices and body aesthetics to its visitors. The same questionnaire was also distributed to participants in two municipal training courses on makeup and facial care.

Multi-sited ethnography was used to follow beauty practices in different hair and beauty salons and clinics in the city, with a focus on residential and commercial sites in socially and politically diverse urban districts, namely Başakşehir, Fatih, Nişantaşı, Beyoğlu, Moda/Kadıköy, and Etiler. In each of these districts, one or two hair and beauty salons and clinics or doctors' offices were selected in which to conduct participant observation during regular, ongoing visits. These districts were chosen as highly contested urban areas for various reasons. They are situated differently in terms of their proximity to the modern city center, with Beyoğlu, Nişantaşı, and Etiler being right in the center, and their residents' socioeconomic status and political sentiments. In the popular imagination, Fatih and Nişantaşı, for example, are located at different ends of the Islamist-secularist axis, with Nişantaşı being a well-off secular neighborhood in the modern city center and Fatih being a rather conservative working-class district on Istanbul's historical peninsula, encompassing parts of Byzantine Constantinople. Whereas Moda, a neighborhood in the Kadıköy district on the Asian side of Istanbul, has a powerful place in the public imagination as the area where the "old" secular Kemalist urban middle class resides in an environment of multiethnic cosmopolitanism, Başakşehir is a more recent addition to Istanbul's imagined city map as a newly built planned city for the emerging conservative middle

---

6. See http://www.guzellikvebakim.com/ (accessed March 18, 2021).

class on the outskirts of the city. Hence, the sites and persons selected are neither representative of nor at the extreme ends of a continuum, but they do draw attention to the urban diversity involved, as well as to some common themes and issues with regard to feminine beauty. By choosing these neighborhoods and districts, I wish to illustrate differences in intimate encounters and concerns in the city, as well as point out that processes like the commercialization and professionalization of beauty work affect various urban spaces in similar ways.

Research took place in an atmosphere of "hyper-politicization" (Kandiyoti 2015, 8) and ongoing public conflict over gendered roles and norms, leading up to a number of mass-scale protests in 2013 and 2014, including the Gezi Park protests, which, according to some estimates, mobilized more than three and a half million active protesters during June 2013 and ended in violent suppression with a number of deaths and thousands injured or arrested by government forces and the police. Due to the rapid political changes in the direction of authoritarian rule in Turkey's more recent past, from today's perspective my main research period, which ended in summer 2014, seems, to borrow Kandiyoti's poignant words, "like a distant memory" (Kandiyoti 2015, 10). However, the encounters, happenings, and conversations in the nail bars, tattoo studios, and beauty salons and clinics that inform this study continue to function as major sites where publicly debated ideals of femininity and sexuality are visibly manufactured and contested.

Embodying Research

Empirically grounded research, especially the kind of ethnographic fieldwork that goes beyond interviewing to engage in participant observation, is highly embodied and involves questions of subjectification, affectivity, and sensuality that turn the bodies not only of those who are researched, but also of the researcher, into sites of mutual reflection. Throughout my research, research participants, especially beauty therapists, reacted to my bodily appearance, with many of the latter encouraging me to "do more," given both their professional interest in encouraging all of their customers to do so and my unfeminine looks when compared to Turkish standards, including short hair and a certain tolerance of gray and body hair. Throughout my research, I received numerous offers to be given hair extensions or Botox injections, to have permanent makeup or body hair removal, or to have my hair dyed bright red or highlighted. I chose to undergo some beauty treatments in order to develop a rapport with beauty workers, preferably those who had the least dramatic and lasting effects on my appearance, in particular blow-dries, manicures, eyebrow shaping, or facial treatments. Having my body hair removed by sugaring over the course of one year by a veteran beauty therapist in a neighborhood salon around the corner from where I lived, I experienced development of the intimate relationship, perhaps even of neighborly friendship, between a beauty therapist and a customer that many interlocutors described.

Observing beauty treatments and being treated myself triggered some conversations on my own bodily foreignness. While my hair was often commented upon as problematic and "Turkish" rather than "German" (being dark and unruly, rather than blond and soft, as was apparently expected of German hair proper), I was often envied for my thinness at the time, though this again was sometimes contrasted with the older Turkish preference for voluptuous feminine bodies that were *balık-etli* (literally, bodies that have "fish-meat"). My light skin was likewise perceived as rather problematic, and one beauty therapist remarked that it was easily irritated due to the fact that I consumed alcohol and pork, substances considered polluting and prohibited in Islam. When I protested, I was told that, even if I did not consume them, these substances were "already in my genes."

Confronted with interlocutors who invest immense efforts to meet or, as in the case of the Brazilian hyperfeminine *travesti* sex workers Julieta Vartabedian (2016) studied, surpass local standards of beauty, many anthropologists doing research on beauty seem to share Vartabedian's experience of being regarded as unsophisticated or even as "ugly" (Vartabedian 2016, 87) when it comes to a beautiful being-in-the-world or to the knowledge and skills of beautification. Sensing my own skepticism and at least initial ignorance in the field of beautification, some research participants opened up by telling me about their own feelings of ambivalence with regard to gendered expectations and beauty standards, while others downplayed their beautification efforts at the beginning of interviews.

Embodying research for me also included a process of becoming increasingly literate not only in the field of beauty, but also in the Turkish language. This process too was relational: while I had some knowledge of Turkish upon arriving in the field—being able to comprehend most conversations, though having difficulties in making myself understood—in the beginning I relied heavily on my research assistant interpreting for me during interviews. Most interviews were conducted in Turkish except when interlocutors offered to speak English, which was mostly the case with cosmetic surgeons who had been trained in the United States.

The question of my religious identity rarely came up during research, though there was one encounter in which it did become an issue: talking to me at length about her beauty practices in her regular women-only salon in the conservative district of Başakşehir, one pious interlocutor eventually became worried that she had disclosed too much to me as a non-Muslim. In spite of being female, as a non-Muslim she reasoned that I might not be part of her *mahrem*, her intimate social sphere. In the more conservative parts of town, namely in Fatih and Başakşehir, my research assistant and I more generally felt we were being treated more with suspicion and mistrust, perhaps for not being veiled and therefore presumably non-pious, or even non-Muslim. In Fatih, we were refused access to several beauty salons due to salon owners being protective of their conservative and pious clientele's intimate social sphere, which should not be intruded on by potentially secularist researchers from other parts of town. Perhaps due to my readiness to make a fool of myself during weekly classes in *oryantal*, the Turkish belly dance offered in a Fatih neighborhood salon, in the end it was here that we spent some of our most enjoyable, sociable, and rewarding hours of research among women, who, contrary to the usual imagination in the neighborhoods where we lived, turned out to be immensely cosmopolitan, open-minded, and good-humored.

Overview of the Book

The chapter that follows, chapter 1, analyzes a particular urban beauty-scape, part of a wider beauty economy in the emerging global city of Istanbul. It shows that, while the global market and media clearly inform everyday practices, there are great differences in the meanings, preferences, and styles of beauty within the city. In a climate of urban development and commercialization, aesthetic body modification and the consumption of beauty services once confined to the upper and highly "mediated" echelons of society have become more easily available and acceptable for a wider group of people and in different parts of the city. This is illustrated by ethnographic descriptions of beauty salons in the modern city center, in a conservative neighborhood in the historical center, and in a newly built Islamic model town on the outskirts of the city. By looking at cosmetic surgery tourism in Istanbul, the urban entertainment industry, local celebrity surgeons, and the discourses surrounding cosmetically enhanced stars—most importantly Ajda Pekkan, a pop star and cosmetic surgery aficionada—the widespread idea of an increasingly beautified Istanbul having beautifying effects on its residents is subjected to a critical reading.

Chapter 2 briefly returns to the event entitled "For a More Beautiful Turkey," mentioned at the beginning of this introduction, to analyze the changing role of beauty and the Istanbul-based beauty sector as a particular location in the global beauty industry and the urban economy. This sector, the chapter shows, promises economic success for an increasing number of entrepreneurial women while also being characterized by long working hours, low pay for employees, and a hierarchical and gendered order of work where working oneself up can take years, even decades. Drawing on a large number of interviews with beauty therapists, hairdressers, and salon owners, this chapter analyzes who performs beauty service work in Istanbul and for what reasons. It analyzes the skills of beauty service work as an intimate labor that relies on manual and emotional skills that are rarely taught by formal training. By portraying one interlocutor, a second-generation beauty worker from a family of rural-urban migrants, it also shows immense changes in the perception of beauty service work as a viable and respectable form of employment for women in Istanbul. It conceptualizes how, amid the professionalization and commercialization of beauty service work, those who engage in it negotiate the complex and affective dimensions of intimacy and distance that arise when intimate body work turns into a commodity.

Like elsewhere, in urban Turkey the construction of femininity is intricately tied up with moral understandings of beauty and gendered norms of what constitutes a proper appearance. Therefore, chapter 3 looks at the varied meanings and practices of beauty by women of different generations and in varied social positions. Beautification, it shows, is linked to understanding of cleanliness, naturalness, and attractiveness, and varies throughout a woman's life course. This is shown by an analysis of the anxieties surrounding the over-investment in beauty by young teenagers and of women concerned about their marriageable daughters "not doing enough." Within a heteronormative context that places great emphasis on the importance of marriage for young adult women, investments in feminine beauty are seen as a prerequisite to married life and marriage itself. The transformation of women into generic bridal beauties on the day of their wedding is described as a social process that prominently involves female kin, including sisters, mothers, and mothers-in-law. Rather than simply being "given," beauty, this chapter shows, is at once a moral achievement and an affective social relationship that relies on one's constant attention to bodily details and general comportment.

The consumption of beauty services is not restricted to younger and upwardly mobile women, as the focus of the scholarly literature on younger women's beauty investments tends to suggest. Much in contrast to cultural conceptions of aging as a process of accomplishment and increasing authority for all genders, in Istanbul too, as chapter 4 shows, a new cohort of middle-aged and younger elderly women has begun to invest in "rejuvenation" and aesthetic "enhancement." Drawing on David Armstrong's concept of surveillance medicine (1995), body-centered life narratives with postmenopausal middle-class women, and participant observation in a private beauty clinic mostly offering Botox injections in the city center, they are described as informed and self-conscious patient-consumers who enjoy a certain level of disposable income and no longer rely on public health provision but pay for their aesthetic enhancement in private medical institutions. The chapter shows how these women commonly reject a fatalistic acceptance of "old age," which they attribute to a more conservative clientele and/or an earlier cohort of women in Turkey.

Instead, they treat the process of bodily aging with invasive beauty work as part of a distinct middle-class lifestyle, also asserting their postmenopausal sexual identities. Lastly, this chapter shows that middle-aged and elderly women in particular need to juggle their desires for beautification with their caring responsibilities within a society that regards their beauty investments as potentially immoral and self-centered.

Some specific bodily concerns in Turkey are the product of history and tie a particular bodily appearance to imaginations of modernity, femininity, and urban citizenship. "Heavy" female breasts and "large" or "hooked" noses, whose surgical treatment is the focus of chapter 5, are clearly among these. In the language of medical experts in Turkey, heavy female breasts and large or hooked noses are national bodily defects, and their treatment is commonly labeled "ethnic plastic surgery." Starting from a critique of this notion, this chapter probes an understanding of cosmetic surgery, in particular nose and female breast reduction surgery, as a gendered and racialized desire for a "normal" body image in Turkey. Drawing on surgeons' accounts of what constitutes a "normal" appearance with regard to nose and breast surgery practices on the one hand and female patients' accounts on the other, it analyzes the multiple and changing meanings of nose and breast surgeries for women in contemporary urban Turkey.

Drawing on interviews and participant observation, including in the hair salon of an international banking headquarters in Istanbul's business district, in chapter 6 I offer an analysis of the role of beauty in women's professional lives in the urban service sector. In the literature, the recent beauty boom has often been linked to the growth of the service sector and the global increase in the proportion of women in paid work. In Istanbul, the growing service sector likewise increasingly relies on female personnel, who are expected to look *prezentabl* (presentable). While attractiveness and beauty may give women an edge in a highly competitive urban job market, this chapter shows that it is not beauty per se that women seek in order to succeed professionally. Beauty work is also shown to be significant for the affective and sensual changes it brings about in women's performance of a self-confident, disciplined self within a competitive urban environment. Finally, against the background of ever more beauty-intensive and feminine norms of women's bodily appearance at their workplaces, individual women's challenges to these norms are analyzed within the context of the precarious working conditions, sexual harassment, and gendered discrimination they are likely to face.

Changing norms of femininity are also the topic of the following chapter, chapter 7. This chapter shows that, by consuming beauty services and making them an aspect of their fashion-conscious feminine selves, young, consciously pious women increasingly question the long-standing hegemonic link between feminine beauty and secular middle-class subjectivity in Turkish society. Accordingly, and in an atmosphere of political tension and the common rhetoric of an increasing secular-Islamic gulf within society, many self-identified secular research participants see the "feminine secular body" as under threat. For them, the fashioning and public performance of attractive feminine bodies through the consumption of beauty services becomes an act of immediate concern. My aim in this chapter is to analyze the relationship between different forms of gendered and embodied middle-class subjectivities and everyday self-fashioning in relation to the "secular" and "Islamic" in Turkey's recent past. In what ways can we speak of "secular" or "Muslim" urban bodies, spaces, or aesthetics in present-day Istanbul? And finally, what kind of self-evident "truths" and everyday distinctions are tied to the fashioning of proper feminine selves in this setting?

These questions lead toward my conclusions on beauty and the making of middle-class femininities in urban Turkey. *Istanbul Appearances* argues that Istanbulite middle-class women's bodily practices and concerns are tied to a wide range of desires and imaginations in a rapidly changing urban space. In present-day Istanbul, beauty practices are about expressing, and sometimes producing, difference and distinction: sporting manicured nails, highlighted hair, or operated noses among other forms of self-fashioning take on identificatory meanings on the background of an increasingly hegemonic Islamic middle class. Within the politicized context of Turkey's recent past, the consumption of beauty services and products has become a marker of women's belonging to the

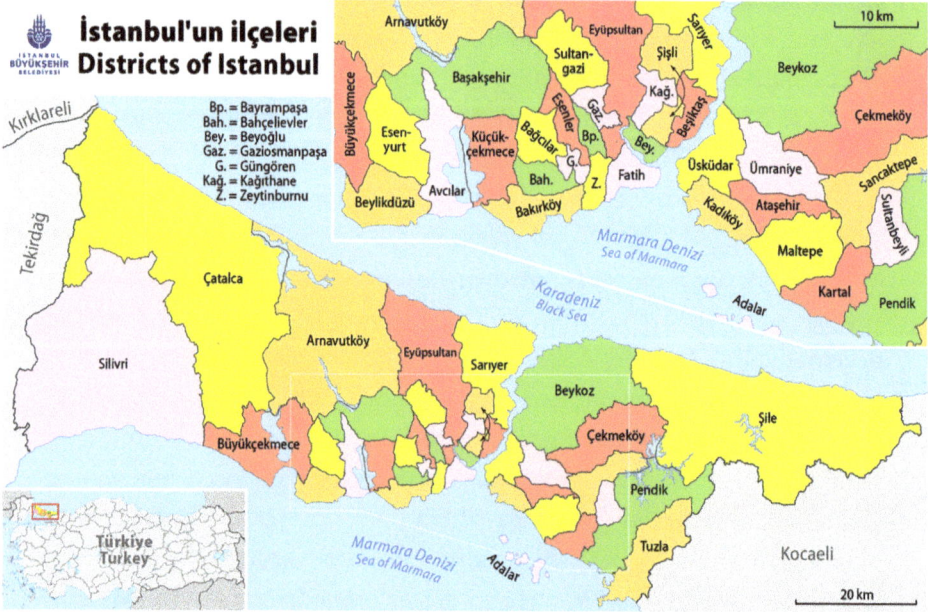

İstanbul'un ilçeleri
Districts of Istanbul

Bp. = Bayrampaşa
Bah. = Bahçelievler
Bey. = Beyoğlu
Gaz. = Gaziosmanpaşa
G. = Güngören
Kağ. = Kağıthane
Z. = Zeytinburnu

1. Map of the districts of Istanbul. (© Maximilian Dörrbecker/CC BY-SA 2.5. https://creativecommons.org/licenses/by-sa/2.5/deed.en)

urban middle classes as a form of citizenship. In framing the condition of being a female citizen in terms of a gendered and racialized materialization rather than formal status, I seek to explore shifts in paradigmatic femininity and female desire. On a more general level, these shifts occur within a transnational, mediated landscape of beauty that draws heavily on beauty's affective force.

1

Istanbul, the "Beautifying City"

In an era of global flows characterized by urbanization, mass migration, and the circulation of mass-mediated images and global brands, it is hardly surprising that the ideals and imaginations of bodily beauty, perhaps like no other industry, are associated with global cities, notably New York and Paris (Jones 2010, 2). Within Turkey, the center of the beauty-fashion industry is clearly situated in Istanbul, an emerging global city and the country's financial and commercial hub. Indeed, some research participants described Istanbul as an emerging center in the global beauty market. This has not always been the case: with no major local brands entering the international market, no commercial television until 1989, and few foreign firms signing licensing agreements to sell their cosmetic products in Turkey, Istanbul long remained marginal within the geography of global beauty (Jones 2010, 203).

As numerous studies of "globalization" and the (new) global economy have shown, global goods and images are never simply adopted or consumed, but are given diverse meanings and are appropriated, refashioned, or rejected in various ways in different local contexts around the world. This chapter seeks to contribute to an emerging anthropological literature on the repercussions of mass-mediated beauty ideals, images, and practices in a particular urban space. As outlined in the introduction, there are great differences in the meanings, preferences, and styles of beauty within Istanbul, hardly surprising for Turkey's and one of the world's most popular cities, with an official estimated population of over fifteen million, home to almost a fifth of the country's entire population (TURK-STAT 2021). Hence, this chapter also serves as an introduction to the urban beauty geography of Istanbul. Thus, in the popular imagination, the urban beauty economy and the consumption of distinctive beauty services are linked to particular central neighborhoods and are commonly seen as new or external to the so-called *varoş* (urban margins), the lower-class settlements on the outskirts of the city.

By profiling three of my research sites across Istanbul, I seek to draw attention not only to the differences between them, but also to the (imaginary) link between the transformation or even "beautification" of urban bodies and spaces. Starting from the focal point of the modern city center, Taksim Square, the narrative moves on to discuss the Istanbul-based entertainment industry and its role in producing particular kinds of mediated beauties across the city. Finally, this chapter includes profiles of research sites in three rather different parts of the city, namely Beyoğlu, Fatih, and Başakşehir, as everyday places where different yet not so different kinds of urban middle-class femininities are manufactured within a particular "beautyscape." I chose these salons and neighborhoods because they draw attention to the urban diversity involved, as well as to common themes and issues across the beauty sector in Istanbul.

"Beautification" in the City Center:
The View from above Taksim Square

> As the city becomes more beautiful, its inhabitants also want to be more beautiful. This is why body aesthetics [*estetik*] in Turkey are becoming ever more widespread.[1]

When in 2011, in one of my first interviews on the topic of femininity and aesthetic body modification in urban Turkey, the well-known cosmetic surgeon Dr. Oskui responded to my question as to why cosmetic surgery and beauty services had recently become so popular in Istanbul, his answer, quoted above, came as a surprise. The longer I studied aesthetic body modifications in Istanbul, however, the more the link between the transformation of urban bodies and space started to make sense. It

---

1. Interview with Dr. Ibrahim Oskui, September 23, 2011. The names of research participants and salons have been replaced with pseudonyms throughout this book, except for those interviewees who, like Dr. Oskui, were interviewed in their role as experts and occupied public positions.

did so from Dr. Oskui's vantage point especially, as his office overlooked Istanbul's central Taksim Square.

Taksim Square and the large Republican Monument at its center are iconic places in the city and for many decades symbolized the European and cosmopolitan face of Istanbul. Designed by the Italian sculptor Pietro Canonica and architect Giulio Mongeri in 1928 to commemorate the establishment of the Turkish Republic five years earlier, they were built amid the ruins of the Ottoman Empire and, at least partly, on the ruins of an old Armenian cemetery (Gül 2012, 106). During my field research, the reorganization of Taksim Square was one of several projects proposed by then Prime Minister Recep Tayyip Erdoğan that became known as the "crazy projects," including a third bridge over the Bosporus and the opening of a new canal between the Black Sea and the Sea of Marmara (Gül 2012, 179). In spring 2013, the Taksim Square project was to begin with the "redevelopment" of the adjacent Gezi Park into a building complex containing a shopping mall and high-end housing. The plan was halted by civil unrest and a series of demonstrations that eventually came to be known as the Gezi Park protests. The square turned into a battlefield after the municipality sent demolition teams, bulldozers, and later the police to evict protesters and demolish their protest camp, after which the protests escalated into a series of antigovernment demonstrations across the country that involved an estimated three and a half million active participants, killed at least eleven, and left more than eight thousand injured (Amnesty International 2013).

Whereas for the protesters the imminent destruction of Gezi Park and the reorganization of Taksim Square were yet more steps toward the commercialization, gentrification, and indeed, the "uglification" of the city center, for the municipality it formed part of an ongoing effort of "beautification" (*güzelleşme*, in Turkish). This beautification was first initiated by the Istanbul Metropolitan Municipality as the *Güzel Beyoğlu Projesi*, the "Beautiful Beyoğlu Project," under the directorate of Kadir Topbaş in the early 2000s with a series of aesthetic interventions, among them the replacement of all store plates on its major pedestrian shopping mile leading up to Taksim Square, İstiklal (Independence) Avenue, with homogenized walnut wood plates (Adanalı 2011, 8n15). Including the removal of street children and beggars, legal pressure, and the forced evictions of unwelcome residents and protesters, the so-called beautification of the modern city center aimed at remaking an area that for many years had been associated with poverty, drug-trafficking, and prostitution. Moreover, both the municipality and the government invested in attracting foreign visitors; for example, through an annual "Istanbul shopping fest," designed after a similar event in Dubai and widely advertised in Turkish Airlines magazines and other media targeting an international audience. Some scholars have interpreted this as a part of Istanbul's transformation into a global city and of its branding as Europe's "coolest" city, a status that received much public recognition when it was elected the 2010 European Capital of Culture (Göktürk et al. 2010).

With almost twelve million international overnight visitors in 2016, Istanbul has indeed become a major global destination, ranked sixth among all destination cities worldwide in 2015 (Hedrick-Wong and Choong 2016, 2). Among them are increasing numbers of tourists from elsewhere in the Middle East, with most visitors flying in from Tehran (Iran) and Jeddah (Saudi Arabia) (Hedrick-Wong and Choong 2016, 44). On its main pedestrian shopping mile leading toward Taksim Square, İstiklal Avenue, signs in Arabic and Farsi have sprung up in shop windows, and Arabic- or Farsi-speaking passersby with bandages on their noses or faces from recent surgery or with the reddish marks from hair transplants visible on their shaved heads have become a common sight. Among Istanbulites, who tend to hide the visible signs of their cosmetic surgery, the fashioning of post-surgery signs by foreigners on their central shopping mile is a topic often commented on and joked about.

For Dr. Oskui, the link between the "beautification" of central Istanbul and urban bodies made sense not least because many of his patients were part of the endless stream of tourists populating Taksim Square and its surroundings, the site of many mid-range and luxury hotels. Born in Iran and trained in Turkey and the United States, he was one of several highly mediatized Istanbul-based plastic-reconstructive and cosmetic surgeons who often performed surgery on so-called "cosmetic surgery tourists." More than half of his up to four hundred patients per annum arrived from abroad, notably from Iran, northern Iraq, Azerbaijan, and the Turkish labor migration diaspora in Western Europe. While we conducted our interview in his stylishly furnished office, complete with a large white leather sofa, extravagant porcelain statues, orchids, and oil paintings of Paris, he received three phone calls from patients calling from Tehran and Dubai whose surgeries were scheduled for the next few days, inquiring about details of their respective journeys to Istanbul and surgery. From where we sat, hundreds of visitors could be seen walking in Taksim Square and taking pictures of the Republican Monument against the setting sun. They in turn could see the large illuminated panel on the top of the building we sat in, inviting them to get in touch with Dr. Oskui, an "internationally acclaimed" cosmetic surgeon.

Debates on cosmetic surgery tourism (CST) relate the phenomenon to a specific form of international travel, typically from west to east or from north to south, to seek medical treatment, in this case cosmetic surgery, at a lower cost with better access, and/or of a higher quality. For Holliday et al. (2015), the cosmetic surgery tourist experience is an interplay of space, place, and travel. Drawing on a large-scale research project on CST in South Korea, Thailand, Tunisia, and elsewhere, they attempt to detach it from the classical model of medical travel, in which "west goes east" or "north goes south," by paying attention to the "specificity of places, people, things, practices, and ideas that come together when someone travels abroad to access a procedure to enhance their appearance" (Holliday et al. 2015, np). Drawing on Appadurai (1990), they suggest the term "beautyscapes" to refer to a specific assemblage of global flows of technical or medical knowledge, mediascapes, finanscapes, networks, and practices of international travel. Likewise, Dr. Oskui described CST in Istanbul as a holistic experience intricately tied to the city's particular service orientation:

> OSKUI: They both travel and have cosmetic surgery. Also, they feel at home here [since] we provide a full service, picking them up from the airport, checking them into the hotel, then performing the surgery, taking them back to the airport. They don't need to be afraid or worry and that's another reason [for them to have surgery here].
>
> CL: Both holiday and treatment . . .

OSKUI: That's it. I like to put it this way: last year, Istanbul was the
World [*sic*] Capital of Culture, in five years' time it will be the
World Capital of Cosmetic Surgery [*estetik*]! (*laughs*)

Rather than simply seeking cheaper prices, here Oskui points to the professionalism of the cosmetic surgery tourism experience in Istanbul, the
future "World Capital of Cosmetic Surgery." Moreover, cosmetic surgery
tourists could feel at home in Istanbul, arguably not only by being cared for
and pampered, but also because they come to Istanbul as a modern Muslim megacity, one that many of them already know from its various media
productions, most importantly its TV soap operas, which are immensely
popular in the wider Mediterranean, Middle East, and Central Asia.

Most of these series, such as the romantic drama *Gümüş* ("Silver,"
in Turkey; *Nur*, "Light," in the Arab-speaking world), are produced and
set in Istanbul and depict a particularly "beautified" image of the city,
including the white upper-class mansions on the shores of the Bosporus and various opportunities for high-end shopping and entertainment.
From chatting with Arabic-speaking patients in Dr. Oskui's office, at
the annual Istanbul Beauty and Care fair, and in a hair transplant clinic
where, during the first weeks of research, I lived on an upper floor next
to cosmetic surgery tourists, it became clear that these series played an
important role in their decision to choose Istanbul as their destination
for surgery and travel. Further research on the topic is needed to analyze whether these series, similar to what has been analyzed for South
Korea (cf. Holliday et al. 2015), not only produce an attractive image of
the city, but also help to popularize a specific "Istanbul" look for foreign
travelers seeking aesthetic enhancement in the city. The fact that they
do impact on their foreign audiences' lives more generally is exemplified
by the documentary film *Kismet: How Turkish Soap Operas Changed the
World*,[2] which shows how young Arab women especially identify with the
television heroines and are influenced by them in terms of how they see
themselves and their role in society.

2. Nina Maria Paschalidou, Greece/Cyprus, 2013, 57 minutes.

Medical tourism has become big business and is a source of national pride for Turkey, with statistics indicating that it ranks high in the number of medical tourists globally. According to Turkey's largest health tourism agency, 662,087 medical tourists visited Turkey in 2019, the year before the COVID-19 pandemic affected global traveling, and earned the country US$1.06 billion in revenue, approximately 60 percent from plastic surgery (*Daily Sabah* 2020). In the Turkey edition of Patients Beyond Borders™, Istanbul is described as a principal "Healthcare City" and "worthy tourist destination" (Woodman 2009, xiv), images illustrated by several pages of glossy pictures, including some of major tourist sights, private hospitals, and "world-class" golf courses. According to Woodman, medical tourists to Turkey sought "a pampered recuperation experience" in "one of the world's first medical travel destinations," its "healing waters" having first attracted travelers "more than two millennia ago" (2009, xiv–xv). Indeed, there is a long-standing healing geography in the city known today as Istanbul, which is historically linked to religious pilgrimage since Byzantine times, namely to the city's numerous healing shrines, hospitals, baths, and cisterns (Talbot 2015). While there is little continuity between the old centers of healing and pilgrimage in Byzantium on the one hand and contemporary medical tourism on the other, the notions of revitalization, healing, and even the healing geography of antiquity all figure prominently in the promotional materials targeting international cosmetic surgery tourists to Turkey today.[3]

Moreover, and in contrast to other medical practitioners, who tend to shy away from such labels, plastic reconstructive and cosmetic surgeons and their agents often self-consciously describe themselves as healers, artists, or, including Dr. Oskui during our first interview, as the more effective psychologists. Within Turkey, private TV channel shows provide cosmetic surgeons with an excellent platform to mediate and indirectly advertise themselves as such. Thus, Oskui and other Istanbul-based

---

3. See, for example, RevitalizeInTurkey, a British company procuring cosmetic surgery in Turkey (https://www.revitalizeinturkey.com/en, accessed March 18, 2021).

cosmetic surgeons have become TV personalities by selling spectacular surgeries on private TV shows such as Seda Sayan's talk show, or *Yeniden Başlasın* (Fresh Beginnings), a so-called makeover reality show similar to *Extreme Makeover* or *The Swan* in the United States and named after a famous song by Turkish popstar and cosmetic surgery aficionada Ajda Pekkan (see figure 6).

Mass-mediated surgery typically combines several types of surgery with the effect of dramatically changing a patient's look in the sense of a bodily makeover. During one of my meetings with Dr. Oskui in early 2014, he presented me with pictures on his smartphone of some of his recently performed combined surgeries, including pictures from abdominoplasty, liposuction, and other kinds of fat-removal surgery on a middle-aged female patient from whose body he had removed 35 kilograms of fat, all performed during the same general anesthetic. Intending to sell this case and its accompanying images to a private TV channel, in one picture he had arranged the tissue removed from his patient's body in a kind of art installation, surrounded by more than a dozen glass bottles filled with the body fat removed during surgery.

Because medical practitioners in Turkey are prohibited from openly advertising themselves, Oskui and several other cosmetic surgeons relied heavily on such shows to reach prospective patients. They subsequently uploaded video recordings of these shows to their personal websites and distributed them via social media. To reach patients abroad more directly, Oskui and others also used advertisements on Turkish-language satellite TV channels in Western Europe and the United States (which were exempt from the prohibition), as well as in magazines and TV channels across the wider Mediterranean, the Middle East, or Central Asia. Competition for cosmetic surgery patients from abroad was indeed fierce in Istanbul, illustrated by the story of another interviewee also working in the cosmetic surgery sector, who one day recounted how in the morning, two of his prospective hair transplant patients from the Gulf had been snatched away from his chauffeur at the airport by an agent who promised to take them somewhere where they could have the same type of treatment for half the price.

The beautyscape of Istanbul as it unfolded itself from Dr. Oskui's office overlooking the modern city center was one of globalized travel and commerce, of the capitalization of mediatized fantasies, of beauty and glamour tied to a particular urban geography that was itself in the process of undergoing often painful operations of beautification. During an era of violent urban restructuring and the privatization of public services, including health and the media, cosmetic surgery has become an increasingly normalized form of beautification in Istanbul. Like Alex Edmonds' (2007) analysis of similar businesses in Rio de Janeiro, the cosmetic surgery sector now forms part of the city's wider neoliberal landscape. Within the brief history of the cosmetic surgery sector, its center has now moved from Turkey's capital, Ankara, where it was rooted in state and university hospitals, to an ever-growing private sector in Istanbul. For another Istanbul-based cosmetic surgeon, Prof. Dr. Gürhan Özcan, this formed part of a wider pattern of urban commercialization:

> The cost of cosmetic surgery is not covered by state insurance, so they [his patients] have to pay cash, or by credit card, or whatever. This [Istanbul] is the centre of the industry, of the economy of Turkey. So most of the money is here, in Istanbul. So most of the people, who will pay for surgery, they are also in Istanbul. This attracts people who do plastic surgery, for the money it brings. . . . It's a business. [At times I ask myself:] "Are you a medical doctor or a businessman?" Many plastic surgeons in this financial service city, they are businesspeople! I am not happy to say this, but that's the way it is. So it is not just the centre of Turkish plastic surgery science, but of business![4]

The amalgam of money, commerce, urban space, and *estetik* (cosmetic surgery) described here becomes especially obvious when looking at the urban entertainment industry and its relation to mediated beauty. With its stories of fame and everlasting beauty, the urban entertainment industry did much to popularize aesthetic body modification in Turkey and to create a particular kind of urban beautyscape.

4. Interview with Prof. Dr. Gürhan Özcan, March 11, 2014.

Mediated Bodies and Fantasies:
Ajda Pekkan and the Stars of Istanbul

Like elsewhere, the fantasy that every woman may be turned into a star through her looks has fueled the Istanbul-based beauty sector, and indeed the local entertainment industry has capitalized on it. This section deals with the role of Turkey's stars and socialites in creating a particular kind of beautyscape in Istanbul, the uncontested center of the Turkish entertainment industry. Their highly mediated and aesthetically enhanced bodies have fueled the urban economy of aesthetic desires and continue to inform urban residents' everyday beauty practices. They do so not by means of direct manipulation or indoctrination, as suggested by earlier studies on media reception, but through a process of affective mediation, one that creates "spaces of possibility and distinction, momentarily centering the body that invokes the representation" (Ochoa 2014, 10).

Any account of the relationship between the Istanbul-based sectors of *estetik* and entertainment has to begin with the so-called *süperstar* of Turkish pop music, Ajda Pekkan. It is her cosmetically altered body that, unlike any other public figure in recent decades, has created spaces of both aesthetic possibility and distinction throughout Turkey. Born in 1946 into an upper middle-class family in Istanbul, Pekkan started her career as a young actress in Turkey's developing film industry in the mid-1960s and is now considered one of the most commercially successful female Turkish music artists. According to her biographer Naim Dilmener (2007), her fame also stemmed from the fact that in the 1960s the Istanbul-based industry was looking for a star who did not shy away from aesthetic body modifications in order to create publicity through spectacular before-and-after tales and photographic collections. Following the motto of "[i]n the entire world, artists go under the knife to become beautiful the way they want to be, to correct their deformations . . . So why don't we?" (Dilmener 2007, 71), Ajda Pekkan came to embody this role like no other.

Under the eye of the public, from the mid-1960s Pekkan transformed herself from a delicate, thin-lipped brunette girl into a tanned super-blonde with feminine curves and plush lips, who never seemed to age. At the beginning of her career, the popular youth magazine *Ses* reported her looks as follows:

> Except for Leyla Sayar, all female Turkish film artists up to 1963 have lifted their nosetips: Muhterem Nur, Pervin Par, Fatma Girik, Belgin Doruk, Semra Sar, Filiz Akın and others. . . . Now we've come across a new star, Ajda Pekkan. . . . her profile and the looks of her nose from the side are of a different quality than those of the stars. In earlier times one would have called her nose "Hellenistic" [*Yunani*]; today one calls it a "Greek" [*Grek*] nose. (quoted from Dilmener 2007, 32)

A few months after the report, Ajda Pekkan began to change her appearance and, so the media noted, her nose stopped looking "Greek" (Dilmener 2007, 37). Whereas up until then Ajda Pekkan had been perceived as averagely "nice-looking" (*hoş* in Turkish), she now turned into a "very beautiful" (*çok güzel*) woman (Dilmener 2007, 37). She was reported to be taking paraffin baths and vibration treatments to slim down her legs and to be working out with the famous physical therapist and aerobic instructor Füsun Önal, a Turkish version of Jane Fonda in terms of popularity; also, her lips changed, as did the color of her hair. According to Dilmener, in the late 1960s and 1970s she "ran from surgeon to surgeon, sparing neither pain nor expense to go under the knife" (2007, 37). In contrast to many other young Turkish singers and actresses of the period, who were said to put on weight quickly after their first success, get married, or else give up their careers, Ajda persisted. She came to embody and was marketed as the "European face of Turkey," in terms of both her looks and her self-conscious choice to pursue a self-determined life as a typical "modern" *İstanbullu* career woman (Dilmener 2007, 32).

From early on in her career, the media reported and commented on Ajda Pekkan's bodily transformations with detailed information as well as dubious rumors, hidden shots, and eventually jokes mediated in the nation's tabloid press, glossy magazines, or television shows. Over the years, Pekkan became both a brand name and something to be avoided for the beauty sector in Turkey, with some interlocutors mentioning her to explain why they abhorred *estetik*, by which they meant creating "artificial looks." As she herself remarked in a talk show on the private television

Kanal D in 2009, "it came to a point where now I am being identified with cosmetic surgery. . . . this topic reached a level where it started to sadden me" (quoted from *Hürriyet* 2009).

In the many decades of her fame, Pekkan came to adopt different strategies for dealing with the media's constant reporting about her body aesthetics, often refusing to talk about the topic altogether, or else downplaying its importance for her looks and more generally her career. In 2000, for example, in an interview she gave to the *Hürriyet* daily, she stated that the only operations she had ever had until after "everybody started having them" were a nose job and fat-removal surgery in the mid-1970s (quoted from *Hürriyet* 2000). Then again, she was quoted as saying that "anyone who has the need and the money, and is not afraid of cosmetic surgery, should do it. For me, cosmetic surgery has always been a necessity" (*Hürriyet* 1998a). More recently, Pekkan filed a lawsuit against the well-known Turkish cosmetic surgeon Prof. Dr. Nazım Durak for compensation for damage to her reputation after he had publicly called her a "weird creation," with "eyes like a frog" and "lips like the bum of a monkey," with a visibly reduced ability to mime, supposedly due to exaggerated Botox injections (*Hürriyet* 2013).

Not least, Ajda Pekkan's story is one of the close link between her own fame (and looks) and that of the surgeons who operated on her. Claiming that her face was "the creation of Mr. Onur (Onur Bey)" (quoted from Süsoy 2000), her look came to be closely associated with the "magic hands" of her cosmetic surgeon and "friend," Prof. Dr. Onur Erol, who, as the owner of his own large beauty clinic in central Istanbul, was himself a public figure often described as the "father" of cosmetic surgery in Turkey. Erol first came to fame in 1982 when he successfully operated on Bergen, a young singer from Izmir and the victim of an acid attack by her jealous husband (Ipekeşen 2006). Surgeons who, like Erol, were publicly known for operating on Istanbul's media celebrities and socialites, were especially sought after and able to demand higher prices than others. As one journalist documented in 2003, whereas a so-called celebrity surgeon could easily ask for US$5,000 (about 7 billion Turkish lira at the time, though charging the fee in the more stable foreign currency) for liposuction or fat-removal surgery, a surgeon in a less exclusive hospital on the outskirts of the city typically charged about 0.8–2 billion Turkish lira (approximately US$500–1,500) for the same type of surgery (Erşan 2003).

In the late 1990s and early 2000s, Ajda Pekkan became one of numerous Turkish media celebrities and Istanbul socialites publicly known to have been "operated" on, including, most prominently, Hande Ataizi, Gizem Özdilli, and Deniz Akkaya. These celebrities' aesthetic body modifications were widely discussed in the Turkish public and imitated, or else cited as negative examples, in ordinary women's beauty practices across the city. In contrast to an earlier generation of celebrities, who typically tried to hide their aesthetic treatments and surgeries, the stars and starlets of a younger generation during the early 2000s were quite explicit about them. Like Pekkan before them, they considered aesthetic enhancements to be part and parcel of their professional careers, as illustrated by Hande Ataizi's dry comment about her multiple tissue injections and nose, breast augmentation, and cheek implant surgeries, all highly mediatized, with the words: "I'm an actress. My instrument is my body" (quoted from *Hürriyet* 1999). In 2001, Ataizi was the first female celebrity to go onstage wearing bandages from her latest facial surgery, a move that shocked the Turkish public at the time. Indeed, until today, few TV personalities have openly shown off their aesthetic body modifications, and when, a decade later, Nazlı Ilıcak, a well-known journalist and politician in her late sixties, went on air shortly after having a facelift in Paris, media commentators spitefully remarked that she had "a face like a balloon," and looked like "Bülent Ersoy" (Terzi 2011).

Like Ajda Pekkan, Bülent Ersoy, a trans person and national star of Turkish classical music in their sixties (Selen 2012), came to be associated with the kind of surgically enhanced beauty that was commonly represented and discussed in urban beauty salons and clinics as both fascinating and exaggerated. When it became known that Ersoy had had yet another round of cosmetic surgery in 2005, namely blepharoplasty, a neck lift, a facelift, the removal of older silicone implants, and a reshaping of her eyebrows, a large number of journalists and photographers waited in front of the private Memorial Hospital in central Istanbul in order to get the first interview or the first shot of her face. Upon appearance, Ersoy hid her face from the public gaze, but the event was nevertheless discussed in the tabloid press for days.[5] Ersoy's diva-like beauty and standing within the Istanbul fashion-beauty industry was publicly honored when in 2013 she was given the role of leading model during the Istanbul fashion week.

While cosmetic surgery is commonly associated with female rather than male celebrities, in recent decades a number of male stars have also become known for having been operated on, among them the Turkish pop stars Tarkan and Mustafa Sandal, as well as the legendary *bağlama*—a stringed musical instrument—virtuoso and former actor Orhan Gencebay. During research, the television personality and actor Beyazit Öztürk, who had himself had surgery, became a popular role model for men seeking to change the shape of their noses (*Hürriyet* 2009c). Similar to what has been reported for Iran (Kaivanara 2016), cosmetic surgery undertaken by male celebrities often has a feminizing effect on their public image. An example is the media image of the Turkish folk singer, actor, and director Özcan Deniz, who changed from hypermasculine "Anatolian hothead" (*Anadolu delikanlısı* in Turkish) to "metrosexual" (*metroseksüel* in Turkish) after his multiple cosmetic surgeries became public knowledge.

In more recent years, and with the discursive trend toward natural beauty, an increasing number of Turkish celebrities have taken a public stand against cosmetic surgery. Among them was Eyşan Özhim, an actress and former model, who had been first runner-up for Miss Turkey in 1990 and, in 2009, criticized the fact that "these days, the understanding of beauty is uniform. With cosmetic surgery everyone looks like everyone else. I can't look at these operated-on faces anymore. I don't know who decided that a small nose, fat lips, and large porcelain teeth that jump out of the mouth are beautiful. I like those who are originally beautiful. This is the way God liked us when he created us" (quoted from Tezel 2009). By the time Turkish celebrities began to pride themselves, more or less convincingly, on the fact that they had never had cosmetic surgery or else preferred a "natural" and "God-given" appearance, their beauty-intensive looks and their consumption of operations had long become popular among a wider public. In the words of one journalist, Mesude Erşan, it

---

5. See, for example, *Aktif Haber* (2005).

had "descended to the people" (*halka indirdi* in Turkish): "Cosmetic surgery used to be associated with film stars, singers or high society. But the number of plastic surgeons has increased and due to the fact that the operations performed by clinics that have opened on the urban margins are offered at much lower prices, these operations have now become popular. Today, salesgirls, clerks, bank employees, secretaries, accountants, fish vendors, retailers and housewives do not regard nose jobs, breast reductions or augmentations and similar procedures as a luxury anymore" (Erşan 2003). This became perhaps most obvious when the "salesgirls, clerks, bank employees, secretaries, accountants, fish vendors, retailers and housewives" described by Erşan started appearing as cosmetic surgery patients in popular magazines and on private TV themselves during so-called makeover shows. In 2014, one of the most popular of these shows on Turkish TV was *Yeniden Başlasın* (Fresh Beginnings), aired on the private channel *Show Turk* and named after a famous song by Ajda Pekkan. It offered women suffering from "aesthetic defects" but of little economic means the opportunity to change not only their looks but, according to the show's motto, their entire lives. The morning shows of Seda Sayan,[6] a TV host and long-haired blonde in her mid-fifties that the tabloid press described as "almost having reached Ajda's record in cosmetic surgery" (*Haberler* 2013), followed a similar script and, as mentioned above, some surgeons were eager to present their "spectacular" operations to it.

Thus, while aesthetic body modification, including cosmetic surgery, was long regarded as the preserve of Istanbul high society (*sosyete*) and its entertainment industry's celebrities, during the late 1990s and early 2000s it became more easily available and acceptable for a wider clientele. Indeed, the aesthetically enhanced looks of Istanbul's stars and their beautyscapes within the city—including prestigious private hospitals and celebrity surgeons—opened up spaces of possibility and distinction for the less famous. They also contributed to the fact that aesthetic treatments that had long been considered shameful, being shunned or hidden, now

---

6. Among them were *Sabahların Sultanı* (Mornings' Empress), aired on *Kanal D* from 2006–9, or *Sabahın Sedası* (Morning Sound), aired on *Show Türk* between 2010–11.

became more public, normalized, and chic, in some cases being a form of conspicuous consumption. This change was played out in different ways in three different settings across the city.

Exchanging (Aesthetic) Differences: The Belladonna[7] in Beyoğlu

Until well into the 1950s, all but a few hair and beauty salons in the city that catered to women were located in the modern city center, in Beyoğlu and the nearby residential neighborhoods of the secular elite, such as Nişantaşı, Şişli, Levent, and Etiler. In medieval times Pera, later renamed Beyoğlu, had been the base for European merchants in the city and, until several waves of persecution and pogroms in the late nineteenth and early twentieth century that effectively "Turkified" Istanbul (cf. Mills 2010, 50–58), it continued to be home to a large population of non-Muslim residents, including Levantine traders, Armenians, Jews, and Greek Orthodox Christians. Famous salons of old Beyoğlu that continue to be remembered by elderly middle-class interlocutors included *George* and *Villi*, both opened by Greek hairdressers in the late 1920s and 1930s. These salons were located in between the famous patisseries, cafés, and theaters on the *Grande rue de Péra*, later to be pedestrianized and renamed İstiklal Avenue, where during the early twentieth century, I was told, one had to dress in European fashion in order to be allowed to walk there.

When the Istanbul Chamber of Women Hairdressers and Manicurists (İKKMO) was founded in 1950, first as a section within the professional chamber of barbers and male hairdressers, and then from 1965 onward as a chamber in its own right, the names of a significant number of its eighteen founding members indicated that they belonged to non-Turkish and/or non-Muslim minorities, including Mosyo Villi, Mosyo Aristokli, Niko Rastapulas, and Edman and Nina Persaje.[8] Following the violent removal of its former residents, in the second half of the twentieth century the neighborhood became associated with decay, visible poverty, crime, drugs, and prostitution until cheap rents and the charm of its dilapidated

---

7. The names of salons in which research took place have been replaced with pseudonyms throughout this book to protect their owner's, employees', and customers' privacy.

8. Interview with Oktay Erkal, April 9, 2015. See also www.ikkmo.org.tr.

art-deco buildings attracted bohemian artists in the 1980s and 1990s. During research the process of gentrification was well advanced, and İstiklal Avenue had become subject to what the urban planner and activist Yaşar Adnan Adanalı (2011) terms a "shopping mall-ization." Over the course of a normal weekend during the early 2010s, several million visitors were estimated to go walking there.

The historical association of the beauty service sector with non-Muslim minorities in this part of the city nevertheless reverberates in the popular imagination today. This is illustrated by the use of the Greek term *kokona*, a word for an elderly (Christian) woman of upper middle-class status much concerned about her external appearance (cf. Nişanyan 2009). The term is still employed to describe a vain and rather unlikable elderly lady, who engages in beautification as a form of conspicuous consumption when she is not busy spreading gossip and intrigue. In Belladonna, one of many hair and beauty salons located in one of the backstreets to İstiklal Avenue, however, the regular clientele was rather unlike the cliché of the *kokona*: in the mornings, salesladies and other professionals working in the numerous cafés, restaurants, schools, hotels, and shops of the area rushed in for a quick *fön* (blow-dry) or manicure; during the day, international tourists and residents arrived from the nearby language schools, international businesses, and organizations, or, alongside local visitors, from a day of shopping on İstiklal Avenue; during the entire day, women arrived with appointments for more time-consuming treatments such as body hair removal, hair coloring, hair extensions, or facial treatments; in the late afternoons, students from the prestigious high schools and training institutes in the area came to have their hair styled or eyebrows shaped; and finally, in the evenings, partygoers or those with a dinner engagement in the many bars and restaurants of the İstiklal Avenue area arrived for professional makeup, a quick haircut or blow-dry—in short, for what one of the Belladonna's owners called "party hair."

The predominantly younger customers of the Belladonna salon liked their looks fashionable, beauty-intensive, and fancy; some came to get what was difficult to get elsewhere in the city, like punk undercuts, pink or blue strands of hair, or hair extensions. Like the hairdressers, who in their usual uniforms of jeans and T-shirts had about them the aura of bohemian rockstars, they sported tattoos, multiple earrings, and even piercings. They arrived knowing what they wanted, but sometimes gave in to the authority of the exclusively male hairdressers, who insisted they had to try out a new cut or color. Many of the more regular clients were upper middle-class fashionistas, who typically arrived with long lists of requests, including the cutting, coloring, and styling of hair, a manicure, a pedicure, the shaping of eyebrows, and the removal of facial hair. Often, up to three persons could be seen working on one customer simultaneously. In early summer, many came for regular tanning sessions to prepare their skin for holidays in bikinis on the beach. Among them was Aytan, a stockbroker in her late twenties, who regularly had her hair dyed blonde and also arrived for tanning sessions in winter and spring to keep her dark suntan. In mid-May 2014 she arrived in her usual salon outfit, branded sweatpants and sneakers, to have braided hair extensions. While two hairdressers worked on her hair, she told me about her recent nose surgery in a private beauty clinic and explained about the numerous tattoos on her upper arms. She confided her anxieties regarding her lips to me, which she thought were too thin and intended to have treated with Botox injections or fillers.[9]

While officially Belladonna was a unisex salon, men rarely entered as customers and, if they did, requested manicures or tanning sessions rather than haircuts. It was a place where the global beauty industry was clearly established in its use of global brands like Wella, Schwarzkopf, L'Oreal, and Kerastase, as well as its media framing, with several international fashion magazines displayed in the waiting area and a large flat-screen TV usually set to the global channel Fashion One. At 30 TRY for a haircut (app. US$15 at the time of research),[10] 20 TRY for a manicure, and 10 TRY

9. Field notes on conversation with Aytan, May 15, 2014.

10. During the main period of field research, the exchange rates between Turkish Lira (TRY) and US dollars (US$) fluctuated between US$1 = 1.75 TRY (February 2, 2013) and US$1 = 2.36 TRY (December 16, 2014). Ever since, the Turkish lira has seen a dramatic devaluation (see statistics of the Central Bank of the Republic of Turkey, www.tcmb.gov.tr). In this book, the average rate during field research (US$1 = 2.05 TRY) has been taken as a basis for conversion.

for eyebrow shaping or a blow-dry, its prices were mid-range and similar to those of other salons in the area.

Entering the Belladonna salon was itself a sensual experience: from one of İstiklal Avenue's dark side alleys, one entered a somewhat dilapidated early twentieth-century building, passed by a rather shady bar complete with fortune-tellers and belly-dancers on the first floor, and then entered a spacious salon with its high stuccoed ceilings and fashionable silver-striped wallpaper behind numerous mirrors reflecting the light of the spotlights above. New customers were helped out of their jackets, led toward the reception desk, and seated in a comfortable black leather sofa in the waiting area. From there, one could observe the hustle and bustle of more than a dozen hairdressers, manicurists, and beauticians working on their customers, with a *çaycı*, a woman serving tea, moving skillfully between them. From the speakers above sounded cosmopolitan pop music, nouvelle vague or salsa, and occasionally Turkish pop music, mingling with the sounds of the hairdryers and the chatter from the manicurists' area. The fragrances of perfumes, hair shampoos, and sprays were in the air, and from the balcony, its doors usually open, came a pleasant breeze and occasionally the smoke of cigarettes from those taking a break.

The salon was opened in the early 2000s by five siblings from Malatya in southeastern Anatolia, with the oldest officially managing it and three brothers working as hairdressers. Once they managed to extend the salon and rent a second floor, the original hair salon became a beauty center proper, with one of their sisters, a trained nurse, working on the upper floor complete with facilities for tanning, body hair removal by waxing and laser epilation, facial treatments, and permanent makeup. Apart from the siblings, there were about ten other hairdressers, ten manicurists, and from two to eight apprentices and assistants, depending on the season, which was low in summer and high in winter and spring. Many of the employees had been recruited through the owners' hometown connections and when in Istanbul lived near the salon. Hierarchies between them were clear and gendered, with the female manicurists and beauty therapists working around and earning less than the male hairdressers.

When in 2013 large-scale protests erupted against the urban development plan to demolish Gezi Park and restructure the adjacent Taksim

Square, Belladonna was in the midst of the turmoil. Several of its hairdressers, including one of its owners, stayed in the communal protest camp that was set up in Gezi Park during the early days of the protest. After the camp was forcefully evicted, the protest took to the streets, including the backstreets where the salon was located. Due to its location right off İstiklal Boulevard, a mere five hundred meters from Taksim as the crow flies, during the street fighting the salon was regularly affected by teargas attacks from the police.

More than a year after the uprising, the letter "u" from the illuminated *Kuaför* (hairdresser) panel outside the salon remained broken where it had been hit by a teargas canister, acting as a material reminder of more revolutionary times. During the teargassing, people had taken refuge on the salon's upper floor or climbed from it onto the roof. One of the owners remembered how, during the protests, salon workers and the few customers who had made it into Belladonna became stuck there for hours or else stayed on for long conversations about the politics of the day, sharing tea and cigarettes. During these and the following weeks and months, politics were often discussed in the salon, with many of the predominantly Kurdish salon workers being staunch opponents of the government.

The salon continued to be affected by ongoing political turbulence and protests in late 2013 and 2014. For example, in the week of what later came to be known as the "December 17 events," when a large number of ruling party members was arrested in connection with a corruption scandal, a mere 583 out of the usual 800 clients during this high season attended Belladonna. The others had obviously decided to avoid the city center or else returned home quickly after work in the area because of the unrest. Indeed, Taksim Square and İstiklal Avenue continued to see demonstrations and other forms of protests during 2014 that were usually violently suppressed by the government forces. In addition, the salon lost many of its international customers when, after several terror attacks and the failed coup attempt in 2016, the number of international Western tourists and long-term residents in the city dropped dramatically. Nevertheless, like earlier salons in the neighborhood, it remained a place for the exchange of aesthetic differences, where customers were styled in the latest cosmopolitan fashions. Like other salons, in particular the Nur salon in Fatih which I will describe in the next section, the large Belladonna salon functioned as a kind of microcosmos of its surrounding center-city neighborhood, as well as wider politics.

Beauty in the Urban *Mahalle*: the Nur salon in Fatih

In her "linked comparison" between beauty salons and practices in Paris, Cairo, and Casablanca, Susan Ossman (2002) makes the distinction between three kinds of salons, namely (1) the neighborhood or "proximate" salon, a kind of "cocoon" that "nurture[s] bodies in formation" and is a space of female solidarity "set off for feminine concerns" (Ossman 2002, 101); (2) the "fast-cut" salon, which is more impersonal and often centrally located, with a clear hierarchy from owner to hairdresser to assistant; and (3) the "special salon," which, located in central or upmarket shopping districts, centers around "famous products, hairdressers, and clients" (Ossman 2002, 121). Given the ongoing processes of commercialization and gentrification in Istanbul city center described above, it is hardly surprising that most salons there oscillated between "fast-cut" and "special" salons within Ossman's (2002) taxonomy. In other parts of the city, many salons more readily qualified for what Ossman terms a neighborhood salon, including the Nur hair and beauty salon, my main research site in Fatih, a district located in the city's historic peninsula; that is, the southern shore of the Golden Horn.

For centuries, everyday life in the city had been characterized by the urban *mahalle* (neighborhood) as the place where neighbors created networks of mutual support and social control (see Behar 2003; Duben and Behar 2002, 29–35). In the neighborhood, collective rituals of washing, grooming, and bathing formed a major foundation of sociability for women in public, gender-segregated baths and later in private homes. The *mahalle*, Amy Mills (2007, 335) writes in her ethnography of a gentrified neighborhood on the Asian side of Istanbul, "is the space of intimate daily life in the Turkish urban context, and narratives of and ways of life in the *mahalle* articulate competing notions of what it means to be a woman in Turkey." While most urban neighborhoods have witnessed an erosion of their social and economic structuring since the 1960s, Fatih continued to be described as "the paradigmatic Muslim *mahalle*" (Gökarıksel 2012, 9) in terms of its historical spatial organization and demographics. In Fatih, public baths indeed continued to cater to residents rather than tourists, and beauty salons were a fairly recent addition.

When Sibel, a trained hairdresser-beautician and former midwife, opened the Nur hair and beauty salon in 2000, it was one of the first in the neighborhood to cater to women. Before opening her salon, Sibel solicited *fetvas* (legal rulings) from three well-known Islamic scholars on the permissibility of the salon and its treatments in order to satisfy her own and her prospective customers' religious scruples. While the rulings stressed the gender-segregated nature of the salon, they did not oppose the idea of a salon in principle. Nevertheless, shortly after its opening, Sibel met fierce resistance from some of her neighbors; a group of women attacked her home, smashing windows and defacing a wall, and for months she was abused verbally by a group of covered women who followed her between her home and the beauty salon. For even longer, people called Sibel anonymously or sent text messages attacking her for opening a beauty salon, which they regarded as sinful, a place of vanity and of the creation of sexual allure that was misplaced in this respectable neighborhood. Sibel remained steadfast, and after she sought the mediating support of an influential Islamic scholar (and, one might add, after she remarried), the hostility subsided. Today she counts many of her pious neighbors among her customers.

The Nur hair and beauty salon was on a little side street just off Fatih's main street, Fevzi Paşa Boulevard. With its small cafés and restaurants, clothing stores selling modest fashions, Islamic financial institutions, and tourist agencies specializing in the *hajj* (Islamic pilgrimage), this street illustrates the Islamic-conservative character of the neighborhood. Diverse styles of Islamic dress dominate the streets of Fatih, and prominent pictures of beautifully arranged and decorated headscarves in the windows of its numerous hair and beauty salons advertise the styling of headscarves (*türban tasarım* in Turkish) alongside the usual services. Following the principle of Muslim gender segregation like an increasing number of salons in Fatih and other conservative neighborhoods, the Nur salon prohibits entry to men and is protected from public view by white foil covering its windows on the inside. Amid notices of special deals and posters of beautiful women, all covered, a large sign at the entrance announces that men are not permitted entry except by appointment. A curtain behind the entrance protects those inside from the gazes of passersby even when the front door stood open, which commonly happened on hot summer or busy weekend days.

When we first met in 2011, Sibel was an energetic, tall, self-confident, and somewhat extravagant woman in her late forties who took great care of her appearance and loved flashy fashion jewelry and glittery shirts and boots. The daughter of migrants from the Black Sea, Sibel grew up in Fatih and lived with her teenage son, her second husband, and, until her recent marriage, her daughter in the adjacent neighborhood of Çarşamba, known as one of the religiously most conservative parts of the city. Like many Çarşamba residents, Sibel became *çarşaflı* a couple of years ago; that is, in public she hides her hair and body shape under a long black coat. In the salon she worked alongside her two "girls," Azra and Elif, who were in their mid-twenties and mid-thirties respectively and who did not cover their hair or dress modestly. Sibel's twenty-one-year-old daughter Sevda helped out in the salon, applying makeup, performing depilation and, until she married in 2015, offering private classes in *oryantal*, the Turkish belly dance. Several times a week, two middle-aged beauticians offered skin treatments, permanent makeup, eyelash extensions, eyelash perms, various treatments for losing weight and rejuvenation, and intense pulsed light (IPL) treatments for permanent body hair removal. Both beauticians described themselves as secular and lived outside Fatih. More recently, amid a growing number of refugees in the neighborhood, Sibel added two young Syrian women as apprentices. Except for the apprentices, all the women working in the salon had known each other for many years and described each other as "like family," preparing meals together and, when business was slack, often drinking tea together or sharing food.

The Nur salon is on three floors, with the main hair salon on the ground floor, rooms for the beauticians and depilation on the upper floor, and a kitchen, a toilet and shower, Sibel's office, a prayer room, and a little gym in the basement. On entry, the customer finds herself in the main hair salon, decorated in white and purple, with three hairdressing chairs and large round mirrors on one side and a waiting area with a black leather sofa and armchairs on the other. A white ornamental folding screen separates the front of the room, reserved for makeup and hairstyling, from the back, where manicures and pedicures are provided in a special chair. The TV above the entrance is usually set to the popular music channel KralPop and plays Turkish pop music at full volume. When the salon is busy, the sound of the music mixes with that of the hairdryers and the lively chatter between the customers and the hairdressers. Those waiting can choose between various promotional flyers, the conservative women's magazine *Ala*, and catalogues of hairstyles, including bridal hair, on the coffee table next to the sofa. Most importantly, the basement extends into the "garden," a large tent in the building's backyard. With its airy atmosphere, large dining table, comfortable armchairs, and stereo, this is a prominent place of sociality for workers and customers alike, and one of the salon's greatest assets.

Thus, in the mornings, before the salon gets busy, Sibel, her daughter, and the hairdressers have breakfast in the garden, sometimes joined by an early customer. At night, the space may be rented for a celebration after someone has given birth or for a henna night, the women-only celebration shortly before a wedding. On some nights during Ramadan, the women break their fasts there, inviting friends and customers to join them. In summer 2014, when Israel launched a military operation against the Gaza Strip, a corner of the garden was devoted to the commemoration of Palestinian children killed during the bombardments. Some of the customers come to the garden to smoke a cigarette or have a chat before or after their treatments, and sometimes Sibel or her daughter serve tea and homemade pastries. While their hair is still wrapped in aluminum foil or their nail polish is drying, women's conversations and gossip revolve around children, common acquaintances, food, cooking, or beauty. Sibel, a clever businesswoman and a great mentor, frequently comments that a customer's skin or hair is desperately in need of a special treatment, one that—what a coincidence—is on offer only this week.

Sibel contributes her knowledge of childbirth, alternative healing, or infertility and its cures, and when she still practiced midwifery she delivered the children of a few of the regulars. Other customers come not only for beauty but also for business, promoting their own services and products, including during my visits a saleswoman for a Japanese firm selling magnet therapy products, a woman from Chechnya on a visit from Cairo who performs *hacamat* (cupping) treatments, and a travel agent who with her husband organizes travel to the Arab Middle East, including pilgrimages to Mecca and Jerusalem. Many of the more regular customers are housewives who live nearby, some of whom arrive with children who play in the garden while their mothers are being treated. Younger women, often in pairs or in groups, arrive for a quick eyebrow shape or a blow-dry in the middle of a day of shopping on Fevzi Paşa Boulevard.

When she started Nur, Sibel had been reluctant to offer pubic hair removal and eyebrow shaping due to the problems they might generate from a religious perspective, her customers themselves long having been reluctant to engage in religiously "problematic" body modifications such as nail polishing or permanent makeup. However, more than a decade after Nur opened, the services demanded and provided increasingly resembled those of salons elsewhere, including those in the modern city center. Sibel nevertheless continued to be concerned with the ingredients of the cosmetic products she used being halal and preferably organic—though she had to drop some of her organic products when she noticed that many of her customers were unable to pay the higher prices for them. Thus, unlike clients in more upper middle-class neighborhoods, those who attended the Nur salon were notably on rather tight budgets. Until recently, many of the elderly and middle-aged clients had done much of the routine beauty work by themselves at home and continued to regard their occasional visits as special. Nevertheless, like elsewhere, there was increasing concern with and consumption of beauty services in Fatih and its female residents, many of whom belonged to an emerging Islamic middle class. As such, they adapt Islamic norms creatively to meet their aesthetic desires (cf. Gökarıksel and Secor 2009, 2010; Sandıkçı and Ger 2010). This became especially clear in Başakşehir, a newly founded conservative district on the outskirts of Istanbul.

Beauty in Suburbia: Arzu and Hayat in Başakşehir

As a result of the massive rural–urban migration that Istanbul experienced from the 1960s onward, Istanbul has been segregated physically along the

lines of socioeconomic status for decades. In her research on spatial contestations in the city, Berna Turam (2013, 2015) describes how the secular,
urban elites in the city center "alienated the pious in the slums" due to their
"elitism," as well as their "unfamiliarity" with these newcomers to the city
(2015, 28). In recent years Istanbul has become more mixed, and many
of the newcomer's squatter settlements have now been turned into large-
scale housing projects by TOKİ (short for *Toplu Konut İdaresi Başkanlığı*),
the Public Housing Development Administration, Turkey's government-
backed housing agency, and luxury housing. Nevertheless, and in contrast
to the usual connotation of suburbia as a rather saturated middle-class
residential area elsewhere, in Istanbul the common notion of *varoş* continues to describe a working- or lower middle-class and pious residential
area on the urban margins (Bora 2010; White 2013, 118). Accordingly, in
the trendy beauty salons and clinics of the upper middle classes in the city
center, Başakşehir was usually mentioned as part of the *varoş*, where residents, as one interlocuter in Nişantaşı put it, were unable "even to match
their handbags and shoes," clearly lacking the style and cultural capital
she attributed to herself.

A one-hour bus ride away from the historic city center to the north-
west, Başakşehir, with its empty streets and high winds, surrounded by
untilled, steppe-like hills, indeed felt as if Istanbul had finally reached its
geographical limits. In 2013, when I first ventured where most of my city-
center acquaintances, including my research assistant, had never set foot,
Başakşehir was still very much under construction, with half-empty gated
communities or social housing complexes located in between large construction sites. Initially begun as a working-class housing project in the
second half of the 1990s during the first period of municipal rule of the
Islamist Welfare Party (*Refah Partisi*, RP), the district had been created
at the initiative of the then acting mayor, Recep Tayyip Erdoğan, later to
become Turkey's prime minister and president. The district was promoted
as an Islamic model city and was widely perceived as an election gift for
his party's supporters. During the first years after its founding, many of
its inhabitants were indeed supporters of the Welfare Party or, after it was
banned from politics by the constitutional court in 1998, of one of the

Islamic parties that succeeded it (Çavdar 2011).[11] With an official population of over 340,000 in 2014, Başakşehir was a rather mixed residential area in socioeconomic terms, with a large number of luxury flats in gated communities and private villas in its fourth and fifth sectors. On its main boulevards, large billboards advertised Turkish brands featuring modest dress for women, and the same brands could be found in its large shopping malls, set up in between the housing projects and functioning as the district's landmarks even more than the local mosques.[12]

In her study of beauty salons in the United Kingdom, Paula Black writes that "[o]ne reason beauty salons are so important to women in a vast range of different cultures is that they represent a socially sanctioned meeting space" (2004, 87). This holds especially true for the urban geography of Başakşehir, where public space considered appropriate for women to hang out in is highly limited. Perhaps not surprisingly, many of the district's beauty salons are situated in its shopping malls or commercial centers.[13] They advertise their services in local magazines or else with the help of posters on the local *sosyete pazarı*, a weekly indoor market for vegetables and textiles used for major outings by women in the neighborhood.

It was in one of the district's smaller malls that we found the first of our two main research sites in the district, the Arzu salon. Arzu was located on the second of four floors in a shopping mall that rose between several high-rise gated communities next to a recently opened subway

---

11. Çavdar (2015, 5) quotes one of the founders of the municipal construction company (KIPTAS) and Başakşehir as saying "[the secularists] were claiming that WP [the Welfare Party, CL] was giving those houses to its own supporters. . . . Supporters of WP and Tayyip Erdoğan saw this project as a matter of *dava* (mission) and struggle."

12. Thus Çavdar (2011, 11) remarks that ironically, in a conservative neighborhood like Başakşehir, mosques have been displaced as central spaces of sociality and function as aesthetic details rather than spaces of everyday sociality. This becomes comprehensible by the fact that mosques are not usually spaces of everyday sociality for women in Turkey, while most men commute elsewhere for work.

13. In the district's online guide of enterprises, thirty hair and beauty salons for women were listed in 2013; see http://www.basaksehirrehberi.com/sektor (accessed March 18, 2021).

station in Başakşehir's fourth sector. On its ground floor was a supermarket; its first floor housed a barbershop, a car registry, and stationer's shop in between several real estate brokers and cheap diners. In contrast to these floors, which catered to a mixed crowd, the second floor catered to women more exclusively, with a total of five hair and beauty salons for women, four women's clothing stores including a shop for children's and baby wear as well as ladies' underwear, and a *davetiye*, a shop where one could order and print invitations and small gifts for weddings, circumcisions, or other festivities. In fact, all the shops on this floor were staffed by women, and during our many visits to the mall we never saw a man shopping or even strolling down this floor's corridors. During the day, Başakşehir more generally had a rather female feel to it, with most pedestrians, salesladies, and even car drivers being women, whose husbands supposedly commuted to work in the city center or to neighboring İkitelli, one of Istanbul's largest free trade and industry zones.

Like all the other salons on this floor, Arzu was a women-only salon, hidden from public view by tinted shop windows and a screen set up in front of its entrance. When we first visited it in October 2013, Arzu was the latest newcomer on this floor and continued to attract clients by means of its promotional offers. It was run by two cousins, both trained hairdressers in their late twenties, Mavi and Arife, who had recently moved to Başakşehir from the Black Sea province of Samsun. Both single, Mavi and Arife lived with their uncle and his family a ten-minute walk away from the salon. They staffed the salon from 9 o'clock in the morning until 7 to 8 at night, seven days a week, occasionally supported by their teenage niece and from 2014 onward by a young apprentice.

Arzu's clients were mostly young or middle-aged women from the neighborhood, often married housewives with children, who typically arrived with their small children in tow. The salon was equipped with a children's room with toys and a children's hairdressing seat. Apart from that, there were four regular hairdressing seats, two stations for washing hair, a station for removing facial hair and applying makeup, a small kitchen, and an extra room for removing body hair by waxing. There also was a waiting area with a red leather sofa and two matching armchairs next to a TV usually set to the Turkish pop music channel Kral

TV, as well as a small bookshelf with Turkish women's magazines and hair model books.

Reflecting the composition of the district's residents, the vast majority of clients covered their hair and sported pious clothing, with some being *çarşaflı*, that is, covering their hair and body under a long black coat in public. While manicures and pedicures, as well as professional makeup, were on offer at Arzu, most clients shunned these services out of moral and/or religious concerns (see chapter 7), arriving instead for services they considered to provide an acceptable standard of appearance, such as the regular cutting, coloring, and styling of hair, as well as removing facial and body hair by threading or waxing. In contrast to Samsun, the only other place where she had worked as a hairdresser, co-owner Mavi noted that her clients in Başakşehir were reluctant to have their hair cut too short, worrying that they would not be able to put it up before covering it, and preferring natural colors to blonde dye or highlights. Exceptions were those whose husbands had explicitly asked them to dye their hair blonde, and Mavi noted with surprise that there were quite a few women among her clients who came to the salon to fulfil their husbands' desires, at least rhetorically. In contrast to most of their clients, Mavi and Arife did not cover their hair in public, though Arife took on the headscarf and a more pious form of dressing in her third year in Başakşehir, at the time she began to consider getting married.

While most of Arzu's clients arrived from the surrounding neighborhood, telling me that they also came to the salon to get out of their homes and away from their daily household chores, for its owners the salon did not (yet) qualify as a neighborhood salon. Perhaps this was due to the fact that it was still new, in a newly created neighborhood where residents still hardly knew each other. Even though the salon was usually busy and waiting clients sat next to each other in the waiting area, conversations between them were rare and were initiated by the hairdressers (or the visiting researcher), rather than by the women themselves. In a similar manner, Ayse Çavdar (2011, 10) observed that residents' living arrangements in Başakşehir, especially in gated communities, made them "invisible to each other" and that "[a]lthough they came to live together with people similar to themselves, they are not very willing to get closer because they don't know the backgrounds of neighboring families." This caused neighboring practices to remain "very formal and distant," unlike in the classical *mahalle*.

A sense of intimacy and mutual support had nevertheless developed between the female shopkeepers and salesladies on the shopping mall floor, with women visiting each other when business was slack or helping each other out with cleaning materials or sugar for tea. Mavi and Arife had formed an especially close relationship with the owner of a store for children's clothes next door, who in the afternoons often brought them lunch from one of the eateries on the first floor, affectionately reprimanding them for not taking breaks or eating enough, while regularly using the salon's kitchen to prepare tea or coffee for all of them.

Across from Arzu and Başakşehir's biggest park, the *Sular Vadisi* (Valley of Water), was Hayat salon, my second main research site in the district. Hayat was located on the two lower floors of a three-floor residential terraced house with a garden in an area named after these houses, the Villas. Its owner, Esma, lived on the top floor alongside her husband and their small daughter. Aged thirty-two when I first met her in early 2014, Esma had been working as a hairdresser and beauty therapist for half her life. A school-dropout at fifteen, she had been encouraged to train in the profession by her mother Hiranur, who in 1996 had opened one of the first beauty salons in Başakşehir and subsequently made three out of her four daughters train in the beauty sector. Hiranur's salon, where all three sisters had eventually worked side by side, had recently been passed on to someone else, and many of its former clients were now regulars at Hayat.

Esma had opened the salon shortly after she got married and moved to her current, newly built residence in 2009. Male clients were accepted as clients' younger sons only, and everyone entering the salon was monitored through the CCTV camera installed at the entrance before being buzzed in by Esma or her assistants. The villa's highly visible security and monitoring system, its architecture, and its several large advertising panels on its street-facing windows displaying women in bridal costumes or being treated to facials or massages created a public aura of exclusivity and exquisite wellness that formed a stark contrast to the familial atmosphere and the intimate relationships between the women inside the salon.

Thus, Esma had opened the salon, she explained, to be able to combine her professional career with her familial responsibilities as the mother of a toddler. The salon seemed to provide an ideal space for that, and when on regular weekdays Esma's daughter played or watched cartoons from the salon's large sofa corner, her young cousin Gamze came to help out, and Gamze's mother, Esma's mother, or Esma's sister came by for a visit, often preparing food or hot beverages for all, the salon indeed resembled a familial space.

While the salon's official opening hours were Wednesdays to Mondays between 10 a.m. and 8 p.m., de facto it was open whenever a client arrived and Esma was at home willing to open the door. She was most busy on Fridays and at weekends, when her clients prepared to spend time with their husbands or had celebrations to attend. On nights in Ramazan, when Başakşehir became unusually lively with cultural events and outings, Esma often continued to work until well after midnight. In contrast, due to the fact that most residents had their extended families living elsewhere in the country, and many of Başakşehir's female residents chose to spend the summer months with them, during July and August the district and with it its salons emptied out. Clients came to Esma's from the immediate neighborhood, as well as from other parts of Başakşehir. With its large sofa corner and a terrace that opened out onto a garden overlooking the green *Sular Vadisi*, protected from neighbors' gazes by high walls to each side, the salon's ground floor and garden formed a space of sociality for women where food, drinks, cigarettes, and the latest neighborhood gossip were shared. Here, rumors of marital problems frequently made the rounds, with the threat of husbands taking a second (Islamic) wife being a popular conversational topic, if not a social practice. In Başakşehir, indulging in cosmetic surgery was considered shameful by many, and few of the numerous customers we talked to confided details of their own cosmetic surgery to us. However, in Esma's garden women openly shared news and rumors about female relatives', neighbors', and friends' latest types of *estetik*.

The salon's first floor consisted of several treatment rooms for more invasive procedures, such as permanent makeup, hair removal using IPL laser, facial rejuvenation, and ultrasonic slimming treatments, which, thanks to Esma's husband being a distributor of medical beauty salon equipment from East Asia, were equipped with a large assortment of the latest machinery. This floor was the realm of Esma's employee Melek, a trained veterinarian and beauty therapist in her early forties who commuted to Hayat salon from the city center three days a week. Having worked in the central upper middle-class districts of Nişantaşı, Levent, and Etiler prior to Başakşehir, Melek described her work there as a process of adjustment: from treating a population that was "developed" and "knowledgeable" about aesthetic treatments to one that had to be educated both in regard to the medical-technical possibilities of treatment and in their ability to visualize and articulate their aesthetic desires.[14] In order to satisfy her pious clientele's religious concerns about products containing lard oil or alcohol—substances that are considered forbidden in Islam— Melek had adapted her assortment of cosmetic products and now worked with herbal products exclusively. Moreover, while before she had relied on cosmetic products from Israel, after a couple of heated debates with Esma she now worked with domestic products exclusively, taking seriously her employer's and clients' political and nationalist leanings. In contrast to Esma and other members of her family, as well as most of her regular clients, who, during the many discussions we had over tea and cigarettes on the salon's terrace, came out as strong supporters of the ruling conservative government, Melek proved more critical of their political outlook and clearly presented herself to us as a visiting outsider to this particular neighborhood.

Conclusion

The "beautifying" Istanbul described in this chapter is a place where the global beauty industry forms part of the city's wider neoliberal economy of consumption and entertainment. In their quest to transform Istanbul into a center of the global (beauty) economy, entrepreneurial actors like the cosmetic surgeon Dr. Oskui employ and contribute to the mass-mediated image of Istanbul as a particularly modern, Muslim, and

---

14. Interview with Melek, December 2, 2013.

consumerist place. The aesthetically enhanced bodies of Ajda Pekkan and other mediated beauties also form part of this particular urban beautyscape, in which the shame commonly associated with active beautification and the presentation of female sexual attractiveness has more recently given way to a sense of women taking care of themselves. Within a climate of sometimes violent urban development and commercialization, the consumption of beauty services and cosmetic products, once confined to the upper echelons of society, has become more easily available and acceptable throughout the city, including among the pious and lower social strata that inhabit neighborhoods hitherto considered marginal in the urban geography of beauty.

As Kathleen Lennon (2014, np) reminds us, the city "plays an important part in 'framing' the body, and its relation to the complex constitution of its inscription, sexual desires, interactive network, projection and its production." Discussing Elizabeth Grosz's idea of a "lived spatiality" of the body (1994), Lennon argues that it is the relationship between the body and the city which "further evokes the idea of multiple forms of management and the political economy of the body bringing it to the evidences of the subjects' positionality in the city's space" (Lennon 2014, np). By describing research sites in three different parts of the city, I have aimed to show residents' varied and embodied positionalities in a heterogenous urban space. In modern central neighborhoods such as Beyoğlu, Nişantaşı, or Etiler, women's hair and beauty salons have been part of an elite space for the consumption of beauty services for almost a century. Indeed, up until today, most of Istanbul's "specialty salons," in Ossman's definition quoted previously, as well as its truly famous cosmetic surgeons, beauticians, hairdressers, or stylists, are located there or in similar districts nearby. In contrast, in the conservative working-class neighborhood of Fatih or the newly built Islamic model town of Başakşehir, beauty salons and clinics are a more recent addition and, according to common understanding, one would probably look in vain for a "specialty salon" there. Given the common devaluation of these neighborhoods as varoş, it is hardly surprising that a beautician traveling there from the city center should conceptualize and indeed fashion herself as a kind of aesthetic vanguard "educating" her clientele in both the medical-technical possibilities of aesthetic

2. From this surgeon's office overlooking Istanbul's central Taksim Square, the link between the transformation of urban bodies and spaces seemed to make perfect sense. (Claudia Liebelt)

enhancement and the ability to communicate aesthetic desires. However, given the emergence of a new Islamic middle class that is increasingly concerned with fashion and aesthetics (see chapter 7), it is only a matter of time before beauty salons in Fatih and other more peripheral or conservative middle-class districts like Başakşehir become an integral part of the urban beautyscape, already offering the styling of headscarves alongside other "special" aesthetic services in gender-segregated environments, with famous stylists, halal brands, and customers of their own.

Each of the salons described here constituted an environment set aside from the public space, yet they also functioned as a kind of micro-cosmos of the surrounding neighborhoods. In spite of their many differences, they are all rapidly changing and mixed urban spaces, where a strict division between cosmopolitan and local, secular and pious, upper and lower middle class, makes little sense. In the beauty salons of Beyoğlu, Fatih, and Başakşehir, relatively pious and more secular women met just like those of different economic means, even if only as customers and workers. Challenging the common assumptions of self-proclaimed cosmopolitans in central neighborhoods such as Beyoğlu, beauty salon workers and customers in Fatih, Başakşehir, and other more peripheral or conservative neighborhoods prove not only well informed about the latest styles and fashions, but they also display a striking willingness to establish new intimate relationships and negotiate the boundaries of moral permissiveness and bodily well-being.

2

"For a More Beautiful Turkey"

The Urban Beauty Service Sector

We [beauty experts in Turkey] produce for our country, we earn, we pay taxes, and we contribute to our family's budget and our country's economy. We want to work in our own country, we want to produce and fight for our rights. Under your leadership [addressing the president, R. T. Erdoğan], within the new Turkey, our women have become stronger, they have access to more qualified education, they join the economy and the workforce to a larger extent, they do their work in a more righteous way. Dear Mister President, we, the beauty experts, are people who deserve their certificates through extended training. [To date] our problem was the following: in spite of our training, [the decision] to work and open up a workplace was taken from us by state legislation; our salons were closed; our trade and artisanship were threatened by imprisonment. (Ayşe Aydın, speech delivered on March 29, 2017, in the Beştepe Congress Center in Ankara)

When, in late March 2017, the Turkish president granted extended rights to beauty therapists by signing new legislation in front of a large audience and in a live rally on national TV in his presidential palace, his speech was preceded by an oration from Ayşe Aydın, the president of İGDESO, the Istanbul Trade and Artisanal Chamber of Beauty Experts and Beauty Salon Employees. In an engaged and emotional speech, Aydın, who had worked for this moment for years, made the proclamation quoted above. She emphatically stressed beauty experts' contribution to creating "a more beautiful Turkey," hence the title of the event, explaining how in the past they had been discriminated against and indeed victimized (*mağdur etmek*). Aydın, a petite and energetic woman in her late forties, herself illustrated the professional achievements and careers of the 300,000 women in the Turkish beauty sector she claimed to represent that day: with no more than elementary schooling, at the age of thirteen she had entered the sector against her parents' wishes to establish one of Istanbul's first beauty salons in 1986. Like the offices of other beauty salon owners, the walls of Mrs. Aydın's office on the first floor of her salon in Istanbul's Üsküdar district bore witness to her long and successful professional career, plastered with numerous training certificates and prizes she had been awarded over the years, especially in the field of makeup art and cosmetics. In 2005, following the introduction of legislation (in 2003) that had devastating effects on the beauty sector and formed the background to her speech in the presidential palace the day it was abolished, she had organized thousands of Istanbul-based colleagues to form their own Trade and Artisanal Chamber, İGDESO, to struggle against it. Finally, she linked the economic success of the highly gendered beauty sector to wider social changes, such as increases in higher education, female entrepreneurship, and self-consciousness, which she also attributed to the conservative leadership of the ruling AKP and its project of a "new Turkey" (Yilmaz 2017).

Taking the perspective and politics of beauty therapists and salon owners as a starting point, this chapter explores the Turkish beauty sector as a particular professional niche for women and, to a lesser extent, men within the urban economy. It shows that the mushrooming sector of beauty services indeed offers economic success for some entrepreneurial women like Mrs. Aydın, quoted above, but it is also characterized by long working hours, low pay for employees, and a hierarchical order of labor, where working one's way up can take years, even decades. To explain the sense of victimization in the speech quoted above, I start by providing the background to the regulatory change in 2017 before then going on to describe the emergence of an urban economy of beauty from the perspective of beauty therapists.

In her book on American nail salons, *The Managed Hand* (2010), Milliann Kang criticizes the feminist writer Naomi Wolf, who coined the notion of the "third shift" to describe the beauty work that women are expected to complete after their first shift as wage earners and their second shift as homemakers, for ignoring "the many women who do not do their own beauty work. Instead, they pass off sizable portions of this third shift onto the shoulders of less-privileged women" (2010, 15). To distinguish between the two, in this book I will distinguish between beauty work and beauty *service* work, the latter referring to the commercialized exchange between a beauty therapist and her customer. In New York, where Kang conducted research on nail salons, these were typically operated and staffed by Asian, particularly Korean, immigrant women, racialized as subservient and caring within the American public sphere. As we will see, in Istanbul beauty service work is likewise gendered and delegated to particular groups of women, who are classified as uneducated newcomers to the city.

Regulating Beauty

Up until the 1980s, the beauty sector in Turkey was barely visible and mostly unregulated, seen as a marginal kind of side business in the male-dominated sector of hairdressing (*kuaförlük*). Thus, I was frequently told that up until the mid-1980s there simply were no beauty salons in Istanbul, and women who wanted to have their body hair removed or their nails done outside of the home resorted to the "ladies" employed in the back rooms of hair salons for women, or the local public bath. It was more common, however, for women neighbors to gather in each other's homes for monthly beauty sessions, where they tended to each other's bodies over shared food, rounds of tea, and the latest neighborhood gossip. Women of somewhat greater economic means had manicurists or body hair removal experts visit them in their private homes to avoid the seemingly unhygienic environment of the hair salon back rooms. In addition, I was told about a female dermatologist and a physical therapist who were considered beauty experts and who were patronized by upper-class women in the center-city elite neighborhood of Nişantaşı.

Parallel to the global boom in aesthetic products and services, the 1990s and early 2000s saw the development of an increasingly differentiated beauty service sector in Istanbul, with private beauty clinics and salons, fitness centers, nail spas, and waxing studios opening up all over the city. Public health officials and the medical profession regarded this boom with suspicion, repeatedly warning about beauty salons as non-medical and nonsterile environments. For example, in 1998 the Ministry of Health warned that beauty salons, due to their "unhygienic environment," were contributing to the spread of infections such as HIV/AIDS or hepatitis (*Hürriyet* 1998). In 2001 a member of the Istanbul Medical Chamber's Honorary Society, Prof. Selçuk Erez, told the national daily *Hürriyet* that most complaints they collected against the "medical" sector were indeed filed against beauticians (*estetikçiler*), some of them of a "truly scary" dimension (quoted from Tuna 2001). Accordingly, in May 2003, partly also to comply with the requirements of the European Union that were demanded from Turkey as part of its integration process, the Turkish Ministry of Health set out to regulate the booming beauty market with state regulation no. 25106.[1]

This regulation first of all introduced a distinction between "beauty salons" (*güzellik salonları*) and "medical centers for body aesthetics," or beauty centers (*estetik merkezleri*), requiring that beauty salon owners were to be state-trained as "beauty experts" (*estetik uzmanları*) and beauty centers were to be established exclusively by medical personnel, that is, physicians or surgeons. Most importantly, the regulation provided a long list of treatments and products defined as "medical" and hence to be performed or prescribed by medical personnel and in medical centers for body aesthetics only, including all kinds of laser treatments, cauterization, and cryotherapy; treatments with alpha hydroxy acids (for facial treatments) of a concentration of over 35 percent, as well as the use of derivatives; the treatment of visible vessels, of acne, of skin peeling procedures, of hair transplantation; and any kind of injection for therapeutic or cosmetic reasons, as well as the treatment of by-effects caused by these injections; and finally weight loss procedures were to be scheduled and handled by medical personnel or trained dieticians. Inspections by Ministry of Health officials were announced, to take place at least every six months (*Hürriyet* 2003).

---

1. See cf. Resmi Gazete, Güzellik ve Estetik Amaçlı Sağlık Kuruluşları Hakkında Yönetmelik, May 12, 2003, Regulation no. 25106.

Regulation no. 25106 shook the neophyte beauty sector to its foundations and a presumably large, albeit unknown number of salons were eventually forced to close down. Only a few of those owners who successfully ran beauty salons actually possessed the required certificates as beauty experts, which necessitated formal training within the recently formed national Education Career and Counseling Center (Merkezi Eğitim Kurumları, MEB), or a state-recognized five-year master craftsmanship (*ustalık*), which—a great hindrance for many practicing beauty therapists—is made available to secondary school graduates only. Some more cunning beauty salon owners apparently started to pay physicians or surgeons to function officially as directors, while unofficially they continued to run their establishments themselves.

It was hardly surprising, then, that accidents and injuries allegedly caused by insufficiently trained beauty experts continued to make the headlines, especially burns resulting from laser treatment used for depilation.[2] Thus, while beauty experts were able to train in the use of so-called IPL (Intense Pulsed Light) technology in salons, some apparently continued to handle more efficient laser equipment, the use of which was restricted to medical personnel under the new legislation. Rather confusingly, however, in the salons, IPL technology was commonly referred to as the "laser" (*lazer*), and few clients seemed to be aware of the difference, not to speak of the legislation. Thus, laser epilation continued to be commonly advertised and demanded by clients in beauty salons, whether the technology actually used was based on laser rays or not. Accordingly, beauticians' continued use of laser technology and their administration of injections for cosmetic use were subject to repeated criticism from the Turkish Society of Plastic Reconstructive and Aesthetic Surgeons (TPRECD). In 2008, the Society's president warned that in the beauty sector things "had gone out of control," with Botox injections and other fillers coming to be applied in "hair salons, massage salons and private homes" (quoted from *Zaman* 2008). Likewise, during an interview in 2014, the

---

2. *Hürriyet*, for example, reported on women who suffered second-degree burns from illegally performed laser depilation in the cities of Antalya (*Hürriyet* 2008) and Denizli (Akkir 2009).

acting president complained that one of the greatest problems in the sector were the beauticians who went beyond their limits:

> I know that some of them use this [laser] equipment. This is a law-breaking activity, and most of all it is very dangerous for the patient. . . . We're trying . . . to tell them [the wider public]: "Please beware of this kind of activity, please make sure they are doctors!" because, they [beauticians] sometimes behave like a doctor and this is another kind of problem! Tell them you are a beautician, and a beautician should behave differently from a doctor, and not exceeding his [*sic*] limits. . . . When people have burns, they approach us to have it fixed. . . . There is no—I mean, there *is* legislation, but there is no control.[3]

In March 2010, the Turkish Ministry of Health renewed its 2003 regulation and required that beauty centers employ at least one surgeon or else employ a physician as the responsible director, and it also announced that it would close down any beauty center that did not comply with these rules after September 10 (*Hürriyet* 2010a). However, as beauty experts repeatedly pointed out, due to their specialized experience, they were often better trained in handling equipment for cosmetic use, and the employment of physicians did not guarantee successful treatment—quite the contrary.

As more invasive aesthetic treatments, including cosmetic surgery, became increasingly widespread in Turkey during the early 2000s, news about aesthetic accidents and mistakes performed by surgeons likewise increased, and the wider public learned about permanent scars, "fallen" nose tips, sagging breasts, and intense pain following aesthetic procedures.[4] One of the more prominent cases was the death of Berna Şallı, a young woman who died of heart failure during fat-removal (liposuction) surgery at a private hospital in Antalya in 2003. It was reported that Şallı had chosen the surgery to enhance her looks shortly before getting married. It later became clear that the surgeon, the father of a former Miss Turkey and Miss Universe, had been inexperienced in this kind of surgery and had hoped to use Şallı to build up his reputation as a cosmetic surgeon

---

3. Interview with Ismail Kuran, July 10, 2014.
4. See, for example, *Hürriyet* 2006, Karataş 2010.

(Tosun and Aktepe 2003). Cases such as Şallı's, sensationalist media coverage of aesthetic accidents, especially if these involved celebrities, and the criminalization of some of the sector's everyday practices contributed to the image of the beauty sector as a shady business, often operating on the edges of legality.

Rather than enforce better treatment, state regulations more often contributed to the beauty sector's public image that it was a dirty business; for example, by forcing salon owners to make arrangements with physicians or surgeons, who more often than not had little to do with the beauty sector. While many salon owners and beauty service workers chose to retrain to become state-recognized "beauty experts" (*estetik uzmanları*), many others, as the following will show, lacked sufficient schooling and remained stuck in the lower segments of the sector instead of working their way up in the hierarchy, which for many had been a major incentive for entering the sector in the first place.

(Wo)Manning the Beauty Sector

Similar to what Kang (2010) describes in her study of Asian, particularly Korean, nail salons in New York, in Istanbul commercial beauty work is structured by differences between beauty service workers and their clients in terms of class and cultural background, with many beauty service workers being first- or second-generation domestic migrants from other parts of Turkey. Not least, the beauty sector is highly gendered, with a clear division of labor between male hairdressers and female beauty therapists, including manicurists, makeup artists, cosmeticians, massage therapists, and those who specialize in the removal of body hair by threading, sugaring, or waxing.[5] While until recently male hairdressers served both

---

5. Sugaring or sugar waxing (*ağda*) is an ancient method of body hair removal in the region, which has recently become rare in commercial settings, but is still commonly used in private homes and some neighborhood salons (figure 4). For this, the sugar paste is heated, applied, and pressed to the skin with a strip of cloth and quickly removed, taking the hair along with it. In commercial salons, the utilized paste is increasingly made of wax products rather than of sugar and other natural ingredients, such as lemon juice. Whereas threading, the removal of hair by a twisted thread, is commonly applied

men and women, although in different establishments, in recent years an increasing number of women have trained as hairdressers for women. Female hairdressers are crucial for the gender-segregated women-only salons that can be found in increasing numbers in more conservative urban neighborhoods.

As elsewhere, and as a particularly feminized and "bodily" kind of service work, beauty service work in Istanbul is socially devalued, with beauty service workers often working long shifts for barely more than the minimum wage.[6] They are commonly seen as school dropouts from the lower social strata of society with little formal education. While beauty service workers normally use the formal form of address with their customers, they are often addressed as "girls," even in the case of married, adult women. The popular imagination of beauty service workers in Turkey is shaped by classical films showing them as beautiful, poor but proud girls who easily fall victim to sexual harassment, for example, by the sons of their rich clients. This is the story of manicurist Nermin in the 1962 Turkish box office hit *Acı Hayat* [Bitter Life], who "eavesdrops on the intimate secrets of the rich but has no place among them" (Dönmez-Colin 2014, 17). Given these connotations of the manicurist in particular as a "girl" of little means and training, it is hardly surprising that women performing professional beauty service work in Turkey today commonly prefer to be referred to as beauty therapists (*güzellik estetisiyenleri*) rather than manicurists, even when they perform manicures almost exclusively.

While the beauty sector was certainly considered respectable for men trained as hairdressers (*kuaförler*), for many decades it was less so for female beauty therapists. This stemmed from a more general discouragement of women's participation in the labor market in a patriarchal society (see chapter 6), but also from the fact that beauty work was seen as shameful for women due to its intimate bodily nature, namely the handling of

---

around the eyebrows and in other parts of the face, waxing or sugar waxing is preferred for removing hair from larger areas of skin.

6. In early 2021, the Turkish minimum wage was 2,826 TRY, approximately the same amount in US dollars, US$400, as compared to December 2014 when the interview took place.

foreigners' bodies. For example, the president of the Trade and Artisanal Chamber of Istanbul Hairdressers for Women and Manicurists (İKKMO), Oktay Erkal, explained that up until the 1990s, "respectable" families would not allow their daughters to work and would definitely discourage them from entering the beauty sector.[7] Given these structural conditions, beauty therapists' routes into the sector at different moments in time are telling of the changes in the beauty sector and its reputation, as well as in the wider society.

For this book, I interviewed eighteen female beauty therapists, including seven beauty salon owners, as well as four male hairdressers, two female salon co-owners without training in beauty service work, and five women formerly employed as beauty therapists. While the male hairdressers had all completed a three-year apprenticeship training (*kalfalık*) that qualified them for the task of cutting and styling women's hair, the professional careers of the female beauty sector workers were more diverse. Even those among them who were trained as apprentices in hairdressing were, in contrast to the male hairdressers, beauty therapists in a more comprehensive way, typically also performing body hair removal, massages, makeup art, and—especially in smaller salons without additional manicurists—manicures and pedicures as part of their daily routine. For some of these tasks they had received training, sometimes in the form of one- or two-day workshops offered by private beauty schools or the companies whose cosmetics or equipment they used, while other tasks they had learned hands-on.

Of the twenty-three formerly and currently employed female beauty therapists interviewed for this book, more than half (thirteen) had entered the sector early on in their lives, as teenagers or children as young as seven years old. Seven of them had started by working in a family salon, typically alongside their mothers (in five cases), fathers or uncles (one each). At least six had dropped out of school after elementary school—that is, when aged eleven or twelve—to support their families economically with what they earned in the salon. Four did so after their families moved to

7. Interview with Oktay Erkal, April 9, 2014.

Istanbul from southeast Anatolia or from abroad, as was the case with Mrs. Hilmiyye, aged eighty-one when I met her, who immigrated to Turkey from Bulgaria alongside her parents in 1951 and considered herself the first female and oldest practicing hairdresser of Istanbul.

These women often described their entry into the sector as something that had "just happened," with some of them explaining that they were attracted to and fascinated by beauty salons from an early age. A case in point was Şule Hanım, a married housewife in her mid-fifties whom I met as the regular customer of a beauty salon in the conservative district of Başakşehir on the urban periphery, where she lived with her son and husband. Şule Hanım had grown up in a family of poor rural to urban immigrants in the Istanbul working-class neighborhood of Aksaray. When she was ten her father died, which left her, as the older of two children, in the position of seeking employment:

> There was a salon on my way to school, and I was always curious about it. Whenever I passed, I sneaked in [and wondered]: "What are they doing there," "What's happening inside," etc. It was a large salon, two floors, they had manicure chairs, and it was always busy inside. Women removed their shoes and scarves, and there was an intimate and chatty atmosphere. It was a very fascinating place for me! So, one day on my way from school, I saw that they had put up a sign in the window looking for an apprentice, something like "helper needed." So I asked myself, "Why not give it a try?" I took my heart in both hands and entered . . .

The quote shows that rather than solely being pushed by dire economic needs, young beauty service workers often actively chose employment in this particular sector, and like Şule, many recounted their initial fascination with beauty salons as places where women were visibly transformed in an "intimate" and "chatty" atmosphere, surrounded by the posters of mundane beauties. Indeed, in many of the salons I visited during research, young girls or teenagers were still helping out with odd jobs, such as serving clients tea, cleaning up, or assisting hairdressers by washing hair or handing over hair clips, especially during school holidays. More often than not they were the salon owners' or beauty therapists' own daughters, cousins, or nieces, who hoped not only to earn some pocket money, pick up skills, or pass the time, but also to be treated to beauty services by co-workers and more generally partake in the salon's atmosphere.

The remaining ten beauty therapists who participated in this study entered the sector later in life, typically in their early twenties. One of them, Sibel Hanım, a salon owner in the conservative neighborhood of Fatih, opened her own salon after changed regulations in the medical sector forced her to close the independent birthing center she had established as a midwife unless she integrated it into a formal hospital structure. Since she refused to work within the gender-mixed environment of a hospital, where she would have been forced to remove her headscarf, Sibel retrained as a beauty expert. As beauty work also dealt with women's bodies in an intimate kind of service work, Sibel considered it close enough to her profession, midwifery. Alongside Sibel worked Sevil, a former makeup salesperson, who entered the sector in her early twenties after her father died and the family could no longer provide for her college education in English comparative literature.

At least four other women entered the sector after a divorce or, as was the case with Fatma Hanım, aged sixty-two when I first met her as a manicurist in Belladonna, a large city-center salon (see chapter 1), after their husbands were no longer able to provide for the family as sole breadwinners. Fatma Hanım and her family had migrated to Istanbul from the southeastern province of Malatya when her husband's small business went bankrupt in the mid-1990s. Job-hunting in Istanbul, Fatma Hanım was able to rely on the two months of training as a manicurist she had received more than twenty years previously, shortly before she got married, as well as on her hometown networks in Istanbul. Belladonna, where she started working, was owned by a team of brothers from Malatya, who also provided employment for several other compatriots, all of whom had moved to Istanbul in the hope of better economic prospects. The fact that Fatma Hanım's story is in no way singular can be illustrated by an observation shared by Didem, a teacher of municipal training courses on beauty service work. Describing her students in Kavacık, a former squatter settlement on the outskirts of Istanbul, she said: "There are those who came from Anatolia, perhaps to get married here, or the husband is unemployed—and they are in economic difficulties, or else think that they can find a part-time job or learn something. [They reason that the training provided in the course is] "something I can rely on when things go wrong," or "something I can do once in a while to earn money," so they think "I'll go there and finish the course, and then I will find a job."[8]

Another reason for women to choose beauty service work, especially in the case of Didem's students, who rarely managed to be formally employed in salons but rather exchanged their services with neighbors, friends, and relatives, was its compatibility with childcare. As Kang remarks in her study of Korean nail salons (2010, 72ff), the fact that women choose entrepreneurship because they expect it to be easier to combine with childcare has largely been overlooked in the scholarly literature. In fact, several beauty salon owners felt that salon ownership provided them with more flexibility in arranging childcare and even allowed them to take their smaller children to work with them. Among them was Elif Karakışla, a former advertising manager who gave up a well-paid position with the prestigious *Hürriyet* newspaper to open a beauty salon close to where she lived. On her website, she describes her decision in the following words:

> It was toward the end of 2007. It was a time when I started wondering what my life was all about. My daughter had just turned two, she was desperately waiting for me to return, while I was commuting between *Hürriyet* newspaper in Güneşli [on the European side of Istanbul] and Erenköy [on its Asian side], struggling like crazy in the traffic, attempting to reach our home without being involved in any accident. . . . [She goes on to explain how much she loved her job; however] all this traffic and the green eyes of this beautiful baby waiting for me led me to take the decision to change my life. So, one morning I woke up, and told myself "Up until today, I learned whatever it takes to start anew, so I will open my wings and start flying." It was like in the story of Hezârfen Çelebi [legendary seventeenth-century Ottoman aviator]: either I do this, or I die. But I don't want to tell myself that I didn't try. So, like anyone who takes care of themselves, I asked myself: "What am I good in?" Facing the mirror, I was looking for an answer: "I don't know . . . I am trained in marketing, CRM [customer relationship management],

8. Interview with Didem, April 3, 2014.

public relations. And I love shoes and cosmetics." So I told myself: Forget about shoes, let's open up a beauty centre![9]

By the time I visited Elif's salon, her daughter was almost ten years old but continued to spend time at the salon after school, chatting with clients, lounging in a corner of the large sofa in the salon's waiting area playing games on her tablet, or watching TV. Like other salon owners, Elif had named the salon after her daughter. Another young beauty service worker, Esma, who had previously been employed in her mother's salon, opened her own salon after giving birth to her first child, reasoning that, given the lack of affordable childcare below the age of three, this was the only way for her to continue practicing her profession.

To sum up, women's life circumstances upon entering the sector are diverse, and to reduce them to the economic alone fails to explain the multiplicity of their reasons. Thus, some research participants stressed their fascination with beauty salons as intimate and mundane female spaces, or simply their love of cosmetics. Despite its stereotypical depiction as an employment niche for poor, uneducated women, the urban beauty sector provided meaningful and viable employment and, in rare cases, a career prospect for women from diverse social strata. As a highly gendered sector that until recently required little formal training, beauty service work offered an employment niche especially for those whose exceptional life circumstances, including migration, divorce, or the death of the family's male breadwinner, forced them to take up employment. This, as the following section will show, has changed little even amid attempts to professionalize and standardize the sector.

The Skills of Beauty Service Work

Contrary to the image of the unskilled, uneducated school dropout, beauty therapists commonly emphasized the specialized knowledge necessary for working in beauty salons. Like Ayşe Aydın's office wall described above, training certificates and prizes were generally displayed prominently in

9. See cf. Karakışla 2014. Kendi Kanatlarımı Denedim; Beni Melissima'ya Uçurdu! http://www.melissima.com.tr (February 3, 2021).

salons, most often in the entrance area right behind the reception desk. While these documents spoke of beauty salon owners' and employees' formal accomplishments, emphasizing professionalism toward clients and legitimacy to visiting state inspectors, in conversations about their profession, beauty therapists typically emphasized skills that could not be learned in formal training, but were highly personal, embodied, and experiential. Thus, long-term salon owners and beauty therapists, who had entered the sector early on in their lives, commonly spoke about beauty service work as a *craft* that was best learned as an apprentice (*kalfa*, from the Arabic *khalîfa*). Indeed, salon owners commonly stated their preference for employees who had been trained as apprentices, in contrast to graduates from recently opened beauty schools. For example, the president of the sector's chamber in Istanbul, Ayşe Aydın, claimed that she would not even consider employing someone if this person had less than four years' experience, no matter whether or not they had a college diploma: "I've seen college graduates who couldn't even hold a thread properly! Every middle-aged woman with some experience knows better how to put on makeup than they do—unfortunately. That's why practice is so important."[10]

Given the formalization in training since the early 2000s and the subsequent mushrooming of private beauty schools offering training within the framework of the national Education Career and Counseling Center, the lack of young apprentices who learned the profession hands-on from a master was widely lamented by hair and beauty salon owners. Among them was Nazan, who sixteen years previously had opened a salon in Fatih, after having herself entered the sector at age nine, first as a helper in her uncle's barbershop and later as an apprentice. Asked how she had chosen the ten women she currently employed, she complained:

> In this sector, things have become difficult. These days, everyone wants to study. Young people, when you tell them "clean up here, do this, do that"—they no longer accept this. They go to school and they think they know everything. . . . But this is not a profession that can be learned through books. In fact, there's no advantage to study this profession at

10. Interview with Ayşe Aydın, April 22, 2014. The following quotations by Ayşe Aydın are also taken from this interview.

school—you need to take things into your own hands. There's a big difference between learning things by doing and by studying things from books, don't you agree? In the books they tell you about one way, but in reality things are much more complex . . . [11]

Similar to what Nazan describes as a kind of impertinence, owners and former apprentices alike typically characterized beauty school graduates as "girls" who "put on airs" and who, as also exemplified by Nazan's statement, could no longer be ordered around. In some salons there were tensions between those who had trained as apprentices and the beauty school graduates, who considered themselves more professional due to their formalized training. This was the case in a nail bar in an upmarket neighborhood, where Saliha, of the ten manicurists there, was the only one trained as a *kalfa*. She claimed:

> Most of the young manicurists today, they are trained in beauty schools, and they put on airs, without really knowing anything about the profession. . . . They go to beauty school carelessly. Nowadays, when you get an assistant girl, they say, "I am a manicurist" after three months of training. I mean, what can you possibly see within three months? . . . In school, most of what you learn is theoretical. I mean, for three years, you have classes like mathematics, religious culture, or moral education. Then, during the last year, they show you like how to hold the tweezers and how things are done in practice! (*laughs*) Except that they don't show you *all* the details . . .

In spite of her greater experience, which was generally recognized by the other manicurists who sought Saliha's advice whenever their clients arrived with a nail infection or fungus, in the everyday workings within the salon Saliha often felt she was treated dismissively. Thus, she had been put in charge of the orderliness of the salon, a task she felt had been given to her not only because she was an orderly and responsible person, but also because she was a veteran in the sector as compared with the others and therefore was above them in the hierarchy within the salon. However, the

11. Interview with Nazan, December 11, 2013.

beauty school graduates, she complained, seemed to think it was her task to clean up after them, and the fact that they often left their open lunchboxes lying around in the kitchen or did not put back the nail polish they had used produced much conflict between them. Against the background of these everyday tensions, Saliha emphasized that as an apprentice,

> you learn from your master, and most of all you learn respect [saygı] toward him and toward the clients. . . . Those who get their training in beauty schools, they don't pay respect to their elders. This was an obligatory thing for us [apprentices]. We were careful about how we acted around them, how we looked, and we could never have spoken back to our master. But people aren't like that anymore. The new generation is really different. Communication between employees and customers is difficult to teach too. When you are trained as an apprentice, you have to do your job, no matter what it is.

In the anthropological literature, apprenticeship has been defined as "the means of imparting specialized knowledge to a new generation of practitioners," especially in the field where this knowledge is based on "implicit knowledge to be acquired through long-term observation and experience" (Coy 1989, xi). As such, it commonly occurs in specializations "that contain some element that cannot be communicated, but can only be experienced" (Coy 1989, 2), and is typically described as a particular "way of knowing" or "learning to see." Not least, it is also described as a way of "structuring economic and social relationships between oneself and other practitioners, between oneself and one's clients" (Coy 1989, xii).

Those who stressed the merits of apprenticeship focused on all of these aspects, and especially emphasized what Saliha calls respect (saygı) toward clients and more generally of the hierarchy within the salon. In some of the larger salons, where an older usta, master, worked alongside other specialized employees and possibly apprentices or trainees, hierarchies were indeed marked. In many salons, new employees who had not yet completed proper training or were not considered experienced enough started from a position as çaycı, named after the çaycı's main task, serving tea (çay). One such çaycı was Deniz, a woman in her mid-forties, who had immigrated to Turkey three years previously from Tiflis, Georgia, and worked in a large salon in the city center. When she was not busy cleaning, serving clients tea, or helping them into and out of their jackets, she could be found sitting next to one of the manicurists, Fatma, watching how she did manicures, pedicures, or facial hair removal. Deniz hoped to one day rise in the hierarchy of the salon to become a manicurist like Fatma, who had been the salon's çaycı for over a year prior to Deniz's arrival.

Like young apprentices, çaycıs are at the bottom of the social hierarchy in salons, earning less and being delegated the most unwanted jobs, such as cleaning. However, once they rise in the hierarchy of the place, their hard work is acknowledged not only by a higher income, but also by their being recognized as properly trained craftsmen. It becomes clear that craftsmanship is therefore not just about learning certain skills, but also refers to a code of normative behavior, what Saliha and many other former kalfalar commonly described as respect.

Another aspect illustrated by Deniz's doings in the salon was that watching, and indeed watching for long periods of time and over and over again, was regarded as crucial for her training. Indeed, experienced beauty service workers commonly emphasized a sensual skill that Cristina Grasseni (2004), in her work on cattle-breeders, calls "skilled vision." Skilled vision, according to Grasseni, is a bodily sense that enables cattle-breeders to assess cattle by looking at them and touching them. Like other senses, she writes, this vision "needs educating and training in a relationship of apprenticeship and within an ecology of practice" (Grasseni 2004, 41). From such a perspective, the skilled vision of an artisan craftsman is an everyday, multi-sensorial practice, a "way of looking at the world" (Grasseni 2004, 41). In a similar way, beauty therapists insisted that their professional practice shaped their everyday views of the world in a very concrete way, namely in the way they looked at their clients and indeed at fellow human beings more generally. This became clear, for example, when one day, toward the end of our interview, a long-term beauty salon owner shared the following observation:

> I mean, you can only do this profession if you love it. For example, I walk
> down the street, and I see everybody's blackheads. Now [turning toward

my research assistant], I am seeing yours. And your hair!—it *needs* to be colored! [*Turning to me*] Your eyebrows need shaping, darling, they're completely disorderly! [*Smiles*] What can I do? It's my profession. Our profession is all about [scrutinizing] people . . .

Indeed, during the municipal training courses I attended on makeup, manicure/pedicure, and facial treatment, the extended analysis or scrutinizing of a test person's skin and nails typically formed a first step in both training and treatment. While for professional beauty workers seeing and remarking upon the flaws on customers' bodies was certainly also part of their sales strategy, the incredible attentiveness to even the smallest bodily details that many of them revealed was indeed remarkable. Thus, beauty therapists we regularly visited and who sometimes treated us with an eyebrow shaping, a blow-dry, or a manicure were especially watchful of any services we might have consumed elsewhere. Thus, when one day I showed up in one of our regular research sites in Fatih, two weeks after one of its employees, Azra, had shaped my eyebrows, the owner, with one critical look at my face from behind her reception desk, shouted out: "Who did your eyebrows, darling?" When I replied that I had been to another salon in the city center, she scolded: "They have no idea about doing eyebrows there! You should have [Azra] do it. They took too much from one side!"

Not least, skills in customer relationship management were crucial for beauty therapists. This was especially true since the gap in the skills and knowledge of beautification between customers and beauty therapists was commonly seen as becoming ever narrower. With an increase in the number of women's magazines in Turkish, YouTube tutorials on makeup or facial treatments, and a long personal history of salon visits, beauty therapists found their customers to be increasingly knowledgeable and indeed picky when it came to beauty service work. Comparing the current situation with the 1990s in the conservative district of Fatih, where she first ran a beauty salon and was now employed as a therapist, Neriman said: "People are much more informed these days! When we opened our salon [in the late 1990s], you had women coming who didn't know a thing about beauty. So, you had to teach them everything. Now they know exactly what they want and what they want you to do."[12]

To sum up, beauty service work relies on specialized skills that are deeply embodied and personal, and rely on long-term experience. Moreover, like any kind of body service work, beauty service work is embedded in social relationships that may be based on respect, trust, and intimacy, but that also contribute to the immensely stressful daily routine of beauty service work. This was especially true, as the following will show, in the emotional work done with customers.

Becoming *Güzin Abla*: Emotional Work with Customers

Dealing with customers was commonly described as the most rewarding, yet also the most demanding and stressful aspect of beauty service work. As a highly gendered service, professional beauty work relies on what Hochschild, in her study of female flight attendants, has analyzed as "emotional labor," namely "the management of feeling to create a publicly observable facial and bodily display" (2003, 7n). While beauty-service workers received no formal training in the management of customers' emotions, all research participants emphasized that their success depended on exactly that; namely, to provide their customers with a sense of being at their ease, properly cared for, and looking their best. This means that, even when faced with difficult, demeaning, and sometimes impossible demands from customers, beauty therapists are expected to repress their own feelings, desires, and thoughts and, as Saliha quoted above put it, "do [their] job, no matter what it is." In most cases this required even more than just keeping one's countenance and performing the requested service, as explained by Tümay, a middle-aged salon owner in the conservative district of Başakşehir:

> People don't come here only to become more pretty. For example, they feel down, and they are like: "I should get a manicure," or "some facial care," and then they come here, and they feel relaxed. There are people like that. I mean, *all* women are like that, including me! For example,

12. Interview with Neriman, June 10, 2014.

you are bored at home, or there is some tension at home, so you go and have your hair dyed, or you get it cut, or you get a facial, or a massage. It's as simple as that. So, in fact, we are like psychologists here![13]

The fact that women requested beauty services when they felt down, bored, or lonely and sought to strengthen their self-esteem through beautification, pampering, and the company of someone to take care of them was common knowledge among beauty salon workers and has in fact been emphasized in research on Turkish hair salons (Cantek 2017). While Tümay, in the quote above, readily identifies with her customers' attempts to use pampering body work to uplift their spirits and indeed naturalizes it as a strategy that "all women" employ, others, especially if they did not possess the means to engage in pampering body work, were more critical of this aspect of their profession. Talking to us about customers who, over a manicure, managed to "pour their hearts out," Fatma, who was rather reticent while working on her customers' nails, jokingly remarked, referring to Güzin Sayar (1921–2006), Turkey's most popular columnist for readers' letters from the early 1960s to the late 1990s, "I've become a kind of Güzin *Abla*!"[14]

Being involved in their customers' lives and listening to their troubles could indeed put an immense burden on beauty service workers. Sitting on the terrace of her daughter's beauty salon, Hiranur remembered the time when she had run her own salon in the newly constructed suburban district of Başakşehir, working alongside her two daughters for over ten years. Running the salon, she said,

you really get to know the people around you. Believe me, you put up with so many people. . . . Sometimes, people who come here, they have so many problems and [when they tell you,] you have to stand upright and continue doing your job. Sometimes you go back home crying because of their problems. We have seen so much in fourteen years. We've gotten

13. Interview with Tümay, November 4, 2013.

14. Interview with Fatma, March 19, 2014. *Abla*, older sister in Turkish, is an affectionate nickname that points to Güzin Sayar's recognized status as an intimate confidante with the Turkish public.

sad and happy with our clients. . . . We've witnessed so many things that we continue to carry around with us. Sometimes we've gone back home and can't sleep. I sometimes appear like I am a very tough person, which is true, of course (*laughs*), but from time to time I really felt depressed because of my job.[15]

Similar to what Hochschild (2003) describes as emotional labor, Hiranur pointed out that, while tending to her customers, she was expected "to stand upright" and continue her job, sustaining an outward countenance even though customers' problems might make her want to cry. While Hiranur had developed the public persona of a "tough person" as the successful manager of an enterprise with several employees, her inability to sleep and her feelings of depression after returning home show that what she witnessed, as well as having to act professional while witnessing it, affected her deeply. During the interview, she continued this line of thought after a brief pause:

I will tell you this: being jolly and able to make other people contented is a very important thing in our profession. I think, as a salon owner, you should *never* reflect your negative feelings onto your customers. I am such a person. No matter what, I am a person who will stand upright while I'm working. I don't give up easily. I have to stand upright so that I can create a connection between the customer and my salon. That's my bread and butter [*ekmek teknesi*]! Running a salon is a very special thing. Your perspective matters. I never underrated anyone. It doesn't matter who she is or how much she has. Each customer is the same for me. I chat with everyone and make them feel contented. And they come again, for sure.

Hiranur's account shows the significance of emotional labor as essential for her livelihood, i.e., for running the salon and making her customers contented. Making customers contented also meant creating long-term relationships with them, relationships that in some instances went beyond the professional encounter in the salon, and in Hiranur's case were

15. Interview with Hiranur, February 20, 2014. The following quotations by Hiranur are also taken from this interview.

intricately linked to the social structure of the newly constructed neighborhood where she lived and used to work. Not least, creating customer satisfaction and long-term relationships depended on her being jolly and never showing negative feelings. Hiranur's repeated use of the phrase "standing upright" points in an almost visceral way to the difficulties and costs of such a posture for her.

Finally, Hiranur's professional ethos required her to treat her customers equally, regardless of their social, economic, or political status. For Hiranur, a fashionista, who in this conservative neighborhood stood out visually, arriving at her daughter's salon in colorful dresses and high heels, this had not been an easy task. It became clear that the tiring emotional labor with customers eventually led her to close the salon and, at the age of forty-nine, retire. Hiranur's account certainly spoke of the human cost of emotional labor and salon work more generally. After the interview with Hiranur, and after the recorder had been switched off, Hiranur's daughter Esma joined us for a cigarette on the terrace of her salon. Hiranur and Esma then recounted one particularly disturbing incident in their shared working life, one they referred to as "the incident with the long-haired woman." This woman had entered their salon in a desperate mood one night and asked to have all her hair shaved off. When Esma, who was serving her, acted surprised and attempted to dissuade her, the customer grabbed a pair of scissors and with a determined look on her face cut a long strand of hair. Then she started crying. Since she was their last customer that night, Hiranur and Esma prepared tea and were eventually told the story behind the woman's salon visit. She had arrived after a violent attack on her by her husband and wanted to have her hair shaved so that he could no longer pull her by it. The night ended with the customer returning to her husband with a fashionable short hairstyle and Hiranur and her daughter unable to sleep. Even years after the incident had happened, Esma and her mother were still visibly disturbed by it.

In an attempt to lift our spirits, Hiranur then recounted a second, this time more comical salon incident also involving a long-haired woman. In fact, it involved the daughter of Hiranur's close friend, who entered the salon one day to have her hair "just trimmed." The daughter, about the same age as Esma, had long and beautiful hair and obviously triggered feelings of jealousy in her. Hiranur laughingly recounted how Esma cut her hair "real short." Esma, who was obviously able to take her mother's teasing, blushingly added, "She had said 'just trim it,' like two fingers-length only!" Even though the women shared the story as a joke, it was obvious that they agreed on the fact that things had gone terribly wrong that day and that Esma, a young apprentice at the time, had violated the code of conduct that was at the heart of their professional practice.

Within this code of conduct, customers were never to be treated as female competitors or rivals with whom one compared oneself or who triggered affective responses such as jealousy or disgust, but rather as persons for whom one subsumed one's own feelings. As Sevil, a middle-aged beauty therapist and makeup artist, put it, the beauty therapist's task was to

> bring out the best in her. Something even the person herself cannot see. For example, someone enters here, saying: "Oh dear, I feel horrible today . . ." and when she leaves, all beautified, she is happy, full of joy. [If they tell you:] "I've been everywhere, and nothing showed any results, I hate all of these treatments," what do I do with such a person? I need to treat her in her entirety. . . . So that she *feels* she is a beautiful person, pleasant-looking [*hoş*], full of self-confidence, happy when she looks into the mirror, [someone, who] knows how to take care of herself. So, you also need to motivate her. What we do is also a kind of motivational training, isn't it? (*laughs*)[16]

While to bring out "the best in her" clearly has to do with one's skill in transforming the customer visibly, it encompasses more than an artistic act, being rooted in a deeper kind of insight into human nature. Professional beauty service work, in Sevil's words, is based on this ability to see a customer in their entirety and to motivate them to feel the change effected by her. As illustrated by a fictive customer entering the salon with the feeling that no treatment could effectively help her, Sevil showed that beauty service work required immense tact and the intuition to effect a change that was not only visible on the surface, but indeed could be felt as a personal transformation. As I will go on to show in the following

16. Interview with Sevil, March 20, 2014.

chapters when analyzing the perspectives of customers as well as of actual customer-therapist interactions, more often than not professional beauty therapists indeed seemingly succeeded in making their customers leave the salon feeling happier, more self-confident, and beautiful.

This required an ability and a personal commitment not everyone was capable of. Numerous times throughout the research I was told that "you cannot do this job without loving it!" Among those who emphasized love as a requirement for beauty service work was Tülay, a middle-aged teacher of municipal training classes on makeup and facial therapy. She repeated the theme of women arriving at salons in need of care and pampering, saying

> Your task is to make these people happy! If you don't *love* people, you should not enter this profession. Also, if you don't like to touch people, this is nothing for you. . . . I *love* to deal with people. When I did my first facial, I said to myself "What a wonderful thing!" I'm removing black-heads, I cleanse the skin and on top of that, I earn money! Also, I like to touch people. I don't have a problem touching people. Some people don't like that aspect, they might even feel disgusted by it, but I'm not like this. Also, because I like being among women, I like to *serve* other women. That's why I chose it.[17]

The love Tülay emphasizes here is not an abstract kind of attachment to one's profession, but an embodied empathy with other people, even humanity, that implies physical touch. The intimate, bodily encounter between beauty therapists and customers, the quote shows, involves strong affects, including happiness, love, servility, intimacy, and disgust. In Tülay's account, the physical aspect of touching other people's bodies that "some people" might find disgusting becomes an act of service. Such positive feelings could only be elicited, in Tülay's analysis, if they are based not on emotional labor as a form of acting, but on an authentic personal preference, an *affective* enjoyment of touching others. Those unable to love their fellow human beings in this encompassing way should rather refrain from beauty service work. One could argue that, due to their lack

17. Interview with Tülay, April 8, 2014.

of empathy, or perhaps of "deep acting" in Hochschild's terms (2003, 38–48), convincing themselves that they loved what they did, some would not be able to overcome negative feelings such as disgust and hence were unable to provide the emotional work required for it.

Some beauty therapists described these feelings when they were forced to treat male customers, especially for massages. While male customers were rare in most beauty salons and some beauty therapists chose to avoid such encounters by working in women-only salons, beauty service work on male bodies was commonly narrated as difficult due to the intimacy and physical touch it implied. Those who were required to treat men as part of their professional routine took care to frame this treatment not in an idiom of love (*sevgi*), but rather within the confines of a therapeutic service (*hizmet*). Tülay's account above also includes a powerful valorization of beauty *service* work as a service directed toward female others, one that contributes not only to the creation of aesthetic norms, but also to the creation of morally proper femininity and bodily states, especially cleanliness.

Aspects such as service-orientation, empathetic care, and dedication, as well as the love of beauty and cleanliness, were sometimes quoted to advance stereotypical views of why women, and indeed *Turkish* women, were "so good" at doing "this type of work." According to one salon owner, Ayşe, Turkish beauticians were simply "the best in the world" because they were "*naturally* dedicated to beauty and cleanliness." This perspective not only naturalized supposedly female characteristics (beauty and cleanliness), it also racialized beauty service work as something that easily came to Turkish women by way of a natural inclination. Given the immense training and human costs that Turkish service workers, like beauty service workers elsewhere, suffered by engaging in this type of work, this statement remains problematic even if its essentializing message is removed. Thus, it connotes a disturbing kind of self-Orientalization, which depicts Turkish women as naturally sensual, caring, and subservient. It needs to be emphasized, however, that this statement was articulated toward a foreigner, one who obviously did not fulfil the standards of a clean and more generally proper Turkish woman, thus clearly also implying a sense of nationalist pride and identity.

The theme of cultural aptness for beauty service work was reiterated from a slightly different perspective by another veteran beauty therapist and teacher of makeup training courses. Asked how she dealt with the intimacy and bodily touch involved in beauty work, Didem responded:

> We work in the service sector, so of course we touch each other, for example, when we apply a mask or makeup. If you have a problem with that, or a sexual problem, this kind of work is not for you. But there's no sexual connotation to it—homosexuality, or lesbianism, these are things that are very remote from our culture. This has to do with our inner feelings, our customs. Homosexuality and all of these things, they are very remote from us here in Turkey.[18]

Didem is arguing here that beauty service work relies on intimate, haptic contact that has no sexual connotations. Assuming an encounter between a female beauty therapist and a customer, this touch is not only nonsexual due to its configuration, but also because "lesbianism" and related things are supposedly remote from Turkish culture and indeed from Turks' "inner feelings" and "customs" more generally. In typical fashion, Didem's statement speaks of a projection of homoerotic desire and sexuality to an elsewhere, one that is commonly located in the West. In its anxiety to emphasize one's own remoteness from sexual, especially non-heteronormative sexual desires—not only from personal inclination, but also because of cultural principles—the quote speaks not least of exactly what it seeks to deny, namely the sexual desire and intimacy that is certainly also implicit in body service work. Given the fact that public baths, the antecedents of today's beauty salons with regard to bodily grooming, intimacy, and homosociality, have long been regarded as primary spaces of homoerotic desire and sexuality, Didem's firm, yet unsolicited response must also be seen within a particular history of the devaluation and stereotyping of beauty service work within the wider Turkish public. It is this kind of devaluation that is at the heart of the often-troubling working conditions in Turkey's beauty service sector.

18. Interview with Didem, April 3, 2014.

Working Conditions

During my first interview with a beauty service worker, which I conducted late one afternoon in the fashionable central district of Cihangir accompanied by a friend who took me to the salon she regularly patronized, the grueling working conditions in the sector became all too obvious when our interviewee, a female beauty therapist in her mid-forties, fell asleep while talking to us. Within seconds, she woke from falling off the manicure stool on which she had been seated, and when she realized what had happened, apologized profusely. The explanation she later offered over a cup of tea was that ever since she had opened the salon at 7:30 a.m., she had not sat down. For 1,500 TRY per month (approximately US$750), she was the main and sometimes sole responsible person staffing the salon from 8 a.m. until 8 p.m. for six days a week. I later learned that her working hours and payment were far from unusual, and indeed our interviewee liked her workplace. This was not because it was a famous place that, as Cihangir's long-term residents liked to say, had been frequented by the popular Turkish classical music star Zeki Müren, but because its current owner covered the payments for her social insurance, which she knew was rare in the sector.

Beauty salon work is strenuous in both the physical and emotional sense even for those who managed to negotiate better pay for fewer hours. Physically, it typically requires the worker to disregard one's own bodily needs while tending to those of others. In smaller salons, where one or two hairdressers and/or beauty therapists were on their own for most of the day, a line of waiting customers meant that they had to delay meals, and even going to the toilet. In a salon run by two young cousins in Başakşehir, this happened so regularly that the neighboring shopkeeper, a middle-aged seller of babywear who also used the salon's washroom and kettle, had taken over the role of a personal "caretaker," as she laughingly commented one day. Thus, every afternoon at around 3 p.m., she popped in to ask whether the "girls" had already eaten their lunch and ordered food from a diner in the same building if they hadn't.

In addition to stressful work routines on some days and times of the week, especially during afternoons and on the weekend, there was

Ramadan, the holy month of fasting, which was widely agreed by the many beauty therapists who kept the fast to be the most exhausting time of the year. In more secular neighborhoods, beauty therapists were commonly expected to continue working on their respective customers even after the muezzin had announced the break of the fast by reciting the evening prayer. In more conservative neighborhoods, such as Fatih or Başakşehir, Ramadan nights were usually spent outside, or else celebrated with family gatherings or cultural events, and customers arrived in large numbers at salons just before or after the breaking of the fast at sunset to have themselves styled. In one salon, which we visited during Ramadan in Başakşehir, beauty therapists worked until way past midnight, and in spite of their own fast during the day, had difficulty finding the time to eat.

Moreover, beauty therapists suffered from a multitude of work-related health problems, including acute or chronic tendonitis from blow-drying hair and backache from standing for many hours each day, or, in the case of manicurists, from sitting hunched over customers' feet and hands. Due to the lack of social security, or because they did not want to close down their own salons, beauty therapists often continued working even when they were sick, trying to hide their colds or flus from customers for fear of losing them. A major occupational health risk, albeit one rarely discussed in public and almost unknown to many younger beauty therapists, was toxic exposure in salons in the form of chemical toxins and other long-term harmful ingredients in hair color, nail polish, nail polish removers, and cosmetics for body hair removal or facial treatment.

From what I was told and observed, occupational health risks from toxic exposure were not usually taught or discussed in professional trainings. While these trainings focused on hygiene and advised trainees to wear disposable gloves to protect themselves and their customers from infections, the fact that chemical toxins in the cosmetic products they commonly dealt with could also be harmful was rarely even mentioned. Moreover, while some beauty salons asked customers to cover their shoes with disposable plastic covers, during research I never encountered any beauty therapist wearing gloves, nor, as is common in some nail salons elsewhere, face masks. Instead, hairdressers usually colored customers' hair with a brush held in bare hands, while manicurists typically showed off different kinds of nail polish by painting them on their own nails, as did makeup artists with different kinds of makeup, thus adding to the constant exposure of their own bodies to chemical toxins. Possibly as a result, veteran beauty service workers often suffered from chronic skin rashes and allergies, migraines, hair loss, and respiratory and digestive problems.

Not least, many of the beauty therapists and salon owners we met as part of this research were heavy smokers. Indeed, a number of research participants had chosen their salon space or workplace depending on whether it allowed them to step outside easily to smoke. While smoking certainly contributed to beauty therapists' health risks, it also afforded a widely accepted, often sole excuse for taking a short break between customers, thus providing relief and relaxation from work-related stress. To explain further why women nevertheless engage in beauty service work and often regard it as a viable and indeed meaningful kind of work, in the following I provide an in-depth portrayal of two generations of beauty therapists, namely Saliha and her aunt.

Two Generations of Beauty Service Workers: Saliha and Aysel

In 2013, when nail art was just about to become popular among some younger, middle-class women in Istanbul, the well-known Istanbul-based fashion-blogger Billur Saatçi posted a recommendation of whom to seek out for the most beautiful and colorful designs in town: Saliha, a manicurist in the exclusive American nail bar located in the central upscale neighborhood of Nişantaşı. By the time the blog had been published, Saliha was already extremely popular among many of the nail bar's regulars, and in order to get an appointment with her, one had to call in at least a week in advance. Despite her busy routine at work, Saliha was supportive of my research from its very beginning, allowing me to watch her work and introducing me to several of her clients, and eventually to her extended family. Most of all, however, she was eager to get across the message that, in spite of its widespread reputation, beauty service work was an immensely significant and therapeutic type of work based on expert knowledge:

> There is a bad impression of manicurists in society. When you say you are a manicurist, people go, like, "I see." They think we are, like—I don't

want to say a bad [*kötü*] woman—but they think you're, like, a simple-minded [*basit*] woman. That's why I avoid looking like one, and when I talk about my profession, I say I am a beauty therapist. I work in a salon, but it is not a simple place—it is a really *disciplined* place, there are lots of rules! . . . I've been doing this job for twelve years now, and I always say that one hand is unlike any other. Every hand has something peculiar to it—they all have different problems. It is different with everyone. And since each hand is unique, the more you see, and the more people you serve, the more you learn. But people don't get this. I mean, they say "It's just a manicure, it's not that difficult: I push the flesh, I rasp and I apply polish, that's it." But it is not like that at all![19]

Reiterating several of the aspects discussed above, Saliha employed various strategies to counter and distance herself from the widespread representation of beauty service work in Turkey. First, she took care that her own self-presentation did not fit the image of the manicurist as a "bad" woman: loose, heavily made up or, as she described during another meeting, dressed gaudily in an attempt to mimic wealthy clients without the means to do it right. Thus, outside the salon she took great care to sport elegant and pious clothes, carefully matching her handbag, headscarf, and overcoat, while within the salon she was dressed more casually, in comfortable sweatpants and T-shirts. In particular she removed her headscarf while working to avoid endless discussions with her secularist clients, who generally considered covered women lowly, uneducated, and oppressed, as she put it. Secondly, Saliha countered the widespread image of the beauty salon as a simple and disorganized place by emphasizing its professional atmosphere as orderly and disciplined, with "lots of rules." Finally, she reframed her work within a discourse of the therapeutic-medical expert knowledge of the "beauty therapist," whose knowledge cannot be taught theoretically, but has to be learned on the job; that is, through the touching and handling of different people's unique hands.

Indeed, the nail bar Saliha worked in when I first met her advertised itself as a space of upmarket pampering and wellness, of beauty as a holistic

19. Interview with Saliha, January 23, 2014.

experience. Signs on the wall asked customers to refrain from using their mobile phones and to keep their voices low. Manicurists were obliged to be attentive and polite, and to refrain from being chatty with clients, which was commonly attributed to more popular salons. Saliha supported this policy and explained it in terms of professionalism. For her, employment in this particular nail bar signified a career she had long worked for. She had entered the beauty sector when she was fifteen years old, helping out by working in a salon to make a living after her mother divorced and took her and her younger sister to live with relatives in Istanbul from Gaziantep, in the Turkish southeast. Her first workplace, a small neighborhood salon in a conservative neighborhood on the outskirts of the city where in 2015 she continued to live with her husband, was a place where women came for standard body grooming rather than aesthetic pampering. Due to its patriarchal structuring, Saliha explained, manicures and makeup continued to be regarded as shameful there, and during her employment she learned little except how to remove women's body hair. Her dream, however, was to do nail art, and thanks to her ambition and skills, she eventually made it into a more upmarket salon in Kadıköy, then a private beauty school, and eventually into the nail bar and other salons in the upmarket central district of Nişantaşı.

The fact that few beauty therapists remain in the employment of one salon for long is well documented in the literature on beauty salons. Thus, in her study of British salons, Paula Black (2004, 127) observes that "[m]any of those who continue as beauty therapists for more than a few years after completing their training will either 'go mobile' (i.e., treat clients in their own homes on a freelance basis), combine 'mobile' work with salon work, or attempt to set up their own salon." Indeed, in 2015, Saliha changed her employer once more and started employment in another salon in the same neighborhood for just two days a week, visiting clients in their private homes as a freelancer on other days (that is, she "went mobile," in Black's words). She did so first of all to increase her income. Thus, while in the nail bar she had earned 1,200 TRY per month for forty hours a week (about 7 TRY or approximately US$3.50/hour), in the new salon, she earned 800 TRY per month for sixteen hours a week (about 11 TRY or approximately US$5.50/hour) and was able to take on more private clients. In this sense, the new position was also a first step toward economic independence and, Saliha hoped, self-employment. Her goal was to open her own salon eventually, and she worked immensely hard for this; for example, she attended evening classes to complete the secondary schooling she needed in order to register for the craftsmanship training (*ustalık*) required to open a salon.

For the time being, though, opening her own salon was still a distant goal, not least due to the high costs involved. Ayşe Aydın, the president of İGDESO, estimated that, given the high cost of equipment, including the standard IPL device for body hair removal, the minimum seed capital for a viable salon was 200,000 TRY (approximately US$100,000), adding that one could "easily spend a million [Turkish lira]." Research participants who succeeded in opening their own salons had typically been able to mobilize their families to support them or had taken out large loans, sometimes mortgaging the family house, like Sibel mentioned in a previous section. Compared to other manicurists, who often earned less and worked more hours, Saliha had been able to negotiate a comparatively good income and a fairly independent work environment. In fact, she earned more than her husband, who was employed full-time in the reception of an international hotel in the city center. Contrary to many other beauty therapists, especially of an older generation, Saliha had not given up employment after getting married, but instead delayed having children until she felt she was in a more secure position professionally. While her initial entry into the sector had been accidental, beauty service work now clearly meant more to her than a temporary means to make a living. The feeling that the beauty sector was indeed a career option for women in Istanbul was shared widely among young beauty therapists like Saliha. This contrasted sharply with the feelings and expectations of an earlier generation of rural to urban immigrant beauty service workers, as became clear when Saliha introduced me to her extended family, among them her aunt Aysel.

I first met Aysel at the house of Saliha's husband's grandmother, who lived in a popular neighborhood in the working-class district of Sefaköy on the outskirts of Istanbul. With both Saliha and her husband Mustafa coming from a region where endogamous marriage was rather common, Mustafa's family was related to Saliha's in a complicated way, with his paternal aunt being married to her maternal uncle, and his cousin being married to an uncle of hers. As we sat to drink tea with the grandmother and two of her daughters—Aysel, who lived in the apartment above her, and Nursel, who had moved in with her children after a recent divorce—we chatted about the role of female beauty, and the women remembered how the first of the family, Aysel, had entered the beauty sector more than thirty years previously.

Like Saliha, Aysel had moved to Istanbul from the province of Gaziantep as a teenager, but experienced economic hardship when shortly afterward her father died and left their mother to take care of seven children, the smallest still a toddler. The family barely survived from the piecework the mother, like many other women in the neighborhood, processed at home for the garment industry. At the age of nineteen, Aysel became the first to leave home upon getting married. Shortly after Aysel's daughter was born, however, her husband died, and without any savings to rely on, Aysel took up employment as a manicurist in a hair salon in an adjacent neighborhood. Her move caused a scandal within the conservative neighborhood in which they lived at the time, with many of their neighbors being rural immigrants to Istanbul and indeed, relatives from Gaziantep, who viewed employment for women, and beauty service work in particular, as "shameful" (ayıp). Her maternal uncle and her in-laws especially tried to discourage Aysel from taking up "this kind of employment," fearing it would reflect badly on the family's reputation. They suggested that she also process textiles on a piecework basis at home as her mother and other women in the neighborhood did. As Jenny White explains (2004), within the rural immigrant communities in Istanbul where during the 1980s many women performed home-based production work for the global market, this was not regarded as work proper, but rather a part of domestic work, being integrated into networks of kinship and obligation and as such not a threat to, but an extension of patriarchal control. Aysel, however, wanted to leave her cramped living conditions to work outside the home, and eventually prevailed against her relatives.

Back then, the women laughingly remembered, anything related to female adornment and beauty work was considered ayıp within the neighborhood. The first, and indeed the only, time Aysel's mother had ever entered a beauty salon was the day before she moved to Istanbul to get a perm, "the fashion of the day," as she laughingly recounted, so as to look properly modern for the big city. Polishing nails, wearing makeup—with the exception of kohl, the black powder village women commonly applied as eyeliner—and for many years cutting off their long braids had been out of the question for the women of the family. Aysel and her mother, her senior by just sixteen years, remembered how, back in Gaziantep one day, they had been scolded by Aysel's grandfather when a neighbor had reported them for putting on rouge in the backyard of their house.

In short, none of their relatives and few of their neighbors had ever entered the salon when Aysel started to work there in 1984. Almost thirty years later, Aysel still remembered her only regular client for manicures, an aunt (teyze) married to a rich man and considered somewhat extravagant among the residents of the neighborhood. During the 1990s this slowly changed, and Aysel's youngest sister Nursel, the first of the family to attend college and considered an Istanbulite through and through within her family, became a regular beauty salon visitor, experimenting, as she laughingly recollected, with every possible haircut and color. Aysel gave up employment in the salon upon remarrying in the late 1990s. At the same time, and like most of the married women in the family, she started covering her hair. By the time I met her, she was leading a pious everyday life characterized by daily prayers, women's gatherings in the neighborhood, and visits to the local mosque.

When, shortly thereafter, Saliha moved to Istanbul and sought employment in a neighborhood beauty salon, her decision was accepted and even encouraged within the extended family, reflecting a change in the perception of beauty service work as viable and indeed respectable employment for women even within more conservative social circles. In this particular family, this change of perception was clearly also related to Aysel's success story. Thus, Aysel had proved to her family that despite its representation as a niche for pretty, morally loose, and sexually vulnerable girls, beauty service work had provided her with a stable income for a limited period of time without affecting her status as a marriageable woman and as someone who was recognized as God-fearing and morally proper within her wider neighborhood community.

Conclusion

This chapter has described the immense changes in the status of beauty service work and workers in Istanbul, and indeed in the structuring of the urban beauty sector over the past few decades. As discussed in the literature on intimate labor (Boris and Parreñas 2010; Kang 2010; Zelizer 2005, 2010), the commercialization of intimate services in the late twentieth century marks an important shift in the relationship between the public and private spheres, as well as in the way that seemingly private matters have become an arena of intimate politics and public debate. Amid globalization and the commercialization of urban life, beauty service workers in Istanbul negotiate the complex, affective dimensions of intimacy and distance with their customers that arise when intimate body work is turned into a commodity.

As an intimate form of labor that used to be situated in the domestic rather than the public sphere, beauty service work has become increasingly regularized and professionalized in both its training and its self-presentation. In today's popular wisdom, beauty service work is no longer a niche of temporary employment for poor, uneducated rural-urban immigrant women, but a viable profession for beauty school graduates in a context of therapeutic care and medicalized wellness. These steps toward professionalization and regularization are regarded with mixed feelings by veteran beauty service workers, many of whom emphasize the embodied, personal skills of beauty service work that are based on long-term experience, including what Cristina Grasseni (2004) has termed a "skilled vision." Moreover, like most interactive service jobs, beauty service work relies on beauty service workers' management of their emotions, which overlaps with the normative expectation of female caring—an aspect neglected in the original formulation of "emotional labor" (see Wharton 2009, 154–55).

This chapter has also described the bad working conditions in Istanbul's beauty sector, which relies on women working long shifts of strenuous work for barely more than minimum wage. The devaluation implied in these harsh working conditions has been linked to the conception of non-productivity that lies at the heart of the social devaluation and silencing of feminized reproductive and service work more generally. Similar to paid domestic work, no surplus value seems to be involved in beauty (service) work: nails and hair keep on growing, no matter how often they are cut; hair color washes out and skin ages in spite of recurring facial treatments. Not least, the association of female-staffed beauty salons with the domestic, reproductive, and intimate spheres of social life, I argue, contributes to their devaluation as nonpublic sites of female care and sharing. In contrast, in many ways similar spaces for socialization for men, such as coffeehouses or barbershops, have been theorized as crucial for the forging of the public sphere (Habermas 1989, 36), as well as in maintaining political subjectivities (Harris-Lacewell 2004).

Against this background, the mass-mediated public demand of respect for beauty service workers voiced by the president of the Istanbul Trade and Artisanal Chamber of Beauty Experts and Beauty Salon Employees quoted at the beginning of this chapter cannot be overestimated in its symbolic, if not political significance. As female entrepreneurs, beauty service workers in Istanbul have partially succeeded in organizing and effecting regulatory changes in their interests. As those who manufacture bodily the normative femininities of the "new" and supposedly "more beautiful" Turkey under the authoritarian leadership of the ruling AK party, in the event described at the start of this chapter they were centerstage, albeit temporarily, recruited for the aesthetic nationalism of the politics of the day. Even when many beauty service workers did not share the political project of the acting president of their professional chamber, they certainly took pride in her speech and savored a moment of rare public attention for their employment niche.

Beauty service workers put up with the hardships and bad working conditions in the sector because they hope eventually to rise in the hierarchy of salons and even perhaps open their own salon. Moreover, beauty service work relies on a deeper affective disposition of beauty therapists, namely their declared *love* of beauty and of serving others so they feel beautiful. In their study of the American retail sector, Williams and Connell (2010) emphasize the hidden "aesthetic labour" that is expected of retail workers, namely to "look good and sound right." According to them, mostly female retail workers consent to the "deplorable" working

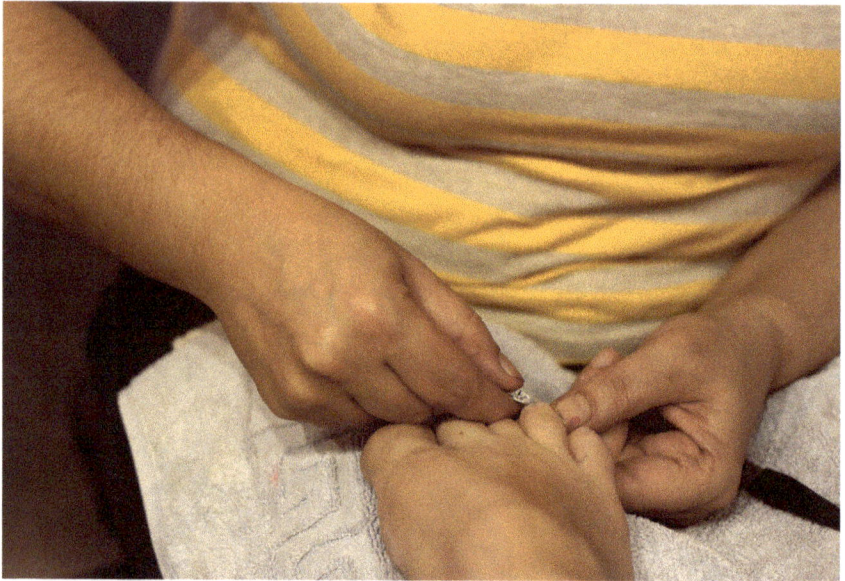

3. Beauty service work in Istanbul is socially devalued, with beauty service workers often working long shifts for barely more than the minimum wage. (Claudia Liebelt)

conditions in their workplaces "because these stores resonate with their consumer interests, not with their interests as workers" (Williams and Connell 2010, 351). They interpret this as a form of "mystification" (Williams and Connell 2010, 368) that obscures social inequality, fetishizes consumption, and keeps working conditions bad. Beauty, as both a promise and an actual service, is certainly also tied to forms of mystification, but in a sense that goes beyond mere commodity interest. Beauty service workers' accounts of their love of beauty speak of desires that transcend the social boundaries between themselves and their customers. Given this insight, it is high time to look at what beauty does and means to different groups of Istanbulite women.

3

The Multiple Meanings
of Feminine Beauty

INTERVIEWER: So what are the most basic things a woman should do
in terms of a well-groomed and beautiful appearance?
İKKMO PRESIDENT: Well, you should go and ask them . . .
İKKMO VICE PRESIDENT: Why, that's easy to tell: she should dress
up nicely, brush her hair, maybe put on some light makeup, like
simple makeup. It's not an obligation to go to the hairdresser all
the time, but it does make a difference if she opens the door to you
at night in her apron, smelling of kitchen. . . . It's a woman's *kismet*
[destiny] to look *hoş* [nice]![1]

Like elsewhere, in urban Turkey the construal of femininity is intricately
linked with social and moral understandings of gender, gender-role conformity, and proper appearances. In the conversation quoted above, the
president of the Istanbul Chamber of Women Hairdressers, Manicurists
and Artisans (İKKMO), like other male interviewees questioned about
beauty and the normative standards of female appearance, was reluctant
to respond. The chamber's vice president, however, was more forthcoming:
a "nice" look, according to him, was no less than "woman's destiny" and
included a wide range of sensual routine practices: the attention to dress,
hair, makeup, and smell. Not least, in the imaginary scene he offers us of
a woman opening the door for her husband returning home from work
at night, female beauty is presented within a particular moral universe,

1. Interview with Oktay Erkal, president of İKKMO, in the presence of İKKMO's
vice president, Necati Çetin, April 9, 2014.

namely within the confines of the heteronormative family home. In this heteronormative space, "she" not only looks nice but does so even after previously having prepared dinner for "him." This chapter will continue to show that within mainstream society investments in feminine beauty are closely linked with imaginations of proper womanhood and, by extension, sexuality and heterosexual married life in Turkey. Thus, the conversation quoted above continued as follows:

> İKKMO PRESIDENT: These days, *every* woman takes care of herself, no matter whether [she wears her hair] open or closed. Turkish men love stylish women! In earlier times, like many years ago, a man used to see his future wife's face for the first time during their wedding. These days are long gone. Young people are not like that anymore, they pay very close attention to good looks. . . . The majority of women are married—if they were ugly, they would not be married! (*laughs*)
>
> İKKMO VICE PRESIDENT: There are no ugly women in Istanbul these days.
>
> İKKMO PRESIDENT: *Çirkin kadın yoktur, bakımsız kadın vardır!* [There are no ugly women, only those who do not take care of themselves!]

This indicates that investments in beauty and bodily self-care are a normative expectation of women, and their failure to become feminine may not only result in "husbands' disappointment," but also in the violation of gendered norms and social etiquette. Adapted from a famous phrase by the cosmetics entrepreneur Helena Rubinstein, "There are no ugly women, only lazy ones" (quoted from Barber 2016, 31), *çirkin kadın yoktur, bakımsız kadın vardır* was an oft-quoted saying in beauty salons and clinics. Its underlying spatial and temporal implications (in Istanbul, anymore) point to an imagined rise in beauty standards and the national pride taken in it.

This chapter looks at the nevertheless multiple meanings of beauty as a social value for *İstanbullu* women and the routine practices employed by them to achieve it. It begins with findings from a survey conducted on women's beauty work and routines of bodily grooming. Presenting two examples of standard beauty practices, namely facial treatments and body hair removal, I will show how feminine beauty is tied to a wide range of sensual, bodily, and moral states and practices, interlinked with cultural notions of cleanliness, etiquette, and more general concerns about bodily matter. By analyzing women's accounts of their first salon visits and their wedding preparations at salons, great differences between Istanbulite women of different generations and social positionings will become clear. Indeed, significant changes have taken place with respect to women's beauty work and routine practices in recent decades, with beauty work being relegated increasingly to professional beauty service workers and engaged in by ever-younger women.

Assessing Beauty Routines and Concerns

In order to acquire a more general idea of women's beauty concerns and practices, in spring 2014 I distributed brief questionnaires to female visitors at the annual Istanbul Care and Beauty Fair (n=30, March 14 and 16, 2014) and participants in two municipal beauty-training classes for women, so-called İSMEK courses, in the lower middle-class district of Kavacık (n=12, May 23, 2014), and the newly established conservative district of Başakşehir (n=4, May 29, 2014), located respectively on the Asian and European outskirts of the city. The forty-six respondents to the questionnaire were between seventeen and sixty-nine years old, with an average age of forty. Almost half the respondents, twenty-one out of forty-five, or 46.6 percent, were married, with thirteen, mostly younger respondents single (35.6 percent); seven respondents (15.6 percent) divorced, and one widowed. Each respondent described her economic situation as middle or middle-class and had engaged in a wide range of professions, with varied educational attainments. While most of the respondents in the İSMEK courses were housewives or early retirees, almost half of the Care and Beauty fairgoers (48 percent, or thirteen out of twenty-seven respondents) were professional beauty therapists, including aestheticians, hairdressers, dieticians, and makeup artists. Given this bias, and the fact that due to my entry into the field all participants were in one way or another interested in cosmetics and beauty, the results were certainly affected. However, unless specified in the discussion of results below, and apart from the time and money spent on beauty—with professional beauty service workers spending more time and less money in salons—divergences in the responses between beauty service workers and other participants in the survey were negligible.

Each of the beauty fairgoers and the majority of İSMEK course participants stated that they regularly attended beauty salons. Ten participants (25.6 percent of the respondents) attended a salon at least weekly, nine (23 percent) did so two or three times per month, and five (12.8 percent) at least monthly. The younger the participants, the more frequently they claimed to attend beauty salons for personal grooming. The overwhelming majority of those who regularly attended salons (79.3 percent) said they had a regular salon that they patronized. Those who responded that they did not have a regular salon but did regularly attend salons tended to be rather young, in their early twenties. The services most frequently requested at beauty salons were, in descending order, the cutting, coloring, and styling of hair (mentioned in thirty responses), manicures and pedicures (mentioned in seventeen responses), facial therapies (in eight responses), and eyebrow shaping, makeup, depilation, and massage (in two to four responses). One respondent stated that she owned her own salon and made her apprentices do "whatever is necessary" for her bodily hygiene and good looks.

When asked what else they did in order to feel good about themselves or even feel beautiful, respondents mentioned "going for a walk" (seven times), doing sports (five times), listening to music, reading books, watching films, or applying facial masks at home (five times each). Others mentioned meeting friends and a healthy diet (three times each). Two each mentioned they liked to try out new nail polish, get a massage, go shopping, or dress up, with one woman also mentioning wearing high heels. Two women in their late fifties, both retired civil servants, who arrived at the Beauty and Care Fair together from Kartal, a former working-class district on the outskirts of the Anatolian side of Istanbul, mentioned the importance of "spiritual balance" (*ruhsal denge*), with one stating that she *always* felt happy and beautiful because she believed in the beauty of God's creation.

Asked what they liked about the salon they patronized, most respondents mentioned hygiene and cleanliness (twelve responses), good and knowledgeable service, and their special relationship with the salon owner or employees (ten responses each). Aestheticians and beauty salon owners were described as cheerful (*güleryüz*) and trustworthy (*güvenilir*), and the respondents' relationships with them were characterized as a form of camaraderie (*dostluk*) based on intimacy (*samimiyet*), with one respondent stating that she had known her regular beautician for more than twenty years. More practical reasons, such as cheap prices, high-quality products, equipment, and close proximity to one's home, were also mentioned, though less often. In several answers, respondents stated that investments in beautification made them feel happy (*mutlu*) and relaxed (*rahat*), even creating spiritual comfort (*ruhsal rahatlık*).

Only three out of forty-five respondents reported having had cosmetic surgery, with two undergoing surgery to reduce scars on their bodies and the third, an attractive woman in her late forties, who arrived at the Beauty and Care Fair with heavy makeup in yellow high heels, mentioning breast augmentation surgery. Given the fact that cosmetic surgery is often hidden, sometimes even from close friends or family members (see also chapter 4), these findings are more telling of the inadequacy of studying such surgery using surveys than providing accurate information on their prevalence.

Asked how much time they had spent on personal care, beauty, and wellness in the past month, almost half of the respondents (seventeen out of thirty-eight respondents, or 43.6 percent) marked the bottom value, that is, fewer than five hours per month. Twelve respondents, or 30.8 percent, stated they had spent between five and ten hours; six, or 15.4 percent, between ten and twenty hours; and four, or 10.3 percent, more than twenty hours on these practices in the previous month. Participants in the survey were also asked about the money they spent on personal care, beauty, and wellness. Of the thirty-eight respondents who answered this question, half said they had spent less than 100 TRY (approximately US$50), with those employed in or owning beauty salons falling into this category; thirteen (or 34.2 percent) said they spent between 100–199 TRY; the remainder (six respondents or 15.8 percent) claimed to have spent more than 200

TRY (approximately US$100) in the previous month.[2] Divided into two equal age groups, those aged forty and above and those younger than forty, the older age group reported spending more time and significantly more money on personal care, beauty, and wellness in the past month in comparison with the younger age group.

All the participants in the survey tended to be quite satisfied with their bodies. It is interesting to note that, in the commercialized and beauty-conscious environment of the beauty fair, participants proved to be slightly less satisfied with their bodies than those who were attending the municipal training courses. Most respondents tended to think that images of beautiful women in the media did not influence the way they felt about their own bodies, though respondents in the professional and commercialized setting of the Istanbul beauty fair were more careful and divided over agreeing on this point. As became clear from both the narrative interviews and the survey, taking care of one's appearance was generally seen as a joyful rather than a burdensome activity; thus, all respondents agreed strongly with the statement that "taking care of my appearance makes me feel happy." Participants in the survey also agreed with the statement that "a woman who wants to succeed should be well-groomed and good-looking," with respondents at the Beauty and Care Fair agreeing even more strongly with this than those in the municipal beauty training courses. This resonates with the findings of my interviews, in which many interlocutors commented that these days high standards of beauty are not only important for career women in professional contexts, but of great importance for women more generally.

While these questionnaire findings are in no way representative of the mainstream urban population, they nevertheless point to the fact that beauty work is commonly seen as a joyful as well as a necessary activity for

---

2. These figures resonate with the findings of the Istanbul Office of the Italian Foreign Commerce Agency, which found that the average amount spent per month and per person on beauty and cosmetics in Turkey was about US$20, as compared to about US$164 for EU members (quoted from *Cumhuriyet* 2016). This relatively low expenditure points to the fact that many beauty services are relatively cheap in Turkey and that investment in them is still rather novel among large segments of the population.

women. Beauty is a deeply social affair, as when it is delegated to beauty service workers described as trusted comrades or intimate friends. Moreover, beauty is associated not only with the visible outcomes of beauty work, *looking* beautiful, but also and very importantly with its affective dimensions and the bodily states it produces, *feeling* beautiful, namely feeling happy, balanced, comfortable, and satisfied with oneself. Finally, it is important to note that for middle-class Istanbulite women, feeling beautiful is not simply an outcome of beauty (service) work, but of a wide range of embodied activities, some clearly being intended to disrupt everyday routines ("wearing high heels"). Within these multiple tropes of feminine beauty as self-care, spiritual balance or playful happiness, beauty as cleanliness is particularly salient.

Beauty as Cleanliness

Shortly after arriving in Istanbul for research in September 2013, in search of sites for participant observation, I entered a women-only club in the secular residential middle-class neighborhood of Moda with the promising name of *Planet Beauty*. Enquiring about the possibility of becoming a member, I soon found myself in the manager's office talking finance. I was offered a "special deal" of eight months membership for the price of six months (900 TRY, approximately US$450), including free use of the club's fitness center and ten sessions of sauna, as well as a discount on all beauty packages on its first floor, and hairdressing services on its ground floor. When the manager sensed that I was hesitant in handing over my credit card, she emphatically addressed me with a promise that initially surprised me: "but you will be absolutely clean (*temiz*)!"[3]

The close link, not to say equation, between *temizlik* and feminine beauty was a recuring theme during fieldwork. Cleanliness created not just by bodily hygiene but by specific treatments on offer in urban beauty salons was commonly seen as a precondition and sometimes as the *essence* of feminine beauty. Whereas Malmström (2015), writing about women in lower-income neighborhoods of Cairo, found that femininity was

3. Field notes, September 27, 2013.

associated with the local tropes of "'sweet,' 'soft,' 'smooth,' and 'pure' femininity" (Malmström 2015, 143), in middle-class Istanbul, the ideal standard was the "clean" female body. The history of cleanliness in present-day Turkey is closely linked to early Republican ideas of urban civility, bodily hygiene, and modernity. In her preface to the *Book of Cleanliness*, Emine Gürsoy-Naskali (2009, 2) evokes how generations of Turkish schoolchildren had to present their hands, nails, and ears to be inspected for cleanliness at morning school assemblies. In the 1940s, the governor and mayor of Ankara, Nevzat Tandoğan, famously introduced public cleanliness inspections, which reportedly also paid attention to people's hairstyles and body hair to ensure that only properly urban-looking citizens adorned the boulevards of the modern capital (Gürsoy-Naskali 2009, 2).

Feminine beauty as cleanliness is both visible on the body and goes beyond the woman's outward appearance, including multisensorial aspects such as smell or language. This becomes clear from the definition of a beautiful woman by Sevil, a beauty therapist and makeup artist in her early fifties:

> A beautiful woman is a *temiz* woman; [she tells] no lies, [she is] respectful, well groomed. For example, I hate it if someone is dressed very chic, but smells of sweat. Or someone who is very chic, but talks foul [*kirli*], in an ugly way. I don't appreciate this. A woman [*kadın*] should be a lady [*hanımefendi*], she should be a proper mother [*anne*], a proper elder sister [*abla*], a proper friend [*arkadaş*]. A beautiful woman should be clever and respectful to those around her. She should stand at the side of her husband. She should be a role model to her children. Otherwise, you might be a 90-60-90 [cm; that is, possessing the ideal measurements], but after a little while it turns into 100-70-120 anyway! (*laughs*) You see, I used to be a beautiful woman myself and sometimes it saddens me. Beauty is ephemeral, but moral values endure.[4]

Here beauty as cleanliness is tied to a wide range of sensual, bodily, moral states, and practices, such as the grooming of the body, a particular way of smelling and articulation, and traits of sincerity, loyalty, and respectfulness.

---

4. Interview with Sevil, March 20, 2014.

It speaks of a certain social status as a *hanımefendi*, whose language should be sweet (*tatlı*), not foul—a warning also commonly addressed to children. Feminine beauty, according to Sevil, is about knowing one's proper place in society. The resulting subjectivity, as her enumeration of various social roles—mother, wife, sister, friend—illustrates, is familial and relational. It is in one's moral relationality with others as a *proper* mother, elder sister, and friend, a *loyal* wife, a *role model* to her children, and a *lady* to be respected by those around her that one becomes feminine. This relates to what scholars of the Middle East have described as a widely shared preference for connective subjectivities or selves, based on a concept of selfhood that is tied to relational experiences (Joseph 1993; Ozyegin 2015, 22–26). In the case of Istanbulite women, relational subjectivity or connectivity is a role expectation, with articulations of autonomy and individuality commonly discouraged in those who are gendered female.

In Sevil's definition of beauty especially, smell plays a major role. In scholarly studies of beauty, the olfactorial aspect of beauty is often overlooked in spite of the fact that concerns with odors are of the utmost practical importance in beauty salons and figure highly in conceptualizations of beauty. As elsewhere, different kinds of fragrances are part of everyday grooming practices and of men's and women's quests for a clean, sensitive, and sensually attuned body in Turkey. In many social and commercial contexts, including in hair and beauty salons, *kolonya* (eau de cologne) is offered as a sign of hospitality. Concerns about odors in beauty salons extend to the selection of cosmetic products, and many salon owners use fragrant sticks or diffusers to create a sensorially more pleasing atmosphere. Foul odors, especially if they emanate from the personal body as the result of metabolic processes such as menstruation, defecation, or sweating, are considered to be to the detriment of beauty, *pis* (dirty), and their management is of the utmost importance in salons' daily routines. Impersonal odors such as cooking smells are considered at least unprofessional, and beauty therapists take great care not to smell of cooking, for example, by changing their clothes after arriving at the salon or after eating out for lunch.

In Sevil's characterization of feminine beauty, the distinction between what is good, moral, and beautiful as a physical-material quality on the one hand and an intellectual-spiritual quality on the other is impossible. Instead, Sevil refers to a contrasting understanding of beauty that clearly makes this distinction, one that presumedly reduces beauty to the measurements of the ideal female body (90-60-90). While she criticizes such a quantification of beauty as superficial and ephemeral, she is not completely immune to it, lamenting that once she too was considered a beautiful woman from this perspective, but sadly no longer is. Sevil emphasizes that beauty cannot be assumed easily and quickly by, for example, dressing up in "very chic" clothes, but relies on constant attention to a broad sensorium of bodily sensations and comportment. Speaking from and as a long-term resident of Fatih, a popular neighborhood that is seen as rather marginal within the urban geography of commercial beauty, Sevil makes it clear that to her (and by extension, to those in her community and of her social position), beauty is not about material wealth—something commonly attributed to the more upper-class aesthetics of the inner-city districts—but more importantly about moral integrity, gendered role conformity, and—once again—cleanliness. This relates to another aspect of feminine beauty, namely that true beauty is "natural" and "pure," in opposition to artificially created.

Natural Beauty

Beauty therapists and hairdressers, and their female customers in Istanbul, commonly emphasized that cleanliness, and by implication beauty, was a process achieved by *ongoing* investments and *holistic* self-care. In contrast to more invasive procedures such as Botox injections or cosmetic surgery, which produced quick and artificial results on the surface, regular treatments, the reasoning went, produced a longer lasting and *doğal* (natural) kind of beauty that went beneath the surface. As the president of the Istanbul Chamber of Beauticians and Tattoo Artists, Ayşe Aydın, remarked:

> Turkish women for me are among the most beautiful in the world . . . because they don't do a lot of *estetik* [cosmetic surgery]. Those [who do have surgery] might look like aliens, with their faces like this (*grimaces*), but they [Turkish women], they're *doğal* [natural]. . . . We need

to support natural looks through cleansing the body. In my opinion, *güzellik temizlikdir* [beauty is cleanliness]![5]

In her endorsement of natural beauty, Mrs. Aydın praises Turkish women for shying away from more invasive body modifications, which make the body look unnatural, potentially foreign, even alien. The beauty worker's task to support natural beauty by acts of cleansing was also at the heart of a book she wrote on the topic of female beauty and makeup art, entitled *Güzelliğin Sırrı* (The Mystery of Beauty; Aydın 2004). It should be emphasized that natural beauty relies on an understanding of the feminine body as an accomplishment that is *made through* the consumption of beauty products and services, rather than something one has been given and is best left untouched.

The distinction between the natural beauty of ordinary (Turkish) women and more artificial or industrial and by implication Western looks has a long history, which was already evident in Ottoman times. According to Ayşe Zeren Enis (2013), it is *the* central discourse on beauty in the most popular Ottoman turn-of-the-century women's magazine, the *Hanımlara Mahsûs Gazete* (Newspaper for Ladies). In the early twentieth century, Enis writes, its commentators commonly emphasized the "mental and sentimental power" of beauty in contrast to industrially produced "European" cosmetic products (Enis 2013, 346). For example, commercial face powders or makeup were contrasted with cheaper, healthier, and more natural homemade domestic products such as spinach leaves, cucumbers, or strawberry water for facial treatment (Enis 2013, 353).

Here, the endorsement of natural beauty as opposed to one manufactured with commercial or industrial products is also fed by reasonable concerns about toxic ingredients in cosmetic products and the resulting health hazards. In her transnational history of skin lighteners, Lynn M. Thomas (2020, 31) notes that toxic substances such as white lead or ceruse have been used in cosmetics across the Mediterranean since classical times. The prepackaged, commercial cosmetics that became available worldwide in the early twentieth century often likewise contained dangerous ingredients

---

5. Interview with Ayşe Aydın, April 22, 2014.

such as arsenic, lead, or mercury (Thomas 2020, 39). While physicians and magazine editors have regularly warned of the dangers involved in using these products, government efforts to regulate harmful substances in cosmetics were limited. According to Thomas, prior to the US Food Drug and Cosmetics Act in 1938, "no comprehensive national law on cosmetics safety existed anywhere in the world" (Thomas 2020, 42).

In recent years, awareness has increased and an entire market of natural-lifestyle (*doğal yaşam*) products has emerged in the Turkish public, with daytime TV shows and advertisements promoting a plethora of natural herbs, organic products, or traditional superfoods for miraculous beauty, wellness, and health. In the global beauty industry, marketing strategies likewise emphasize cosmetic products' capacity to put into effect a healthy and natural look. Istanbul's beauty salons offered a variety of treatments that promised beauty in such a "detox" sense of natural beauty, including organic hair coloring, pineapple- or lemon-juice treatments instead of chemical peels, or newly rediscovered traditional cupping treatments (*hacamat*; see also chapter 7). The discussion shows that the tropes of feminine beauty as based on naturalness and cleanliness are interlinked. This also becomes clear by looking at two of the most common beauty treatments among middle-class Istanbulite women, namely facial treatments and depilation.

Deep Cleansing: Facial Treatments

Regular facial treatments in beauty salons, I was told, became chic in the urban (upper) middle classes during the late 1990s. Several middle-aged women in a regular Pilates class that I attended as part of my research in the exclusive and private women-only club *Planet Beauty* told me that a monthly beauty salon session for facial treatment was considered an absolute must among their circles of female friends and neighbors. Given the steep prices of such facials in beauty salons (1–200 TRY, app. US$50–100), however, most women preferred to treat their faces at home. The declared goal of facial treatments was deep cleansing, that is, a clean and smooth skin that was free from wrinkles, blemishes, freckles, and blackheads.

Whereas in earlier times, according to Ayşe Zeren Enis's analysis of the Ottoman *Newspaper for Ladies* magazine, "the softness and whiteness of the skin was very important for the beauty of a woman," and "when the skin got darker because of the sun, this was not desirable for women" (2013, 359), during my research women did not shy away from the sun, and sometimes even desired a suntan, though were usually concerned about the blemishes or other damage extended exposure to the sun might create on their skin. While most beauty therapists were opposed to using bleaching or toning products on their clients, several did report applying such products when clients demanded them. These reportedly did so because they desired a smoother rather than a lighter complexion. Moreover, in spite of the generally sunny climate in Istanbul between spring and autumn, women did not commonly use sun creams or blockers on their faces, claiming that their skin was used to the exposure of the sun, a fact much lamented by beauty therapists, who frequently warned their customers of the negative effects this might have on their facial skin.

Instead, many women in lower middle-class neighborhoods treated their faces with water and simple olive oil or milk-and-honey soap, a staple product sold in rectangular bars in the traditional *baharatçı* (herbalist) drug stores and open-air markets. The common use of soap for the cleansing of facial skin, already the subject of warnings in the Ottoman *Newspaper for Ladies* (Enis 2013, 349), was another source of concern for beauty therapists. Thus, Tülay, a teacher of municipal training classes on facial care and makeup in the conservative district of Başakşehir on the urban margins, explained:

> The skin of women here is especially dry because they clean their skin five times a day for prayer. Most usually, they use soap. That's why their skin becomes easily irritated, chapped, and dehydrated. Also, in this district, the weather is rather arid and windy, further harming the skin. So [in my classes,] I tell them how to treat their skin: "All right, cleaning your skin is important, but don't wash your face with soap all the time! If you do so, at least use a moisturizer. When you leave the house you also put on pants, so do something to also protect your skin." This kind of knowledge . . . [6]

6. Interview with Tülay, April 8, 2014. The following quotations by Tülay are also taken from this interview.

To learn more about facial treatment practices, I attended Tülay's class on the topic. In the mid-morning course, offered by the municipality free of charge for resident women, Tülay Hanım, a resolute and energetic woman in her late forties, taught about ten female students, most of them married housewives or, in two cases, recent high-school graduates from the neighborhood, how to prepare and apply facial masks and makeup. Proper facial treatment, the women learned, included a multitude of steps, such as cleansing the skin with hot steam and cotton pads; the application of tonics, creams, and masks—in the class, mostly homemade mixtures based on traditional formulas that included yeast or yogurt; and peelings, possibly with electronic equipment such as "vibrating spoons" or "e-massages," which were popular in beauty salons during field research. While performing or supervising the application of facials on her students, Tülay Hanım repeatedly lectured them about the importance of bodily cleanliness for women: "We also clean our houses at least once a week, so why not our faces?" In an interview, she explained further:

> Cleanliness is a precondition for beauty. . . . I always tell my students: "Before you leave the house for a meeting, you are cleaning your house. So now, your house looks first-class, but you yourself, you look second-class." In my opinion, it should be the other way round: you should take care of yourself first and only secondly of your home. . . . I look at women's hands, and they're all worn out from cleaning their homes. [When you leave your house,] "You don't take it out with you—but [you *do* carry] your body!" So the first thing is to take care of your facial skin, your hands, your body. No one outside will know how clean your house is, but they will see *you*, and no one will enjoy the sight. Also, it's disrespectful. You should love yourself and respect yourself!

By linking the cleaning of one's house to that of one's body, especially one's face, Tülay was making a moral statement by referring to common expectations of (married) women's roles. Regularly cleaning one's house or having it cleaned certainly is a major gendered role expectation. Instead, investing time in taking care of one's own looks and body, especially if this came at the expense of domestic chores and duties, could easily be considered narcissistic and selfish, especially if engaged in by married women with younger children and highly regulated time regimes.

According to Tülay, care responsibilities commonly led women to neglect their own bodily needs and desires to an extent that reflected on their moral personae. Teaching women the techniques of facial cleansing and more generally beautification, Tülay also made sure they internalized her underlying message on the ethical value of bodily cleansing and encouraged them to reshuffle their priorities. In this sense, taking care of and cleaning one's own body was not a vain or selfish act in making oneself attractive, but a prerequisite to creating a respectful (*saygı*) and pleasant (*hoş*) outer appearance, a major norm for diligent wives and self-respecting women. Moreover, given the fact that divorce rates in Turkey, for many decades among the lowest among Muslim-majority countries, have recently been rising, the threat of others, in particular husbands, "not enjoying the sight" was certainly perceived as real by Tülay and her students. Criticizing women's tendency to sacrifice themselves for the needs of their families to the extent of neglecting their own bodily self and well-being, Tülay's somewhat polemical comparison between women's clean houses and their unclean faces and bodies never failed to make an impression on the course participants.

Desiring Hairless Bodies

Bodily cleanliness in Turkey is also manufactured, and very crucially, by depilation, the removal of body hair. In Turkish, a clear distinction is made between *saç* (head hair) and *kıl* (body hair). Whereas women's head hair is expected to be long and shiny, body hair is unacceptable on any part of the body of an adult woman, and historically also on men (cf. Delaney 1994, 160). Drawing on field research in an Anatolian village in the 1980s, Carol Delaney (1994) noted that full body hair removal, including the removal of facial and pubic hair, was a central part of the beauty ritual of young women in preparation for weddings. In present-day Istanbul, body hair removal likewise routinely forms part of the "marriage packages" that are on offer in hair and beauty salons. As Laura Miller notes in her study of Japanese body aesthetics, in Turkey too, "[t]o not remove body hair is not a matter of personal inclination but rude behaviour and an affront to others" (2006, 110).

Body hair is tied to intense bodily affects, namely shame and disgust, and its removal, albeit painful, was commonly described as an almost visceral form of desire. Many interlocutors reported suffering from intense body shaming in relation to facial and body hair during puberty. Accordingly, women often described their first visits to beauty salons as having been triggered by the desire to have their body hair removed and their "bushy" eyebrows cleaned up or shaped. Many did so by saving up money and sneaking out of family homes to beauty salons secretly, in defiance of their mothers' attempts to delay their daughters' investments in beauty and feminine attractiveness. Working women or young mothers, who had little time for regular beauty salon visits, reported being plagued by severe feelings of guilt for not being able to conform to the standards of bodily etiquette, especially with reference to body hair.

In recent years, many younger middle-class women have undergone permanent body hair removal by laser or IPL treatment, often paid for by their parents after graduation or just before marriage. Other women have their body hair removed at least monthly by sugaring or waxing (*ağda*) their legs, armpits, bikini zones, and mustaches. In beauty salons, facial hair was often removed by threading. Few women, mostly elderly, continued to frequent public baths for body hair removal or met up with female relatives and friends for the purpose of collective *ağda*, as was reportedly common in earlier decades. Shaving, I was repeatedly told, was out of the question for all but a handful of research participants, often those who had been socialized abroad. Similar to what Malmström (2015, 151–52) has reported about female depilation in Cairo, "[t]he idea of a woman using a razor was unthinkable because the skin of a woman should always be soft and smooth." Shaving was commonly understood as something that men did and that gave them a "stubbly, masculine appearance" (Malmström 2015, 151–52).

Due to the intimate nature of body hair removal, especially pubic hair, those who relied on beauty salons for regular body hair removal formed close relationships with their beauty therapists based on trust, but more often than not also on social distance, given the typically lower social status of beauty service workers in relation to their customers (Liebelt 2016). One interlocutor, Özge, recounted how, in the *mahalle* (neighborhood) where she came of age in the 1980s, it was considered "weird" to attend a beauty salon to meet standards of bodily grooming such as body hair removal. "Why should a woman who has plenty of time at home have her bodily grooming performed by somebody else?"[7] the women in this neighborhood reportedly wondered, and Özge recounted how her mother and her female friends and neighbors had monthly gatherings in each other's homes for body hair removal sessions through sugaring and the shaping of eyebrows through threading alongside tea and biscuits. When Özge started to work and eventually moved out of her parents' home, body hair removal became increasingly problematic for her. Entering a salon and delegating the job was difficult for her not only because of the financial costs involved, but also because of the shame of revealing her body to a foreigner. By the time we first met, fifteen years after her first salon visit at the age of twenty-two, Özge had attended the same salon for at least a facial hair threading biweekly and a full-body waxing monthly, claiming that by now her regular beauty therapist had turned into a friend. What eventually persuaded her to have her body hair removed professionally was the time she saved by doing so.

It is interesting to note that *not* removing body hair seemed never to have crossed her mind. When I suggested this to her, Özge reacted in an amused fashion and at our next meeting introduced me to a self-identified queer friend of hers, who did not remove her body hair. The two explained that perhaps more than anything else—her masculine dress, her short haircut, etc.—the fact that she did not remove her facial and body hair contributed to the frequent perception of her as a transgender and non-feminine person. In her classical study *Purity and Danger*, Mary Douglas (2002 [1966]) shows that what is considered clean and unclean or dirty is never absolute but defined in a social process linked with broader conceptualizations of morality and order in any given society. According to Douglas, objects defined as dirty are typically ambiguous in their symbolic doings. As "matter out of place," (Douglas 2002 [1966], 50) they disturb the boundaries between cultural categories and thus threaten the symbolic order. From this perspective, the strong desire to remove body hair from female bodies becomes thinkable as an act intricately linked to the binary

7. Interview with Özge, January 21, 2014.

conceptualization of gender. The removal of body hair is one of the central acts, indeed a necessary act in making the female-gendered body proper, clean, and feminine. Whereas in Cairo women also commonly referred to the Qur'an and cited hadiths to legitimize depilation (Malmström 2015, 153), in Istanbul the link between bodily cleanliness (*temizlik*) and Islamic purity (*taharet*) was less explicit, though it certainly existed.

Within more devout Islamic circles, eyebrow shaping was sometimes problematized as prohibited, because it is listed in a well-known hadith as one of several bodily practices that alter the appearance of the God-given body. While the prohibition was common knowledge in hair and beauty salons, especially in more conservative neighborhoods such as Fatih or Başakşehir, it rarely prevented beauty salon owners from offering this kind of service or clients from demanding it. Thus, consciously Muslim customers sometimes justified shaping their eyebrows as acts of bodily "cleaning," closely related to purity and actually prescribed in Islam, rather than as changing their looks or increasing their female attractiveness.[8]

The practice of eyebrow shaping or cleaning also draws attention to the fact that some beauty practices are rather ambivalent in respect to their bodily "doings": on the one hand, they may contribute to a clean, pure, and more generally proper female body; on the other hand, they may also be seen as undermining one's appropriate appearance by disrupting bodily integrity or, in the case of eyebrow shaping, accentuating female

8. In its exegesis (*tafsir*) of the Qur'anic *Surat An-Nisa'* (The Women, 118–21), the Turkish Directorate of Religious Affairs (*Diyanet İşleri Başkanliği*) offers the following commentary: "In regard to eyebrow plucking, donning hair [as in wigs or extensions] or tooth fillings it is narrated that they are threatened with 'a severe and harsh penalty,' however, the hadith should not be taken to be concerned with such small things. These kinds of applications were rather the characteristics of lewd women or unbelievers or the behaviour of those driven by the devil who exhibit a devilish purpose." The original reads: "Kaş aldırma, saç taktırma, dişleri düzeltme konusunda rivayet edilen ve 'sertlik ve ağır ceza tehdidi taşıyan' hadisler yalnızca bu küçük şeylere yönelik olmamalıdır. Bu tür uygulamalar ya o zaman iffetsiz kadınların veya müşriklerin özellikleri idi ya da şeytanın tesiri bulunan, şeytanî maksatlarla sergilenen davranışlardı." (Diyanet, "Nisâ Suresi—118–21. Ayet Tefsiri," https://kuran.diyanet.gov.tr/tefsir/Nis%C3%A2-suresi/611/118-121-ayet -tefsiri; accessed March 19, 2021).

attractiveness, which some see as utterly disruptive if displayed within the wrong social context. This also lies at the heart of public anxieties over female teenagers' increasing investments in beauty.

Teenage Aesthetics Anxieties

> "Turk: Be (full of) patriotism, zeal and confidence" for me is a
> saying I still believe in. But they have turned it into something like
> "Turk: beautify, get noticed by everyone and always take the easy
> way out." (Yazıcı 2010)[9]

There is a moral conception of beauty in Turkey that links it with the bodies of young adult women, especially around the age of marriage. The idea that a preoccupation with beauty and fashion is inappropriate or shameful for schoolgirls due to its sexual connotations is widely shared, especially within conservative circles. Recent years have seen a growth in the consumption of commercial beauty services by teenage girls, accompanied by public anxiety about schoolgirl or teenage aesthetics. This anxiety is partly linked to a nationalist fear that the beauty and cosmetics industry is affecting young Turkish girls not only in terms of their appearance, but also, as a global and ultimately foreign force, in their values and identities as good citizens in the making. In a contribution to the popular daily *Hürriyet*, the Turkish TV presenter and author of numerous books, including a volume on makeup and facial treatments, Ayşenur Yazıcı (2010), criticizes Turkish schoolgirls for wearing makeup too young. In the statement quoted above, she refers to a famous saying by the founder of the Turkish Republic, Mustafa Kemal Atatürk, which Turkish elementary school pupils are made to recite during official ceremonies—"Turk: be (full of) patriotism, zeal and confidence"—claiming that contemporary pupils and youth have turned this aphorism into "Turk: beautify, get noticed by everyone and always take the easy way out."

Along similar lines, in a comment likewise published in *Hürriyet*, the columnist Cengiz Semercioğlu (2010) wondered: "Where do all those

9. The original reads: "'Türk, öğün, çalış, güven' benim için yürekten inanılan bir söz. Ama onlar 'Türk güzelleş, herkes seni fark etsin, kolay yoldan hayatı kotar' olarak değiştirdiler."

operated seventeen- and eighteen-year-olds walking down Bağdat Boulevard [an upper middle-class neighborhood on Istanbul's Asian side] or
in Etiler [a central upper middle-class neighborhood] come from?" and
"What will a young woman who has her lips done at seventeen, her nose
at eighteen and her breasts at twenty do in her thirties, forties and fifties?" In conclusion, Semercioğlu warns that "[i]f we as the media do not
restrain ourselves, we will come to a state where in ten years' time we will
not recognize our own children." In both contributions, the increasing
consumption and the popular promotion of beauty services and aesthetic
body modification is framed as a threat to national identity; children may
become unrecognizable, even foreign to their own parents, and they may
trade in the most sacred values of the Turkish Republic (patriotism, zeal,
confidence) for the superficial and narcissistic pleasures of a global consumer culture.

In the United States, psychologists like Rita Jackaway Freedman have
long studied the preoccupation of teenagers, especially adolescent girls,
with beauty work. Speaking from a critical feminist perspective, Freedman (1984) argues that social norms of feminine beauty create particular adjustment problems for adolescent girls, including a "negative body
image" and "lowered self-esteem," during a time when all teenagers
undergo a phase of "narcissistic self-obsession." Like feminist writers on
anorexia in Western societies (Orbach 1986, Bordo 1993), Naomi Wolf
(2002, 203–17) links the prevalence of intensive dieting and anorexia
among adolescent middle-class girls in the United States to a form of resistance to social norms of feminine beauty. While in my own research I did
not tackle teenagers as research participants—my youngest interviewee
was twenty-two years old—many research participants did talk about
their own as well as their daughters' or granddaughters' beauty concerns
and practices during adolescence. Whereas many middle-aged or older
interlocutors remembered their first preoccupation with beauty and their
first salon visit just before their public engagement party or wedding, this
was noticeably different for younger women, who more usually claimed
to have engaged in beautification practices from their early teenage years
and to have entered beauty salons of their own accord or in the company
of mothers or older sisters at a much younger age. Several of the younger

women but none of the middle-aged or elderly women I talked to reported eating disorders, including anorexia and bulimia, during adolescence.

Women from urban upper middle-class families often prided themselves on the fact that their mothers and even grandmothers had already regularly attended salons, yet in less wealthy or rural–urban immigrant families regular beauty salon visits before the 1980s were reportedly rare and, if they occurred at all, were usually delayed until the wedding or other extraordinary celebrations became imminent. Thus, many middle-aged or elderly interlocutors from lower social strata recalled that their first visit to a beauty salon was in preparation for their own or an older sibling's wedding. None of them reported entering a salon as a paying customer while still in school, and few recalled their mothers going to salons except for special occasions, such as a close relative's wedding.

One of my interlocutors, Fatma, a middle-aged beauty therapist of southeastern Anatolian origin employed in a fancy hair and beauty salon near Istanbul's central shopping boulevard, shared the observation that "nowadays, mothers bring their daughters to have body hair removal at a very young age, when they are twelve or thirteen, rather than when they are about to get married, like it was back in our times. At the age of fifteen, these girls come on their own for a *fön* [blow-dry], or to have their facial hair removed! This would have been unthinkable ten years ago! People are not ashamed anymore!"[10]

When interlocutors expressed themselves scandalized by contemporary teenagers' increasing investments in beauty services, they typically compared them to their own beauty work, or that of other female relatives in earlier decades. In comparing their own acts of beautification with those of their mothers and grandmothers or, depending on interlocutors' age, their daughters or granddaughters, great differences became obvious, not only between the generations, but also between women of urban vs. provincial and lower vs. more elevated social backgrounds. In simplified terms, whereas in more provincial and conservative families of lower social status a visible engagement in beautification and the consumption

10. Interview with Fatma, March 19, 2014.

of beauty services was considered potentially shameful, especially if indulged in by unmarried girls of their own accord, in more upper middle-class Istanbulite families female members' regular beauty salon visits were more of a standard practice, and interlocutors more frequently reported having been taken along to beauty salons from an early age. In contrast, regular beauty salon visits were out of reach for women of less economic means in earlier decades in Istanbul.

Women's accounts of their first visits to beauty salons often reflected their fascination with this particular social space, permeated by both homosocial intimacy and cosmopolitan otherness. For example, Şule Hanım, also mentioned in chapter 2, grew up in dire economic circumstances in the working-class neighborhood of Aksaray in the 1960s and remembered the beauty salon that she passed on her way to school as a "very fascinating place." Şule recounted how during puberty she developed a serious inferiority complex about her small body height, her black mustache, and her bushy eyebrows, and fantasized about having her facial hair removed. However, as with Fatma's opinion quoted above, her mother considered visiting beauty salons and indeed facial and body hair removal as shameful and morally inappropriate for schoolgirls. Attending the salon as a paying customer was out of the question for Şule and her mother for economic reasons. It was only when Şule started earning her own salary from a secretarial post that she was finally able to consume beauty services regularly.

In contrast, interlocutors born in the 1980s, when the global beauty boom started to affect the urban landscape and beauty services became more easily available even in the more popular neighborhoods, often recalled going on salon visits of their own accord during puberty. They likewise reported feelings of uneasiness about their bodies during puberty, especially with regard to body and facial hair (thick or bushy eyebrows), as well as their height and weight. In contrast to earlier generations, younger generations seemed to fantasize more easily not only about body and facial hair removal, but also about hair coloring, makeup, and professional manicures, and in some cases cosmetic surgery.

For example, İlkay, born into an upper middle-class family in the mid-1980s, first visited a beauty salon of her own volition when she was thirteen years old. She remembered being disturbed by her "thick eyebrows"[11] and followed up on her older sister's recommendation to "go and get them fixed." She recounted that she "sneaked out secretly" to a salon her older sister had recommended, paying for the treatment out of her own pocket money. When her mother—a frequent beauty salon-goer—noticed, she was disturbed not by the outcome, but rather by the fact that İlkay hadn't consulted her, ending up at a "random place" that might have been unhygienic and unprofessional. She was furious, however, when at the age of fifteen İlkay had her dark brown hair dyed bright red, telling her: "You're destroying your hair! At your age, you can have highlights at most, but not this kind of color!" İlkay remembered that at the time, in the early 2000s, having one's hair colored was still unusual among schoolgirls, giving her the reputation of a "wild" girl. In contrast, "today," she reported, "you can see much more of that." Once İlkay had finished her education and started employment in her family's company, her mother's attitude toward her daughter's beautification efforts changed once more. Now that she considered her daughter to be of the right age and situation to marry, she encouraged her to do more in terms of styling and recently, while shopping for a dress for a cousin's marriage, even suggested paying for İlkay's breast enlargement surgery, just in case she wanted it.

In some cases, first salon visits were narrated as part of a revolt against parents, particularly mothers, who sought to retain control of their daughters' outward appearance and, closely related to it, their sexual and gendered identity. For example, Dicle, a performer in her early forties, recounted her first salon visit as the result of a pubescent conflict with her mother. During her early childhood years, her mother would regularly cut her hair. While this was quite usual at the time, Dicle's mother was especially good at it as a trained hairdresser, who, because of what Dicle called "the classical Turkish family norms," was forced to give up employment once she got married. At a fairly young age, however, Dicle started having disagreements with her mother over the length of her hair, with

---

11. Personal interview with İlkay, November 8, 2013. The following quotes from İlkay are also taken from this interview.

Dicle wanting her hair very long or very short, whereas her mother made her wear it at a neat shoulder-length, much in conformity with the gendered norm for primary and secondary schoolgirls. Subsequently, from early puberty on, Dicle refused to have her hair cut by her mother and eventually entered a hair and beauty salon ("supposedly a famous one") of her own accord to get a fashionable haircut. She remembered that during this first salon visit

> they treated me like a stupid little girl. They seated me somewhere in the corner and after they washed my hair, they combed it with a disgusting plastic comb, forcefully pulling my hair. I saw the cracks in the plastic comb and was in pain because I understood that I wouldn't be treated well in there. . . . So, I ran away from there with wet hair, saying something like "Oh no! I forgot—I need to be somewhere," and I simply ran away. I went home and dried my hair by myself.[12]

Other women likewise reported being mistreated when they went on their first salon visit of their own accord by older beauty therapists or hairdressers, who by all appearances did not regard them as full clients, or else disapproved of their beautification efforts as silly or inappropriate.

Middle-aged women, who were in their teens and early twenties when the beauty boom took effect in Istanbul outside of upper middle-class circles, saw great differences between their own and their daughters' consumption of cosmetic products and beauty services. One of my interlocutors, Salma, a divorced artist in her mid-forties whom I interviewed close to her home around Bağdat Boulevard—an area considered particularly prone to the performance of teenage aesthetics—talked about her shock and helplessness in trying to confront her thirteen-year-old daughter over the latter's beauty practices. Her daughter had recently taken to applying makeup, namely eyeliner, concealer, and lipstick, on a regular basis:

> I try to stop her, but it's difficult. Young girls are like that now. They all style their hair, some even coloring it; they put on makeup, they dress

12. Interview with Dicle, February 19, 2014.

up. . . . She [her daughter] has friends who started coloring their hair at fourteen. That's so wrong! What is going to happen to their hair once they grow older? But that's the environment they grow up in. It's very hard even to talk to her about these things. She spends hours in front of the mirror and it takes her up to an hour to style up in the morning before she is ready to leave the house. They're influenced by media images. They feel fat even though they're not. All those celebrities she adores, they're foreigners. She and her friends, they collect magazines and images of women whose eyebrows they like, saying, for example, "I want my eyebrows to be shaped exactly like hers."[13]

Like the authors of the newspaper articles quoted at the beginning of this section, Salma is clearly alarmed about her daughter's and other young female teenagers' beauty practices with a mixture of moral and health concerns. Moreover, she is also disturbed by the notion of a foreign influence on her daughter mediated through the images of non-Turkish women in her daughter's fashion magazines. Like other mothers or grandmothers who lamented their young daughters' or granddaughters' intense beauty practices, Salma at least partly attributed her daughter's beautification efforts to the competitive urban environment she had grown up in. Commenting on her preschool granddaughters' frequent requests to paint their nails, another interlocutor, a beauty salon owner in her sixties, said: "They want it because they see others [doing it]. If they lived in the village I grew up in, they simply wouldn't see that [i.e., kindergarten kids with their nails polished]."[14]

Women in the age and situation of being grandmothers were more generally critical of girls' beauty concerns and frequently blamed mothers, including their own daughters and daughters-in-law, for introducing young girls, including their granddaughters, to the world of beauty at a far too early age. Asya, an upper middle-class woman and grandmother in her late sixties, remarked: "Today, thirteen-year-old *kızlar* [girls, daughters]

13. Interview with Salma, June 12, 2014. The following quotes from Salma are also taken from this interview.

14. Interview with Tümay, November 4, 2013.

get manicures, highlights, etc. I mean, *gençler* [teenagers] can get those things much easier than before. Mothers take their *kızlar*. At our age, mothers usually didn't because they themselves didn't do much. Also, mothers used to see thirteen-year-olds as *çocuklar* [children] and didn't *want* to take them."[15]

What is worth underlining in this quote is Asya's repeated switch from the gendered term *kız*, plural *kızlar* ("girls," but also "daughters") to the gender-neutral terms *çocuklar*, children, and *gençler*, teenagers, to reinforce her statement, namely that thirteen-year-old girls are inappropriate consumers of beauty. In her study of sexuality, love, and piety among young Turks, Gul Ozyegin (2015) notes that the classification of female persons into the "two [distinct] categories of '*kadın*' and '*kız*' on the basis of the status of their hymen is still pervasive in Turkish culture and clearly reflected in Turkish vernacular" (Ozyegin 2015, 47). According to this vernacular, "[t]he *kız* becomes a *kadın* . . . when she is married and her hymen is broken" (Ozyegin 2015, 47). Implicit in this distinction, Ozyegin notes, is "the desexualization of unmarried women and the normative expectation that the transition from girlhood/nonsexual to womanhood/sexual should occur within the institution of marriage" (Ozyegin 2015, 47). The investments of teenage girls in beauty and, by extension, sexual attractiveness, clearly disturbs these normative assumptions.

Beauty for Marriage

Adult men and women are generally expected to marry, and in spite of rising divorce rates and an increase in the age at which people marry in Turkey, weddings continue to be seen as "the focal point in the life of a person and his or her family" (Delaney 1991, 124). A large-scale study of marriage and divorce in Turkey from the early 2000s found that 95.4 percent of respondents had married at least once, with the age at first marriage being 19.9 years for women and 23.5 for men (Demir 2013, 83). According to more recent statistics (TURKSTAT 2021), in 2020 91.2 percent of the population aged between 30–59 had married and the mean age at first

---

15. Interview with Asya, January 29, 2014.

marriage was 25.1 years for women and 27.9 for men. While divorce rates have been increasing in the past two decades, at 1.62 divorces in a thousand marriages (TURKSTAT 2021), the crude divorce rate in Turkey is still low by international standards. Changes in marriage and divorce statistics are heatedly debated by the Turkish public and for the family-based gender ideology of the AKP, which elevates marriage and motherhood for women, the annual release of the Turkish Statistical Institute's marriage and divorce statistics is a neuralgic political moment. After the president publicly commented on the latest statistical trends in early 2019, urging young people to get married and have children, many of these same young people, Hikmet Adal (2020) observed, reacted by posting their views on the topic under the hashtag #EvlenmiyorumÇünkü (#Iamnotgettingmarriedbecause), making it a trending topic in Turkey.

The imaginative link between beauty and sexuality outlined above becomes especially obvious around the time of marriage. A beautiful body—in the wider sense of beauty outlined above—is commonly seen as a prerequisite for heterosexual marriage and sexual life, the two being expected to overlap in the dominant heteronormative order. The most important qualities men seek in future wives, according to a study by the Turkish Statistical Institute in 2006, "are being beautiful and getting married for the first time" (quoted from Demir 2013, 84). In the media, the importance of (hetero)sexual attractiveness for marriage and married life is readily stressed and often sensationalized, as in headlines such as "In the Southeast, No Marriage without Cosmetic Surgery" (*Hürriyet* 2003a), or "Marriage of Twenty Years Rescued by Combined Cosmetic Surgery" (Erşan 2010). To repeat, although kept away from beauty practices while not yet considered of marriageable age, girls considered to be the right age for marriage are typically encouraged to engage in beauty practices by mothers and other female relatives to make more of themselves and attract a husband.

In preparing weddings—their own, but also their friends' and female relatives'—young women invest (or are made to invest) in beautification and typically attend a beauty salon. In Istanbul, beauty salons and clinics frequently offer marriage package deals that include full body and facial hair removal, manicure and pedicure, bridal hair and makeup, as well as, less commonly, facial treatments, lip fillers, Botox injections, and tanning sessions. Indeed, on a regular Saturday morning during spring and summer, bridal preparations can be witnessed in practically every larger beauty salon in central Istanbul. In some districts, for example on Fatih's Fevzi Paşa Boulevard or Kadıköy's Bağdat Boulevard, such beauty salons cluster in areas with a variety of other services relevant for weddings, such as wedding-gown tailors, wedding halls, and photographic studios.

In the scholarly literature, the importance of attractiveness and beauty for the marital market and marriage has been reported widely, with Jha and Adelman (2009) writing about skin color preferences on Indian matrimonial and mate-seeking websites, Laura Miller (2006, 157) noting the heightened aesthetic expectations of men for marriage in Japan, Bonnie Adrian (2003) analyzing the transformation of women into generic bridal beauties in Taiwanese bridal photography, and Wen Hua (2013, 93) describing an obsession with female beauty in Chinese marriage markets. Rather than engage in the debate on beauty and the marriage market, in the following I will focus on observations and personal accounts of beautification on women's wedding days. I will begin with the accounts of two elderly interlocutors, Memduha and Feride, born respectively in Istanbul in 1926 and in southeastern Anatolia in 1941. These illustrate that while actual bridal aesthetics have undergone significant changes in recent decades, especially in the transition from rural contexts to more urban ones, the underlying notion of the immense importance of an active *making* of femininity through investment in the bridal body on the day of the wedding (*düğün*, as opposed to *nikah*, the official wedding ceremony) is not called into question.

One day over tea at her home in the popular neighborhood of Küçükçekmece on the outskirts of Istanbul, Feride, the grandmother and great-aunt of Saliha, introduced as a beauty therapist in chapter 2, recounted the story of her marriage. Feride grew up in rural Gaziantep and at the age of thirteen entered an arranged marriage to a relative in her extended family. The day before the traditional henna night, just before the wedding, Feride was taken to the bathing house by a group of female relatives, including her mother, aunts, and her future mother-in-law, for her first complete body and facial hair removal. On the day of her wedding, the process of "making me into a bride,"[16] as Feride put it, continued. Her long black hair was combed, braided, and decorated with colored bands, and powder and rouge were put on her face. Her eyes were emphasized with black kohl eyeliner and she was dressed in a long gown her mother had sewn herself, as well as elegant shoes that had been borrowed from elsewhere in the neighborhood. While she claims to remember little of the wedding itself, she still remembers the excitement that resulted from these acts of beautification: "it felt," she recounted, as if she had been "given a new face."

Compared with other outlines of bridal preparation in rural Anatolia described in classical ethnographies, the bodily transformation of Feride into a bride, including the removal of body hair, the braiding of her hair, and her adornment with henna and eyeliner, was fairly standard and served to make her body not only beautiful, but more generally "proper" in gendered and sexual terms. In this rural context, not all forms of beautification would have been considered appropriate. As Feride recounted, the application of Western makeup, especially lipstick and nail polish, was considered *ayıp*, shameful, for respectable women, even during weddings. Similar to what Delaney (1991, 86) reports from a central Anatolian village during the early 1980s, where "[v]illagers were shocked to learn that women in the city go to beauty salons where men see, as well as cut their hair," in Feride's village during her youth, pubescent girls and women were expected to guard their modesty, not least by not cutting or publicly displaying their hair. It was not until the day she moved to Istanbul in 1978 that Feride, now in her mid-thirties, had her braids cut and her hair permed during her first-ever beauty salon visit. While her eldest daughter's wedding preparations, which also took place back in the village, differed little from her own, her youngest daughter's were already marked by the urban context in which they took place; namely, in an Istanbul beauty salon. There, she was transformed into a bride of the latest global fashion in terms of dress, hair, and makeup. In Feride's account, narrated to me in the company of daughter and granddaughter, access to beauty and the urban beauty salon signified a process of becoming urban.

16. Field notes, June 23, 2014.

Whereas regular beauty salon visits were uncommon among all but a few middle-class families in the first half of the twentieth century, even in Istanbul, older interlocutors who had grown up in wealthier, urban families more readily recounted attending beauty salons in preparation for their weddings. For example, Memduha, born into an urban family of early Republican state officials in 1926, entered a beauty salon for the first time in her life at the age of twenty in preparation for her wedding. The salon, located on Istanbul's modern strolling boulevard, İstiklal Avenue, was owned by a non-Muslim hairdresser whose regular clientele were the fashionable ladies of the urban bourgeoisie. Memduha remembered being excited about this salon visit, but when she came out of the salon with her hair styled in a complicated chignon hairstyle of the latest fashion, she felt "utterly uncomfortable," her head feeling "heavy" and "huge." Apart from having her hair done, Memduha also had her body hair removed and wore some light makeup, including rouge and lipstick. Her overall unpleasant wedding-day beauty experience made Memduha shun subsequent beauty salon visits, except for special events such as balls or close relatives' weddings.

Like Memduha, many younger women reported feeling uncomfortable at being turned into a generic bride on the day of their wedding. In her attempt to subvert the norms of the generic bridal look, which she perceived as "exaggerated," my research assistant reported that she told her makeup artist that she would be attending a friend's wedding, rather than her own. By the time of my research, the standard bridal beautification routinely included an elaborate hairdo that did not leave one errant strand of hair, artificial eyelashes, and heavy (ağır) makeup that created the impression of immaculate, flawless skin and gave faces the look of immobile masks, making people appear quite different from their everyday selves. For consciously Muslim brides, who covered their hair during wedding celebrations that are mixed-sex affairs in Turkey, many salons in more conservative neighborhoods like Fatih and Başakşehir routinely offered the arrangement and lavish adornment of headscarves with pearls and other decorative elements (türban tasarım; see figure 8). Observing the making-up of a befriended bride, Ebru, a human resources manager in her late twenties, in a large salon in Caddebostan, a trendy (upper) middle-class residential neighborhood on the Anatolian side of Istanbul on the day of her wedding, I jotted down the following conversation:

> EBRU: I'm not sure about these artificial lashes . . . Perhaps we should put on the thinner ones?
>
> MAKEUP ARTIST: During the rehearsal last week, you wore the thick ones.
>
> EBRU: Yes, but don't they look exaggerated?
>
> MAKEUP ARTIST: Come on, darling, this is for your wedding! It has to be as exaggerated as can be! (*starts to attach the thick lashes*)
>
> EBRU (*ADDRESSING ME LAUGHINGLY*): Look what they're doing to me? They're talking me into all these things, telling me: "But it's for your wedding!"

The feeling of being talked into an exaggerated form of beauty for marriage, Ebru felt, also held true for her wedding gown, her shoes, her hairdo. The act of being talked into it was an exclusively female affair, and apart from the beauty therapist, included in Ebru's case her mother, mother-in-law, sisters, and female friends; her future husband, on the other hand, had had little say in these matters. During their bridal preparations women often tried to insist, typically unsuccessfully, on what they perceived as less eccentric or exaggerated looks. The experience of intense beautification on the day of their weddings could be utterly uncomfortable, with brides suffering from burns under drying hood machines or headaches due to tightly pinned up and unremovable hairdos or headcovers. Neda's account of her wedding preparations speaks of such a deeply disturbing experience:

> I was very young when I got married, I was twenty-three. So I did everything they [her in-laws] wanted to make them happy. They took me to a beauty salon, and they made my hairdo into that of a Barbie doll. They made me get married the way they wanted. So, as a result, I hated my own wedding. I don't have any wedding pictures that I kept! (*laughs*) That was the only moment in my life when I had no chance to oppose. . . . Right up until today, I feel claustrophobic in beauty salons. . . . They put me under this [drying hood] machine, and due to the pain [resulting from the heat it created], I cried like a baby.

The experience of suddenly lacking control over one's own body and looks, bereft of any possibility to oppose it as described here by Neda, clearly resonated in other descriptions of *being made* into a bride. The bridal beautification that beauty therapists aim at was clearly about producing a generically rather than individually beautiful bride, what Neda described as the aesthetics of a Barbie doll. However, in contrast to her, many married female interlocutors did cherish the aesthetic transformation that was the outcome of beauty salon visits on the day of the wedding. They proudly presented their wedding pictures in living rooms or on social media, not in spite of but because of the fact that their appearance as brides differed so significantly from their normal everyday selves. Nevertheless, in contrast to more regular, everyday visits to beauty salons, which were generally described as joyful and relaxing, the intense beautification and personal transformation that took place on the day of their weddings were described in terms that highlighted the pain, tediousness, and loss of control also implied in making the body beautiful, feminine, and proper.

Hairdressers and beauty therapists, on the other hand, typically enjoyed the preparation of brides, not only because it paid well, but also because it afforded them the opportunity to create more extravagant and demanding hairstyles and makeup art than in their usual everyday routines. Hairdressing, the president of the Chamber for Women Hairdressers, Manicurists and Artisans, Oktay Erkal said in an interview, was "unlike any other profession," precisely because of the bridal preparations:

> If you prepare the hair of a bride—for all hairdressers in the world, that's probably the one thing that makes them most happy! It's a very *hassas* [sensitive] situation. And perhaps years later, the same woman will arrive with her children and tell them: "You see, this *amca* [uncle] here, he did my bridal hair!"—it is something very emotional. She will never forget. You will be a part of the family forever.[17]

The narrative of the hairdresser-becoming-family through the act of bridal beautification describes an affective investment in the romantic mystique of the wedding day as the most extraordinary day in the life of

17. Interview with Oktay Erkal, April 9, 2015.

a young woman. The act of beautification on this special day makes him imagine a particular heterosexual utopia: one in which the former bride visits her "uncle," the hairdresser, with her children in tow to recount the happy day of her wedding in beauty.

Conclusion

This chapter has highlighted the importance of beauty (service) work for the making of proper feminine selves in urban Turkey. Beauty, it has shown, is a highly sensual and affective affair that includes not only the looks, but more generally the multisensorial styling and bodily comportment of a person gendered as female. In its close relationship to ethical conceptions of cleanliness and sexual subjectivity, the material-physical aspects of beauty cannot be divided from its moral-social aspects. Rather than simply being "given," natural beauty has multiple meanings. It is a moral and social achievement that relies on the constant attention to bodily details and matters such as the growth of body hair, impurities of the skin, or foul smell, to make the body clean. Cleanliness is widely regarded as a prerequisite for and equivalent to feminine beauty. In spite of its normative character, women do not commonly perceive the production of femininity in regular beauty salon visits as a form of social pressure, but instead narrate it in terms of comfort, joy, and more generally satisfaction with oneself.

Women's investments in beauty are embedded in relational definitions of female subjectivity and relations between mothers and daughters, as well as between sisters, female friends, and neighbors. Whether taking place at home or in beauty salons, they are social affairs tied to gendered role expectations that are widely shared among women of different social strata. Engagement in beauty requires time away from family duties and other socially imposed routines. With the exception of bridal preparations, time spent in beauty salons is perceived as time spent for oneself and needs to be negotiated carefully with husbands and other close relatives. In her study of Istanbulite women's engagement in sports, Sertaç Sehlikoglu found that her interlocutors had to integrate their exercise routines into tightly organized time regimes that circled around their "gender roles and family life . . . marked by clocks, calendars, timetables, and fixed work, school and gym hours" (2021, 200). Women's visits to the gym broke up their monotonous daily routines of serving their families' needs. Like the women visiting beauty salons and doing something "for themselves," the women studied by Sehlikoglu spoke about the "joy" they felt as a consequence (Sehlikoglu 2021, 202–4). Their desire for sports works against some of the gendered and cultural norms in Turkey in that women are seen as "trespass[ing] into a masculine zone of physicality, strength, and activity" (Sehlikoglu 2021, 42). Accordingly, the exercising women studied by Sehlikoglu usually downplayed their enthusiasm by speaking about their mere "curiosity" or "interest" in sports (*spor merakı*, Sehlikoglu 2021, 54–61). In contrast, women's desire for beauty seems to confirm and strengthen normative assumptions of Istanbulite middle-class femininity. Nevertheless, I noted that many of my interlocutors likewise downplayed their potentially disruptive, erotic, and glamorous desire for beauty by speaking of beauty in moral terms as "cleanliness."

Sehlikoglu interprets her interlocutors' sporting activities, many of them stay-at-home moms or retirees, as a sign of the emergence of less familial and relational, *desiring* subjectivities, which "lack a cultural vocabulary and imagination in Turkey" (2021, 61). This relates closely to what Ozyegin found in her study of *New Desires, New Selves* (2015) among young, upwardly mobile university students in Istanbul, who reject notions of "selfless femininity," struggle for more personal freedoms, and desire "to stop seeing themselves through the eyes of the other" (2015, 26). These findings resonate with the statements of beauty therapists such as Fatma and Sevil quoted above. Emphasizing the moral value of cleanliness rather than outright attractiveness, beauty therapists lectured on the importance of beauty work and bodily discipline for adult women. They performed being knowledgeable educators, who teach women not only about the right techniques and materials of beautification, but also about the selfhood and discipline this implies. Shifting priorities from a self-sacrificing household and family caregiver to a more conscious role-model of bodily self-care, they argued, furthered women's position not only within families, but also within the wider society. In popular neighborhoods, beauty therapists like them often functioned as harbingers of the contemporary urban (beauty) economy and, in some cases, of the aesthetic nationalism

4. A pot of *ağda*, the lemon and sugar syrup traditionally used for removing hair from larger areas of skin. (Claudia Liebelt)

of the day. "Clean" and feminine urban middle-class women thus contribute to the image of a modern and beautiful nation.

Not least, feminine beauty is part of an etiquette that positions one's body within a particular urban topography, nevertheless characterized by great differences with regard to social status and (assumed) urban belonging between different groups of women. It is both an egalitarian promise available to anyone ready to subject herself to particular body routines—as is implicit in the saying that there are no ugly women anymore (in Istanbul)—and a requirement that involves continuous, multisensorial attention and considerable investment in terms of financial resources and time. Those who fail to meet these gendered standards of beauty are not only considered ugly or unclean, but they also trigger strong moral and affective responses, including shame and disgust. They draw attention to themselves as disrespectful others who lack bodily discipline and knowledge about their proper place in society.

Finally, concerns about the commercialization of beauty products and services as foreign and unhealthy, the discussion has shown, are hardly new. When it comes to teenage aesthetics, the common discourse of pride in the natural and unspoiled beauty of Turkish women changes into anxiety about a recent loss of control over immature girls who prefer the global consumer culture to more patriotic values and styles. The common shift of concerns over teenage beautification to a fear that marriageable girls are "not doing enough" demonstrates once more the close links between beautification and the creation of sexual female selves. It is this sexualized reading of beautification practices, the following chapter will show, that makes them problematic once again when women grow older.

4

Aging "Well" in Urban Turkey

There is the common understanding that beauty, care, and cosmetic surgery are for young ladies only. Once you give birth to a child, and especially once you become a granny, there is no need for these things.[1]

In the anthropology of aging or what has been called geroanthropology (Cohen 1994), little has been said about experiences of aging in relation to beauty or bodily aesthetics, especially among older persons, compared to age stratification, grandparenthood, the life course, and the medical, political, demographic, and economic concerns of aging societies. Moreover, in the literature on beauty work and aesthetic body modification, the focus is clearly on young and middle-aged women, with the beauty practices and perspectives of older middle-aged or elderly women being surprisingly absent. Perhaps this is due to the fact that, according to international statistics, cosmetic surgery patients tend to be younger or middle-aged, between nineteen to thirty-four and thirty-five to fifty years old respectively (ISAPS 2019, 49). While there are no statistics on the age distribution of cosmetic surgery patients in Turkey, this chapter points out that the consumption of invasive beauty services in Istanbul is not restricted to younger and upwardly mobile urban women, as suggested in much of the literature. In spite of the common conception, quoted above, that in Turkey, "once you give birth to a child," and especially "once you become a granny," there is no need for beauty and bodily self-care, anti-aging and rejuvenation products and treatments now form a major segment of the urban beauty and cosmetic market. For urban middle-class

1. Interview with Nureddin Yıldız, October 13, 2013.

145

women, aging well has become a major concern, and it typically implies a long list of invasive and noninvasive beauty practices.

One of the few ethnographies to focus on the relationship between aging and beauty is Frida Kerner Furman's *Facing the Mirror* (1997), about an American neighborhood beauty salon catering to mostly elderly Jewish women. The elderly clients described by Furman act within an age-segregated society that devalues older people by giving them the feeling that both their looks and their knowledge are no longer up to date or relevant. Closely related to what Furman argues is a widespread reduction of women to reproductive and sexual ends in American society, for women aging is tied to a loss of status (1997, 107). By rejecting the labels "old" or "elderly," these women claim a younger inner self within an older body. This, according to Furman, "may be interpreted as a form of resistance [to dominant beauty ideals], not coyness or denial" (Furman 1997, 108). Through their regular visits to beauty salons, where they have their hair dyed and styled and have their hands and feet manicured and pedicured, these women affirm their style and class and hence defy common stereotypes of the elderly as being in a state of bodily decay and neglect. Their beauty practices can be read as a demand for recognition and respect in a situation where "being yourself . . . is insufficient to ensure respect" (Furman 1997, 121).

Turkey, by contrast, has been described as a society where respect and loyalty to the elderly of both genders are major social norms and where authority, especially for women, increases with age (cf. Delaney 1991). Moreover, as also outlined in the previous chapter, the preoccupation with beauty is regarded as the preserve of younger marriageable or newly wed women, being considered shameful (*ayıp* in Turkish) if indulged in by either teenagers or older women. During research, this was most clearly expressed by the conservative Islamic scholar Nureddin Yıldız quoted at the beginning of this chapter. Looking at the relationship between cultural concepts of aging and middle-aged and older urban women's investments in bodily attractiveness, this chapter describes the major changes that have been taking place in these fields in recent decades. It portrays a new cohort of middle-class women, those whom medical practitioners in Istanbul commonly call the "self-conscious menopausal woman" (*bilinç sahibi menopozlu kadın*, in Turkish). Confronted with the first negatively viewed signs of aging during the beginning of Istanbul's beauty boom in the late 1980s and 1990s, these women feel the need to invest considerable amounts of time and resources in ongoing bodily attractiveness and body maintenance.

Moreover, these changes, I argue, are also related to changes within the wider medical field, namely the medicalization of aging (cf. Zola 1991) and the emergence of what Armstrong (1995) called "surveillance medicine" in the second half of the twentieth century. Similar to the transhumanist conception of aging as a disease (Hainz 2014), in the age of surveillance medicine aging becomes a risk, in this particular case an aesthetic-medical risk to be treated with aesthetic upgrades and bodily rejuvenation. In Turkey as elsewhere, as a result aging middle-class women are confronted with heightened expectations in terms of aging well, and practices of aesthetic self-surveillance have become women's responsibility as individuals, especially after menopause.[2] Thus, cosmetic interventions for body maintenance or rejuvenation, as I show below, are tied to critical markers in the female life course, most importantly childbirth and menopause, rather than biological age per se. In what follows, I introduce the concept of surveillance medicine in the context of aging and bodily aesthetics. I then describe the relevance of pregnancy/childbirth and menopause for women's anxieties over aging. Finally, I present ethnographic material from a day of participant observation in a private beauty clinic in the central middle-class neighborhood of Etiler, where aging well turned out to be a major concern for patients.

Aging Well in the Age of Surveillance Medicine

Among plastic and cosmetic surgeons within the growing private medical sector in Istanbul, the fact that patients at specific stages of the life course prefer particular cosmetic treatments is common knowledge. As one interviewee, the plastic and reconstructive surgeon Dr. Ismail Kuran, put it:

---

2. See Brooks (2017) on this for the United States.

> I can separate my patients into the older and the younger ones. The younger ones, the most common operations I perform [on them] are rhinoplasty and breast augmentation [surgery], [and patients are] always between eighteen to twenty, twenty-five [years old]. Their main concern is to change their looks, sometimes also their body shape— liposuction is also common—but rhinoplasty is usually the most common. If I divide the other group, those older than thirty-five or forty, some have deformities following their pregnancies. Breast surgery is very common among them, [that is,] breast lifting, breast reduction, and most also have abdominal surgery. Then, after menopause, [patients request] face surgery; they first start with Botox injections, fillers, laser or radio frequency treatments, and then move on to have facelifts and other kind of lifts.[3]

In the quote above, Dr. Kuran differentiates between younger cosmetic surgery patients, who desire to change their looks, and older ones, who seek particular treatments to deal with the visible signs of bodily aging, namely those tied up with feminine biological processes such as pregnancy and menopause. Accordingly, nose jobs, full-body depilation, and breast enlargements are regarded as younger women's procedures, typically engaged in by those around the age of marriage; breast augmentations and different kinds of liposuctions, most importantly the so-called "tummy tuck," engaged in by younger middle-aged women, are subsumed under the notion of *annelik estetiği*, literally "motherhood aesthetics," a translation of the term "mommy makeover"; and finally, face-, eyelid-, or neck lifts, as well as Botox and other facial injections and rejuvenation treatments, are commonly associated with older middle-aged women around the time of menopause. Hence, surgery and other invasive procedures in the treatment of bodily "deformities" among younger patients are seen and marketed as body "enhancement" and among older patients as body "maintenance," "repair," or "rejuvenation."

From this perspective, female aging is perceived as a medical-aesthetic risk in need of preemptive cosmetic treatment. It can also be linked to the medicalization of aging that allegedly emerged in the second half of the

3. Interview with Ismail Kuran, June 28, 2014.

twentieth century in what the medical sociologist David Armstrong (1995) termed an age of "surveillance medicine." Derived from the French word *surveiller*, "to watch over," surveillance can be defined as "the focused, systematic and routine attention to personal details for purposes of influence, management, protection or direction" (Lyon 2007, 14). It includes a great variety of social and mediated interactions that depend on an ever-increasing range of information and digital technologies. Surveillance studies often present surveillance as intrinsically ambiguous in that it may entail the care and safety of the surveilled on the one hand and their control and discipline on the other (cf. Lyon 2007). This can also be said of surveillance medicine.

Proposed in an attempt to analyze the process of a "fundamental remapping of the spaces of illness" (Armstrong 1995, 395), surveillance medicine describes a new form of medicine that began in the early twentieth century and extended the medical eye over the entire population, targeting "everyone" (Armstrong 1995, 395). Drawing on Foucault's concept of "political anatomy," Armstrong suggests that the medical gaze shifted from the interior of the patient's body to its relationship with its exterior, as well as with the collective body. Within surveillance medicine, tools such as sociomedical surveys and profiles and height and weight growth charts are employed to measure the health and determine the characteristics of a "normal population," thereby dissolving distinct boundaries between the clinical categories of healthy and ill, normal and pathological. The result is the creation of a world in which all bodies are relative to each other and "everything is normal and at the same time precariously abnormal" (Armstrong 1995, 400). Those subject to surveillance typically reconfigure their identities within the process. In the age of surveillance medicine, this reconfiguration of identity manifests itself in "the dissolution of the boundary between health and illness" (Armstrong 1995, 400) in which specific populations at risk are identified and spatially mapped. Thus, the ordinary categories of health and illness are reworked into a scale in which "the healthy can become healthier, and health can co-exist with illness" (Armstrong 1995, 400). Within this regime, everyone, especially those "at risk"—due to their "abnormal" body weight in relation to height, for example—are expected to engage in self-surveillance. Its ultimate triumph, writes Armstrong, "would be its internalization by all the population" (Armstrong 1995, 400).

As will become clear from the presentation of my ethnographic data below, the conceptualization of aging as a risk factor within the cosmetic medical practice opens up a space for patients and medical practitioners alike to promote and consume all kinds of beauty treatments that focus on specific "healthy" lifestyles and preventive treatments. The future of bodies is clearly envisaged in this process as a process of deformation that at this stage cannot be halted or reversed but can nevertheless be slowed down in an attempt to age well.

Motherhood Aesthetics

In 2010, the popular daily *Hürriyet* proclaimed a new fashion in the world of cosmetic surgery, namely the so-called "mommy makeover" (*annelik estetiği*, literally "motherhood aesthetics"). The report explained that women living in Turkey's larger cities no longer accepted negative changes to their bodies after pregnancy, childbirth, and breastfeeding "as fate," but were running to cosmetic surgeons in great numbers to regain their pre-pregnancy bodies. A cosmetic surgeon from the Plastic, Reconstructive and Aesthetic Surgery Department at Istanbul's Cerrahpaşa Hospital, Prof. Dr. Akın Yücel, is quoted saying: "Every pregnancy brings with it a big belly, flabby skin, fallen breasts and especially problems with abdominal stretch marks. With a mommy makeover, it is possible to remove all of these emerging problems" (quoted from Erşan 2010a). The article continues almost like an advertisement, suggesting that women could have a combined mommy makeover surgery with hospital stays as short as one night and prices starting at around 3,000 TRY (approximately US$1,500).

Given numerous media reports on the matter, it is perhaps surprising that, in my own sample of sixty-two female cosmetic surgery patients and beauty salon clients, the vast majority of whom had given birth to children, only three related the consumption of invasive cosmetic procedures to the bodily effects of pregnancy, childbirth, and breastfeeding. Procedures mentioned in this regard were liposuction, breast augmentation, and sleeve gastrectomy (stomach reduction) to fight a post-pregnancy weight gain. Moreover, while many mothers of small children I met or interviewed as part of my research reported feelings of disaffection and unhappiness about the changes their bodies had experienced after giving birth and breastfeeding, they rarely felt the need to undergo cosmetic surgery in the form of a substantial bodily makeover. Nevertheless, the bodily changes related to pregnancies, childbirth, and breastfeeding triggered concerns about bodily aging among many of them. This was also the case for Dicle, who decided for breast augmentation surgery after a severe loss of breast volume resulting from breastfeeding when she was in her early thirties.

Dicle, in her early forties when I interviewed her, remembered how she felt "like an old woman" due to her fallen breasts and had the vision that cosmetic surgery would turn her into a "young girl" again.[4] While the surgery did indeed relieve some of the urgent dissatisfaction Dicle had felt about her body, the concern about aging remained, though it remained tacit in everyday life. More precisely, her anxiety over aging resurfaced every year around New Year:

> In everyday life, you don't realize a thing. You go to sleep, work, go to sleep. Next thing you know is like, 'It's New Year's Eve again!' So [you realize:] one more year is gone, another one is gone. And you say to yourself: 'Just a minute, the year before, I used to do exercises, I was not in such a bad shape.' However, this year you couldn't do it, so then you start to see the difference. But, I mean, taking care of yourself—it's a race against time, it's impossible.

As a singer and performing artist, for Dicle a youthful and fit body is a professional prerequisite. In the past, she said, she has struggled "like crazy" to remain and, after pregnancy, regain a fit and attractive body. The existential and even fatalistic way in which Dicle talked about aging (a race against time) has to be seen from the position of someone whose economic survival ultimately depended on the state of her body, or, in her words, who "need[s] the body to make money." Reflecting on her own

---

4. Interview with Dicle, February 19, 2014. The following quotations from Dicle are also taken from this interview.

attempts as a single, divorced mother to limit or contain the signs of aging on her body, she described the dilemma over what to prioritize:

> [As a performing artist,] you need to run from work to work, from music set to music set, trying hard to make your body stay young. To engage in bodywork, especially if you also have the responsibility to take care of a family, feels like a big selfishness. I mean, you need to be living in a very narcissistic way if you want to look and feel like you're not aging! Other than that, everybody my age will feel they're aging. For example, there are friends who get all irritated about their facial lines. Some started injecting Botox at the age of thirty so that their lines won't be so visible at the age of forty-five. It's endless! (*laughs*)

It is clear that for Dicle the process of aging is not seen as a natural or linear process, but as one that can actively be formed and even halted with "bodywork." However, the amount of time and money required for this kind of bodywork is unattainable for most, including herself, not least due to familial care responsibilities, which are typically greater for mothers than fathers in Turkey. There also is an underlying moral judgment of intense bodywork in her account that hints at the idea that women who prioritize bodywork over spending time with their children or their domestic chores possess a narcissistic and selfish character. Finally, similar to what has been analyzed for the United States (Berkowitz 2017), Dicle recounts that some of her friends use anti-aging treatments, most importantly Botox injections, as a "preemptive strike" in the hope that "they won't develop deep crevices in their face in the future" (Berkowitz 2017, 2). Studying Istanbulite women's engagement in sports, Sertaç Sehlikoglu (2021, 229) has likewise noted that young women take preemptive measures and conceptualize their bodies as "prenatal." Highly influenced by images of the "celebrity mum," they seek to prepare their bodies for giving birth and breastfeeding by exercising.

Like Dicle, who related her post-breastfeeding surgery to subjective feelings of aging, many professional middle-aged women juggled with the conflicting expectations and time constraints of their roles as mothers and women at a critical phase in their professional careers. While most experienced aging and dreaded it, few managed to invest in halting the visible process of aging on their bodies the way they would have liked. As the following will show, given that she had the financial means to do so, this often changed at a later stage in a woman's life, when care responsibilities subsided as the children grew up, got married, or otherwise left the family household. Whereas invasive cosmetic treatments after pregnancies and childbirth were less common than the public discourse on so-called "mommy makeovers" might imply, those around menopause have become increasingly normalized, at least within particular segments of the urban middle-class.

"Retaining Shape" after Menopause

In my guideline interviews, I asked sixty-two female cosmetic surgery patients and clients of beauty salons how they felt about aging, *yaşlanmak* in Turkish. In a second step, I asked whether they noted any signs of aging on their bodies, and if so, which. While women of all ages answered the first question along rather similar lines, typically by listing negative emotions such as fear (*korku* in Turkish) or sadness (*üzüntü* in Turkish), responses to the second question were more varied and depended on the respondent's age. Thus, while all women listed what they perceived as their bodily problems, younger women's answers were clearly less specific, including gray hair or facial lines. In comparison, postmenopausal women provided longer and more detailed lists of visual, biological, and medical changes, including increased body weight, flabby skin, hanging breasts, and gray and dry hair, as well as sleeplessness and other health-related problems. Postmenopausal respondents typically linked these changes to the ending of their monthly menstruation. Moreover, a number of middle-aged women who had not yet experienced menopause talked about their apprehension of its arrival, not least because they had heard about the aesthetic problems allegedly resulting from it.

Rather than a mere medical fact, menopause has been analyzed as an influential, yet highly contingent cultural concept. In her comparative study of aging and menopause in Japan and the United States, Margaret Lock (1995) shows that middle-aged women's experiences and conceptualizations of aging vary considerably across the globe. Thus, the Japanese women who appear in Lock's study attach relatively little importance to the ending of their monthly menstruation and use the polysemic term *kōnenki* to describe bodily discomforts during a specific life passage, rather than the Japanese equivalent of the medical term "menopause." Likewise, in Turkey, the "invention" of menopause is fairly recent (Erol 2011). Thus, from interviews with a large number of middle-aged women in Turkey, Maral Erol (2011) learned that they did not remember their mothers or grandmothers suffering from what is now commonly termed the *menopoz*, perhaps also due to the shame attached to talking about sexual matters with one's children. Nevertheless, local conceptualizations of menopause clearly vary from the biomedical model typically presented as a universal medical fact. Introduced as a medical concept in the Netherlands in the 1930s, in Turkey menopause did not enter the public sphere until the late 1980s (Erol 2011, 137). According to Erol, it took at least another decade before it became common knowledge beyond a small circle of medical practitioners and their patients in Turkey, and even longer before it was widely debated, with numerous media publications appearing between 2005 and 2008 (Erol 2011, 137). For Abigail Brooks (2017), who studied cosmetic surgery among elderly women in the United States, the promotion and marketing of menopause as "a 'deficiency disease' with 'symptoms' that require medical intervention" (Brooks 2017, 6) is part of a wider medicalization of aging and a new commercialization of medicine in the United States. In Turkey, the public debate on menopause is framed in a narrative of women's "second spring," *ikinci bahar*. It stresses the fact that with the right medical treatment, and in contrast to cultural conceptions of aging, women's social and sexual lives are "not yet over" just because their monthly menstruation has ended (Erol 2011, 137).

Indeed, many of the self-identifying postmenopausal women interviewed for this study conveyed a sense of being among a first generation of Turkish women who did not accept their fate as elderly but instead claimed a sexually active and younger self. Ongoing beauty practices, and even intensified self-care, were seen as crucial for this new understanding of old age. One of these respondents was Jale, a retired academic and translator in her early sixties whom I interviewed in her stylish apartment on the sixteenth floor of a posh, newly constructed high-rise in the central middle-class neighborhood of Fulya. Jale, a slender and athletic woman with tanned, even skin, blue eyes, and shiny bronze, shoulder-length hair, was the yoga friend of two other interlocutors whom I had interviewed about their cosmetic operations. Against the background of a breathtaking view of the Bosporus, Jale explained her main motivation for combined eyelid and facelift surgery eight years prior to our interview: "Being old (*laughs*)! When I looked into the mirror back then, all I was seeing was a drooping face. Especially the part above and around the lips [disturbed me]. Well, I can say that it was the desire to see myself younger and more beautiful that motivated me."[5]

When I asked Jale about aging, she instantly distanced herself from those who are "really old" ("old age makes me think of medical issues, like Alzheimer's, etc.") and pointed to the fact that she still felt "kind of young," she also pointed out that what she wore—a gray corduroy blouse and branded jeans—was not usually worn by women her age in Turkey, thus also distancing herself from a more conservative majority populace. For Jale, the arrival of menopause had triggered an anxiety of aging that within a few months had led her to undergo multiple "rejuvenation" operations:

My size changed. Some upper parts of my body became fatter. . . . It's about yourself, you say to yourself, "What have I become!" To anyone else you look just normal, but you have this image of your past self on your mind. At this age, aging is the most distinctive thing about your appearance. Your skin becomes flabby, your body loses its shape, you get wrinkles everywhere, etc. These changes are like, hmm, I mean, hmm . . . (*throws up her arms up in the air in a gesture that suggests helpless despair*).

For Jale, menopause is seen as the quasi-natural cause of an entire range of negative bodily changes and indeed of an identity crisis. During the interview, Jale continued to talk about her "past self," that is, her younger and more beautiful self, which she compared against her current postmenopausal state of "deformation." She described how, during her

---

5. Interview with Jale, January 23, 2014. The following quotations from Jale are also taken from this interview.

teenage years, she was generally considered beautiful and felt at ease with her looks. She laughingly recalled that, when going to movie theaters as a young college student in the late 1960s, she compared herself favorably to the main actresses and dreamed of becoming an actress herself ("in order not to waste my beauty!"). Being beautiful (*güzel* in Turkish) was so intricately tied to her identity that, when her looks started deteriorating "dramatically" after menopause, this created immense pressure for her to maintain her looks by cosmetic intervention: "They say '[Jale] is *güzel*,' and you are getting used to that description, so you always strive to suit that description, . . . I mean, I even think my husband would have divorced me if I had not retained my shape."

As a consequence, aging for Jale became tied to a process of gaining knowledge about how to "retain shape," investing the necessary time and effort to do so while also adapting psychologically and emotionally to a new self that was no longer tied to common understandings of beauty such as freshness and youth. Retaining shape clearly formed part of Jale's everyday routine and discipline, comprising a long list of beauty and health practices such as regular massages, daily yoga lessons, walking, and exercises, as well as a great deal of attention to what she called a healthy diet (organic rather than processed food, water instead of soft drinks, etc.). In addition to the standard practices of bodily grooming that Jale was already consuming during her monthly beauty salon visits, she now also started visiting a dermatologist twice a year for Botox injections, fillers, and other treatments for facial rejuvenation. She regularly sought her dermatologist's advice on the latest anti-aging treatments and described herself as open to whatever he suggested was needed.

To communicate what, apart from divorce, was at stake for her with aging well, Jale described a scene that took place every summer when she and her husband traveled to their private seaside resort in Bodrum on the Aegean Sea. Sitting on her own or one of their neighbors' terraces overlooking the private beach, Jale recounted, the women usually discussed the bodily state of their mutual female acquaintances:

> They say things like: "Oh my, did you see her? She's become so deformed!" Women are always talking in this kind of way about others,

and you certainly don't want to be seen like "her." Like (*she changes her voice to emulate a gossiping voice*): "She's become so *old*! You should see how *decomposed* she looks!" (*laughs*). You hear them say things like that about somebody else, and you wonder what they say about you when you're not around . . .

In Jale's account the private beaches of Bodrum, generally known as the place where Istanbul's upper middle-class vacations between June and September, becomes a stage for the public performance of aging feminin-ity, presented before the critical eyes of a likewise aging female audience. Jale's account of this spectacle suggests a world full of social pressures and ambivalence with regard to aging for urban (upper) middle-class women. On the one hand, she obviously gives in to these pressures and shares the common expectation of middle-class women's obligation to age well, also participating in the gossip about women's use and rejection of cosmetic interventions. On the other hand, she also distances herself from those who seem over-concerned with their own as well as other women's looks, obviously desperate in their attempt to look young and attractive forever. Drawing on the popular image of the *kokona*, an elderly, upper-class woman overly concerned about her outer appearance (see chapter 1), dur-ing the interview Jale continued to tattle about the "women from [upscale] Nişantaşı," who at her age were artificially blonde, bejeweled, "and all made up with lipstick and stuff." While she was convinced that her own style was more natural and tasteful, it must be admitted that, for an out-sider less trained in the minutiae of style in central Istanbul, she might well have been mistaken for a "Nişantaşı woman" as she defined it herself, living in a neighborhood that bordered on Nişantaşı and likewise making up and dyeing her hair.

The concern over having "natural" rather than "exaggerated" looks was indeed great among postmenopausal women who consumed inva-sive cosmetic surgery treatments. Another research participant, Neslihan, an upper middle-class woman in her mid-sixties and one of Jale's friends from yoga, likewise distanced herself from the beauty-intensive "exag-gerated" looks of some of the elderly women in her social environment. Since the beginning of her menopause in 1995, Neslihan had had three combined cosmetic operations, namely a breast lift and two subsequent rounds of face and neck lifts, as well as eyelid surgery. In our interview, Neslihan emphasized her anxiety over "unnatural" looks as the outcome of surgery, triggered by the "exaggerated" looks of one of her cosmetically altered friends. Such exaggerated looks frightened people off, she claimed, recounting an encounter with a lady at a funeral she recently attended:

> There was a lady who was all done up, like this—(*curls her lips in an exaggerated way to imitate her*). This woman, she almost looked like an alien, in a really scary way! You shouldn't be able to discern cosmetic surgery, and this kind of *estetik*, the very exaggerated kind, it's not right. It makes me think that these people have mental problems. Beauty should look natural![6]

Elderly women who consumed invasive cosmetic treatments obsessively in their attempt to fight the signs of bodily aging were obviously anxious and indeed "mentally troubled" in their attempts to look young. Moreover, they had chosen forms of surgery that were discernible, rather than natural-looking, which Neslihan judged in moral terms to be "not right." The consumption of such surgery was conspicuous in that the patient obviously wanted to show, in Neslihan's words, "that she can afford it." Neslihan in contrast aimed for a *hoş* or "pleasant-looking" surgery outcome in an attempt to "please people," including her husband, who supported her in her desire for cosmetic surgery and had accompanied her to numerous doctors' consultations. Moreover, like Jale, she regarded her invasive cosmetic procedures as just a small though indispensable part in her struggle of "aging well," which on a more quotidian basis included a healthy diet, yoga and fitness classes, and a general interest in health and well-being.

The subsumption and downplaying of cosmetic surgery within a daily routine of "aging well" in the accounts of Jale and Neslihan point to its ambiguous meaning for elderly women. Within a competitive urban environment, elderly women who consumed invasive cosmetic treatments

---

6. Interview with Neslihan, March 12, 2014. The following quotations by Neslihan are also taken from this interview.

could never be sure whether and when their attempts to maintain their feminine attractiveness at an advanced age were judged exaggerated and desperate, rather than pleasant and effective. Thus, while cultural conceptions of aging have clearly been changing in recent decades, at a certain point urban middle-class women were still considered "too old for beauty," or, as the following will show, considered themselves too old at least for the more invasive cosmetic practices that they had consumed until recently.

"Too Old for Beauty"

In Turkey maturity for women is closely related to their reproductive and caregiving tasks in relation to different generations of family members, most importantly their children, husbands or spouses, and parents. It is widely agreed that women born in the early Republican years of the 1930s and 1940s were expected to devote their lives to their families, no matter whether they lived in villages or cities, or whether they also chose to have a career. Telling the anthropologist Esra Özyürek (2006) about their lives, this cohort of secular, middle-class "children of the Republic" stressed the personal discipline and sacrifice that was expected of them as the vanguard of a new type of emancipated women, who combined their professional and family lives to serve the newly founded Turkish Republic.[7] While these women took great care to look well groomed, proper, and fit, the dominant moral values of national and familial service, discipline, and sacrifice went against intensified individual investments in self-care, appearance, and attractiveness that were under the strong suspicion of being narcissistic, wasteful, and vain.

Most of the postmenopausal middle-class women interviewed for this study were younger than the cohort interviewed by Özyürek in the late 1990s and early 2000s. In fact, they were the grandchildren rather than the children of the Republic. When in the 1990s Istanbul experienced a boom in the personal care, beauty, and fitness market, most of my older interlocutors were married mothers in their late thirties to fifties and, as shown so

---

7. Interestingly, Özyürek does not analyze the gendered aspects inherent in women's narratives, which I argue are crucial for their deeper understanding.

far, many of them experimented with various aesthetic treatments offered by an increasing number of beauty salons and clinics in the city. They did so in contrast to an earlier generation of women, including their mothers, whom they often described or remembered as well-groomed and proper looking, but who rarely if ever entered a beauty salon when they were their age, let alone engaged in cosmetic surgery. In contrast to the postmenopausal women described so far, their mothers had come to downplay their sexual identities after menopause, which was symbolized by the fact that some of them had adopted a loosely tied headscarf.

The new cohort of beauty-conscious elderly middle-class women likewise felt that a time came when one was simply too old for beauty. However, in contrast to an earlier generation of middle-class women, this did not mean that they stopped consuming beauty service work; instead, as we learned from the outline above, they eventually came to choose less invasive, supposedly "natural-looking" treatments and emphasized aspects of well-being and health instead. A case in point was Nehir, a retired teacher in her mid-sixties, who reflected about her beauty practices from the position of someone who considered herself "too old for beauty," as she jokingly remarked at the beginning of our interview. Born into a staunchly Kemalist middle-class family of early Republicans in the capital Ankara, shortly after marriage Nehir moved to Moda, a secular middle-class neighborhood on the Asian side of Istanbul where we met as the participants in a mid-morning Pilates class at a private women-only beauty and fitness club. She continued to be married to her husband of over forty years, and was a mother of two and a recent grandmother.

Asked about her beauty practices, Nehir recounted how, ever since she got married, she regularly attended hair salons for cutting, styling, and coloring her hair, and for manicures, pedicures, and body hair removal. At the age of forty, in the late 1980s, she had had her first facial treatment after venturing into a clinic she saw advertised in a women's magazine. For many years afterward she returned there once a month to have various aesthetic treatments, including permanent body hair removal, facials, and rejuvenation treatments. After menopause, when she turned fifty, Nehir opted for cosmetic surgery and had her face and cheeks lifted, as well as eyelid surgery to treat her drooping eyelids. In an interview, she explained her motivation as follows:

> At that age, you feel that you're getting older and [start] looking bad, and you want to look younger and more beautiful. But at my [current] age, you don't feel that—you accept your age. But at fifty—between forty-five and fifty —when everybody around you is young and good-looking— the lines around here (*points to her temples*) feel—they make you feel depressed. I felt like that. But now (*laughs*) I'm okay, I accept everything. The only thing [that matters to me now] is my health. . . . But before, it was different. You have a husband, and you want to be attractive. You want to compete with other women. To challenge the other women— you know what I mean?[8]

Here Nehir distinguishes between a time when she was still anxious about her looks and her present age, which she describes as health- rather than beauty-oriented. Once again, the imagined link between female attractiveness and heteronormative sexuality becomes obvious here in that until recently Nehir felt the need to "compete with other women," not least with respect to her husband's attention. More recently, however, the feeling of competitiveness had subsided to one of acceptance. Thus, when asked whether she considered any other cosmetic intervention in the future, Nehir responded vehemently:

> No, not at my age. I advise this to women aged fifty. After the age of fifty, it becomes weird [*komik*]. But when you turn sixty, from old to older (*laughs*), you should feel like you have accomplished something! I felt like this, at least. All my friends felt like this. But shortly before that, all my friends tried to do something—I mean, they all did some kind of [cosmetic] surgery. All women my age did. You cannot understand this at your age. In order to understand it, you have to be that age . . .

Whereas at the age of fifty bodily changes signaled for Nehir the beginning of an old age that caused negative feelings for her and that she

---

8. Interview with Nehir, May 19, 2014. The following quotations from Nehir are also taken from this interview.

was not yet ready to accept, at the age of sixty, having fulfilled the social expectations of her as a mother, namely to marry off her children successfully, and having also become a grandmother, old age turned into an accomplishment for Nehir that lessened its negative aspects. Whereas ten years earlier for Nehir beauty work and attractiveness had come with the pressure of not losing her husband to more attractive and younger women, today, from the social position of an accomplished grandmother and a wife who had obviously aged well, she felt beyond that pressure. She now related her ongoing beauty practices to personal pleasure and well-being. This was also reflected in her changing preference for particular beauty treatments, namely from invasive cosmetic surgery to treatments more commonly subsumed under wellness, such as regular spa visits, massages, or aromatherapies. Cosmetic surgery at her age, Nehir was convinced, was considered weird. Nevertheless, a well-groomed appearance continued to be of great importance to her and was tied up with her own understanding of femininity: "Even if I'm over sixty years old, I'm still a woman!"

Another research participant in her early sixties who described herself as too old for beauty was Sakine. When I first met her, Sakine was working as a director's secretary in an international financial institution in central Levent. An energetic, outspoken, extroverted woman with a great sense of humor, Sakine likewise described herself as being at peace with her aging body and even mentioned some positive aspects of aging for women. For her, these were related to her own experiences of sexualization as a young divorcée in a provincial patriarchal setting and as an urban immigrant. As the oldest daughter of nine children born into a lower middle-class family from Samsun on the western Black Sea coast, Sakine married young and gave birth to a daughter in her early twenties. Soon afterward her husband abandoned her and, aged thirty-one, Sakine filed for a divorce, a highly unconventional move for young women in the province at the time.

In earlier times, Sakine, who continued to look attractive at her age, had been a stunning beauty, a fact that was supported by old family pictures and the accounts of her younger sisters. She described her former attractiveness as a burden in the conservative small town she grew up in because she felt especially prone to unwelcome sexual advances by men and, closely related to this, subject to restrictions on her movements that she partly imposed upon herself for protection. Moving to Istanbul made life easier for Sakine in this regard, but posed different bodily challenges. While in her hometown, due to the imminent threat of sexual assault as a young woman without the protection of a husband, she had downplayed her attractiveness and hidden her body under layers of loose clothing to the point of becoming alienated from it, in Istanbul, as a young woman in search of employment in the service sector, she felt the need to show and invest in her bodily attractiveness. Accordingly, Sakine started to visit beauty salons regularly and during the 1990s underwent multiple cosmetic treatments and surgery to reduce her body weight. Her beauty work proved so successful that at the age of fifty Sakine was approached by a well-known event manager who asked whether she would participate in a "Miss Fifty-Year-Old" beauty contest that he was organizing for a private TV channel. The offer coincided with Sakine's menopause, and when she heard that the event included a bikini contest, she refused, saying that it was inappropriate for women "in this stage of life to appear in a bikini in public."[9]

In contrast to some of the women quoted above, Sakine did not intensify her beautification efforts in search of a "second spring" after menopause, but rather began downplaying her sexual identity, mostly by the way she dressed. For example, she no longer dressed in tight pants or wore low necklines. Similar to the women quoted above, for Sakine aging eventually removed some of the pressure in relation to maintaining her good looks and attractiveness: "Now I am aged sixty, thank God! I don't care about my age these days . . ." This indicates that the desexualization implied in aging for women may first come as a threat, but eventually, and for some, it may also turn into relief. Claiming not to care about her age, Sakine nevertheless continued to invest in her body. Thus, in contrast to older female family members, she continued her regular beauty salon and clinic visits for manicures, pedicures, Botox injections, and other rejuvenation treatments.

9. Interview with Sakine, December 26, 2013. The following quotations from Sakine are also taken from this interview.

To sum up, like earlier generations of women, the new cohort of urban postmenopausal middle-class women described in this chapter eventually began to downplay their sexual identity after the end of menstruation, describing themselves as "too old for beauty." However, they did so later, typically after first intensifying beautification at the beginning of menopause in an attempt to stay competitive or in search of the so-called "second spring." Moreover, despite describing themselves as "too old for beauty," they usually continued to invest in body aesthetics, if not in treatments seen as boosting sexual attractiveness such as cosmetic surgery, then at least in those seen as maintaining the body or reducing the (visible) signs of aging. Finally, while Nehir and Sakine differed in their personal experiences and conceptualizations of aging, they both described a process of coming to terms with one's body. In both cases, this process was closely monitored and guided by various therapeutic and medical actors in the commercial urban beauty economy. The following section changes the perspective to show how this plays out in one of the sites of the urban beauty economy, namely a private beauty clinic in the center city district of Etiler.

Waiting for Rejuvenation in Etiler

Arriving one Thursday morning in early April 2015 for another day of interviews and participant observation at İlke and Serhat's private beauty clinic in Etiler, my research assistant and I were greeted by the carefully made-up doctor's receptionist in a white tunic. We slipped on disposable overshoes from a box next to the entrance and settled in the large, white waiting room, decorated with a Greek-style female nude sculpture beneath a wall of medical diplomas collected by İlke and Serhat over the past three decades, to wait for their patients to arrive.

A married couple in their early fifties and both medical practitioners, İlke and Serhat first opened their clinic in 1994 after İlke, a trained dermatologist, returned from additional training as a cosmetologist in Germany. Back then comparable professional training was not yet available in Turkey, and the clinic, located on two upper floors of a residential building, soon gained a reputation as one of the first professional beauty clinics in this upmarket center city neighborhood. By the time I was first introduced to Serhat and İlke by a family friend, İlke's sister, and visited the clinic in 2011, numerous beauty salons and clinics had opened in its vicinity. Serhat and İlke's patients arrived for treatments from both the urban vicinity and abroad, namely the entire Middle East and Europe, to choose from a long list of aesthetic services, including fillers, eyelid surgery, laser depilation and, in another facility run by the couple, hair transplants. The most common treatment at the clinic, however, was the injection of botulinum toxin for facial rejuvenation.

The regular injection of the neurotoxic protein botulinum toxin (Botox) to treat and prevent the development of wrinkles by paralyzing facial muscles was quite common among specific segments of middle-aged and older upper middle-class women during my research in Istanbul. It was generally seen as one of the first steps taken by middle- and upper-class women to deal with the visible signs of aging. First documented in 1989 by an American plastic surgeon following clinical trials and the approval of the American Food and Drugs Administration in 2002, botulinum toxin has become a popular cosmetic treatment worldwide, marketed by several pharmaceutical companies under various brand names, including Botox by Allergan, a global pharmaceutical company headquartered in Dublin (Berkowitz 2017).

In Turkey, botulinum toxin injections and other facial rejuvenation procedures are extremely popular even in comparison with global statistics. In 2017 the International Society of Aesthetic and Plastic Surgeons (ISAPS) estimated that 221,808 botulinum toxin injections were administered in Turkey in 2016, alongside more than 70,000 other nonsurgical facial rejuvenation treatments and injections, including the injection of hyaluronic acid and autologous fat, so-called fillers. This meant that, when it came to botulinum toxin injections, Turkey ranked number four of all countries listed, with a staggering 4.5 percent of all such injections globally being administered there.[10] According to national regulations,

---

10. Due to the increased popularity of other injectables such as hyaluronic acid, in 2019 the share of botulinum toxin injections in Turkey had decreased to 49.6 percent of all nonsurgical procedures, even though at 199,506 injections its number was still high. (ISAPS 2019: 21)

injections for facial aesthetics and rejuvenation are to be administered by medical doctors in medical office facilities, free-standing surgicenters, or hospitals only;[11] most patients seem to have them performed in private medical offices or surgicenters every five to six months. In 2015, facial Botox injections cost from 300–350 TRY (approximately US$110–30) per session in Istanbul. Accordingly, beauty therapists often criticized the treatment as expensive, with only limited and temporal effects, and recommended their own, noninvasive rejuvenation treatments instead.

On the day of our visit at the beauty clinic in Etiler in 2015, a woman in her early sixties, a regular patient of İlke and Serhat, arrived with her thirty-seven-year old daughter shortly before noon. While Serhat administered the injections into the daughter's face, the mother told us that she had been "doing Botox" for almost ten years to alleviate the glabellar frown lines between her eyebrows that run in the genes of her maternal line. After menopause, when her body started "deteriorating," she began to be bothered by these lines and was haunted by the vision of developing the same stern facial expression her mother had. When she noticed the same lines develop in her daughter's face a few months ago, she persuaded her to get the injections as soon as possible to prevent them from developing further.

After the treatment with botulinum toxin, the two women were in a hurry to leave because they were already late for a lunch with friends in a nearby shopping mall. As soon as the door shut behind them, Serhat came to join us in the now empty waiting room, asking the receptionist to serve us tea. He complained about the patient, telling us that she insisted on having botulinum toxin injections between her eyebrows only, out of a concern to "look natural." Serhat found this strange because "she is already doing something." According to him, she clearly did not do enough to prevent visible aging, and when he met her, he suggested treating other facial wrinkles with botulinum toxin injections too. In addition, her sagging eye

---

11. Resmi Gazete, Güzellik ve Estetik Amaçlı Sağlık Kuruluşları Hakkında Yönetmelik, May 12, 2003, Regulation no. 25106.

bags and a deepening nasolabial fold needed "urgent treating," preferably with fillers. Nevertheless, the patient remained what Serhat describes as "fixed on her frown lines."

Those who "did Botox" in Etiler and elsewhere were typically concerned about looking natural. Thus, due to the treatment's high cost and limited availability in the first years after its discovery as a cosmetic product, for many years it was, and in some respects still is, regarded as a *sosyete* (elite or high-society) procedure in Turkey, one that celebrities and public personalities or those who wish to be recognized as belonging to this exclusive social group regularly undergo. Thus, "doing Botox" has a certain chic to it, which makes it attractive beyond its actual bodily effects. On the other hand, those publicly known for their botulinum toxin injections are often described as exaggerating its use, and the Turkish tabloid press abounds with images of celebrities with awkwardly swollen faces bereft of the ability to mimic, or with pouty lips obviously resulting from recent injections. Accordingly, when I asked Sakine, portrayed in the previous section, whether she was happy with the outcome of the treatment, she responded: "Yes, because they didn't turn me into a monkey." Her expression obviously referred to a remark by a well-known aesthetic surgeon during a private TV channel talk show several weeks earlier, describing the aging yet never aging Turkish superstar Ajda Pekkan as having "no mimic in her face" and with lips that looked like "the bum of a monkey" due to her allegedly excessive use of the drug.[12]

The next patient at the clinic that day was a woman called Günay in her early forties. She arrived from nearby Şişli for Botox injections. More than four years ago, and inspired by her employer, the owner of a wig store in upmarket Nişantaşı, Günay started to "do Botox" regularly. At around the same time she started having "problems around the eyes," with lines developing between her eyebrows and on her forehead, which she attributed to her genes. She explained that after she had her face treated,

12. Pekkan later filed a lawsuit against the surgeon to claim compensation for reputation damage (Hürriyet 2013).

it "looked much nicer, my eyebrows were lifted, and this really opened up my facial expression."[13] When the effect started to show several days after the injection, she said, "I felt extremely happy, and that's why I continue doing it." While we chatted with Günay, her close friend Miray arrived alongside her older sister Tülin also to have botulinum toxin injections. The women gave each other a warm welcome, and the newcomers apologized to Günay for arriving late from their Pilates class at a nearby fitness studio. This was Tülin's first time to "do Botox" and Günay, who introduced Miray to the clinic several years ago, now introduced Tülin to Serhat. While Serhat left to treat Günay on the clinic's upper floor, Tülin was handed a patient questionnaire and information sheet about the procedure to read, fill in, and sign. The receptionist also took a picture of her face, the "before" photograph, later to be compared with the photograph to be taken a week after the treatment, when the result is expected to show. Checking his photographic files, Serhat later presented us with Günay's before-and-after-photograph, which the sisters commented on as "not looking like Günay at all," especially in its "before" version.

While waiting for Günay to return, the sisters started chatting about Tülin's recent stay in a luxury hotel on the Mediterranean coast with her family. Miray, a woman in her early forties, was dressed sportily, with tanned skin, and a bird tattoo showing on her chest. Tülin, about ten years her senior, carried herself with an upper middle-class chic. She was wearing gold jewelry, shouldered an Yves Saint Laurent handbag, and possessed the latest model of an expensive smartphone. In our interview she told us about her anxiety regarding the injections, which she felt were long overdue. All her friends did these injections, and she had been reluctant for "too long." She was especially concerned with the facial wrinkles on her forehead, her crow's feet wrinkles, and her upper lip, which recently started looking like "an old lady's lip." Other than that, and with the exception of some excessive fat on her belly, she was rather satisfied with her body. She talked at length about the different kinds of classes she took in her fitness

13. Interview with Günay, April 2, 2015. The following quotations from Günay are also taken from this interview.

salon to stay in shape. Like Günay and in fact many other interviewees, Tülin usually did not tell her husband about the aesthetic treatments she was planning to have and had not told him about her appointment today. Moreover, she was prepared to cover the treatment from her own savings, in contrast to products for the family's day-to-day needs which she paid for with her husband's credit card. Telling us about this, Tülin realized that she had not even inquired about the costs of the treatment; however, she trusted her sister and Günay to negotiate a good price for her.

In the meanwhile, Serhat had finished Günay's injections, and she re-emerged, only to disappear again into İlke's office to discuss an eyelid treatment that Serhat had suggested. The receptionist summoned Tülin. In the treatment room, Serhat asked her to lie down on a chair that bore a resemblance to a dentist's chair and without further ado started with three injections each into Tülin's left and right temples. Every time he pulled out the syringe, he quickly pressed a cotton ball to her skin and showed the cotton ball to Tülin to prove that there had not yet been any blood. Blood eventually did emerge after another round of injections between the eyes, into the forehead, and in the upper lip, but Serhat quickly changed the cotton ball and Tülin didn't seem to notice. Instead he reprimanded her for smoking, telling us that smokers' lips always looked "worse" than nonsmokers'. After less than five minutes the procedure was finished, and Tülin sighed with relief. "It wasn't such a big deal," she said. "Of course not," responded Serhat. "What about this one," Tülin asked him, pointing to her nasolabial fold. "It's still okay," he said, adding, "We will treat it with a filling once it's become deeper, in about five years from now." Telling her not to massage her face in the next twenty-four hours or to sleep on either side of her face for the right result to show in a few days, he then directed her to come back for a checkup the following week and went downstairs to call up Miray.

The doctor-patient interaction shows that Serhat clearly took seriously his patient's anxiety by attempting to simulate the treatment's "bloodless-ness" as a supposedly "petite" surgery. Reprimanding her for smoking, he promoted not only a healthier lifestyle, but one that actively engaged with the aesthetic rationale of his patient's medical consumption, namely to slow down the visible signs of bodily aging. Tülin, on the other hand, proved to be an informed consumer-patient engaging in self-scrutiny as part of her self-surveillance and willing to do more if need be. Not least, the medical interaction established a temporal axis in which the treatment of Tülin's nasolabial fold was already envisaged as being necessary "in five years' time."

The final patient to arrive at the clinic that day was Ayzer, a stylish blonde in her late fifties made up with lipstick and eyeliner, and dressed in tight black pants, heeled boots, and a red lady's suit jacket. Ayzer had been a regular of the clinic for ten years, from when her menopause began. She reported having regular botulinum toxin and vitamin injections twice a year as well as occasional fillers, and eyelid surgery to treat her drooping eyelids. That day at the clinic, Serhat treated her with hyaluronic wrinkle-fillers to reduce her facial lines, which cost about 500 TRY (approximately US$185 at the time). During our conversation in the waiting room, Ayzer told us that the treatments she had had at the clinic and their results made her happy (*mutlu*), while the thought or sight of her own aging appearance usually made her feel depressed (*umutsuz*) and sad (*üzüntülü*). Facing the mirror naked these days, she confided, she hardly remembered her former attractive and fit self, and especially detested the flabby skin and excessive fat on her thighs and belly. Like many other female patients at the clinic, Ayzer seemed anxious about her attractiveness as the wife of a public figure (according to what Serhat hinted at after she left) and as someone whose identity had for many decades been tied to being considered a beautiful woman.

To sum up, many of the regular female patients at this private beauty clinic formed a specific type of middle-aged to younger elderly patients concerned about their looks and bodily "deformation," who were well informed about the latest trends and treatments. While generally fit and healthy, they arrived at the clinic for regular check-ups and the *latebost* (preventive) treatments, closely monitoring their bodies and—setting aside their own money, and in spite of bargaining hard—investing "as much as it cost" to reduce the visible signs of aging. These women clearly rejected the idea of fatalistically accepting old age, which they attributed to a more conservative or earlier cohort of women in Turkey, using aesthetic body modifications to assert their postmenopausal identities as women in their "second spring." They did so in contrast to an earlier generation of women, including their mothers, whom they often described or remembered as well-groomed and proper looking, but rarely if ever entering a beauty salon, let alone an office or clinic for aesthetic procedures when they had been their age. In contrast to them, and in spite of their different conceptualization of the ending of their monthly menstruation, their mothers had come to downplay their sexual identities in this period of their lives. By the time my research took place, the discourse of menopause as a major marker of bodily changes—that is, bodily deformation, in the language of beauty therapists and medical practitioners specialized in aesthetics—had been firmly established in elderly women's body-centered life-course narratives. Many of the postmenopausal women in the higher social strata I was often referred to by acquaintances or else encountered in beauty salons and clinics in the urban center like that described above chose to invest in aesthetic body modifications to treat subjective feelings of ugliness and depression that for them were tied to menopause.

The women who entered the clinic in Etiler in search of rejuvenation and aesthetic "upgrades" demanded respect not so much due to their maturity, but due to their ongoing attractiveness, self-care, and competitiveness with other women, including those younger than them. Against the background of a wide range of standard routines to keep the body fit, healthy, and attractive, they obviously felt the need once in a while to "pull themselves together" through invasive, albeit "natural-looking" cosmetic procedures.

Conclusion

Confronted with the first negatively viewed signs of aging during Istanbul's beauty boom in the late 1980s and 1990s, a period in which menopause became public knowledge and soon thereafter was medially invented as marking women's "second spring," the postmenopausal women described in this chapter chose to actively invest in rejuvenation and aesthetic "upgrades." While some women are ready to do "whatever is needed," following the advice of commercial beauty therapists and medical experts in private salons and clinics, others are troubled by very specific visible signs of aging; for example, those they find disturbing in their mother's aging bodies. As a social practice, the injection of botulinum toxin and similar (often presumably "bloodless") aesthetic body modifications observed at the clinic described above offer an interesting example of what has been called "surveillance medicine" (Armstrong 1995).

Within the shift from hospital medicine to surveillance medicine described by Armstrong, an increasingly informed and self-conscious patient who enjoys a certain level of disposable income and is, strictly speaking, healthy no longer relies on public health provision but pays for his or her own treatments, often in private medical institutions. Treatments are undertaken not necessarily to improve one's health, but to prevent it from deteriorating. From this perspective, it is aging itself that is considered an aesthetic-medical health risk or even a disease, to be treated by rejuvenation procedures as part of an entire lifestyle that also includes a healthy diet, sports, recreation, and wellness, things all widely talked about in the waiting room area of the clinic described above, as well as in interviews with postmenopausal middle-class women across Istanbul.

Looking at their mothers and grandmothers, who were unable to consume similar kinds of cosmetic treatments due to the shame associated with investing in one's sexual attractiveness as a woman later in life and to the unavailability of such treatments, new cohorts of aging women in Turkey see in their faces their own futures in the form of aesthetic "deformation." Whereas cultural conceptions of aging emphasize social accomplishment and increasing authority for all genders, the female patients of private beauty clinics seem to have internalized a conceptualization of aging as risk, not least an aesthetic one. Earlier conceptualizations of aging, however, do not simply disappear. Heteronormative middle-class women in urban Turkey are still valued for their social accomplishments as the main caregivers in private households of children, grandchildren, and aging parents. Efforts in respect of body maintenance, beauty, and self-care that exceed the standard routines of bodily grooming are still considered potentially vain and narcissistic. They are justifiable only insofar as they do not impede on women's care responsibilities and are pathologized if engaged in by women who are considered "too old for beauty." Being judged as such is—just like aging itself—dependent upon one's

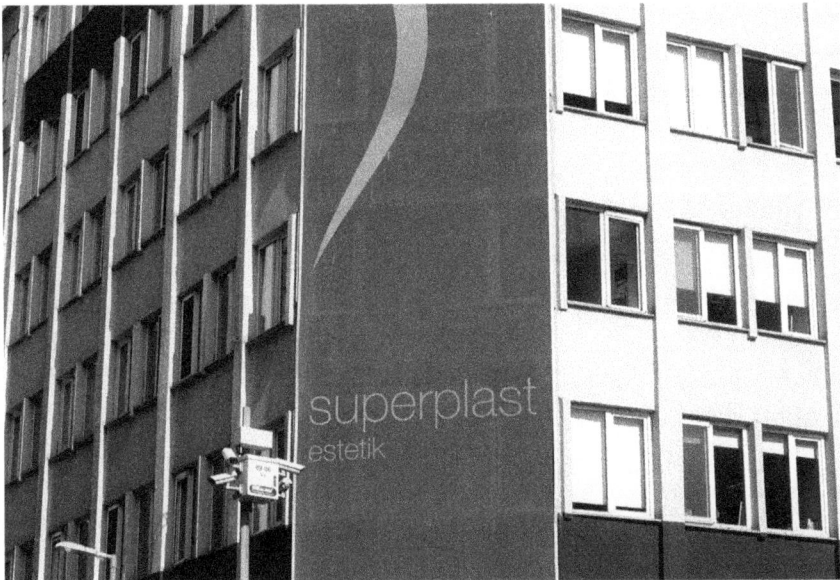

5. In front of a private beauty clinic in Nişantaşı: in the age of surveillance medicine, aging becomes an aesthetic-medical risk to be treated with aesthetic upgrades and bodily "rejuvenation." (Claudia Liebelt)

social positioning, rather than biological age. Thus, in her landmark essay on "The Double Standard of Aging" (2018 [1972]), Susan Sontag notes that aging varies according to social class. Sontag observes that, whereas wealthier people may look younger, "anxiety about aging is certainly more common, and more acute, among middle-class and rich women than among working-class women. Economically disadvantaged women in this society are more fatalistic about aging; they can't afford to fight the cosmetic battle as long or as tenaciously" (2018 [1972], 21). This certainly holds for Turkey, where the ongoing consumption of beauty treatments and services, particularly the more invasive ones, is commonly seen as the preserve of urban, upper middle-class and secular women, at least for the time being.

In her ethnography of elderly Jewish women attending an American neighborhood beauty salon, Frida Kerner Furman describes three strategic responses by elderly beauty salon clients to their declining bodies, namely resentment, acceptance, and compensation (1997, 102). Acceptance of aging, Furman stresses, is not a passive activity, but "requires reflection and courage" in that it represents "a struggling of the soul to affirm what is yet possible, to let go of what is not" (Furman 1997, 102). For the women described above, acceptance of aging was likewise tied to an intense process of coming to terms with their changing bodies in times of heightened expectations of "aging well." It required the juggling of different, somewhat competing social valuations of themselves as respectable mothers and grandmothers on the one hand, and attractive wives and sexually active lovers on the other. In contrast to earlier conceptualizations of aging, this chapter has shown that, in the contemporary urban economy, aging well in accordance with gendered and classed expectations has become a challenge for postmenopausal middle-class women, extending well beyond menopause.

5

Reshaping "Turkish" Breasts and Noses

Shortly after I distributed questionnaires on beauty practices and cosmetic surgery in a municipal training course on makeup in Kavacık, a lower middle-class neighborhood on the outskirts of Istanbul's Anatolian side one afternoon in May 2014, Hülya, one of the thirteen female course participants, blurted out: "How could cosmetic surgery possibly be regarded as something 'positive and important'?" She was paraphrasing one of the statements in the questionnaire that I asked participants to agree or disagree with. This comment by Hülya, a middle-aged housewife, like most of the course participants, triggered a lively debate on *estetik* (cosmetic surgery in Turkish) that soon came to circle around the reshaping of breasts and noses. The first to respond was the teacher, a former marketing manager in her early fifties, who shared the story of her sister. Her sister, she said, had recently overcome a serious depression by undergoing breast-reduction surgery, something she should have opted for "many years earlier." For decades, she had hidden her breasts under baggy clothes and refused to wear bathing suits or go swimming out of shame about her large breasts, afraid that men would stare at them. Other stories of nose and breast-reduction surgery surfaced, and the women, many of whom were rather critical of cosmetic surgery when this was merely a matter of boosting attractiveness, eventually agreed that, if one was suffering from big noses or heavy breasts, cosmetic surgery indeed potentially offered a cure. They expressed sympathy with those who opted for surgery because they felt uncomfortable (*rahatsız*) with their bodies in public and obviously sympathized with women who experienced bodily discomfort

175

triggered by public staring. Whereas in this particular social environment cosmetic surgery tended to be considered sinful for permanently changing one's God-given appearance, as well as shameful because of its sexual connotations, after some discussion nose and breast-reduction operations were clearly treated as exceptions. These cosmetic surgery procedures, among the most prevalent in Turkey, were commonly seen as based on the perfectly understandable desire for a normal body image.

The most common cosmetic surgery procedures in Turkey are, in descending order and according to the statistics gathered by the International Society of Cosmetic and Plastic Surgeons (ISAPS 2019), rhinoplasty or nose surgery, breast augmentation, liposuction or fat removal surgery, eyelid surgery, fat grafting (face), and breast reduction for women. While this list is similar to the global average, as well as the ISAPS listings for the United States, Brazil, Japan, and Mexico, who currently top the list of countries with the highest number of plastic surgery procedures worldwide, nose and breast-reduction operations are more frequent in Turkey than in any of the countries listed. This chapter seeks to contribute to the debate on the standardization of bodily features through cosmetic surgery by probing an understanding of its procedures, in particular nose and female breast surgery, as a classed, gendered, and racialized desire for a normal body image, or, in the case of breast-enlargement surgery, a sexy body image in urban Turkey. There are specific bodily concerns in Turkey that are the product of history and are interlinked with imaginations of modernity, femininity, and urban belonging. "Large" or "hooked" noses and, sometimes, "heavy" female breasts, whose surgical treatment is the focus of this chapter, are clearly among these; as the following shows, they are seen as problematic among particular groups in Istanbul.

In the language of medical experts in Turkey, heavy female breasts and large or hooked noses are national bodily defects, their treatment generally being labeled "ethnic plastic surgery." Developed by US-based cosmetic and plastic surgeons, the term "ethnic plastic surgery" is usually employed with reference to the specific physical characteristics and different anatomical features of "minority patients," that is, non-Caucasian plastic surgery patients (cf. Mann 2014, Slupchynskyj 2005). In societies in which ethnic features are tied to marginalized minorities, correcting these features has been characterized as a major motivation for cosmetic surgery. For example, in his comprehensive cultural history of cosmetic surgery, Sander Gilman (1999) foregrounds "racial passing," that is, the desire to pass visibly from a negative category to a positive one, as "the basic motivation for aesthetic surgery" (Gilman 1999, xvii). According to Gilman, the rise of cosmetic surgery at the end of the sixteenth century in Europe rested on attempts by those constructed as dangerous, namely the syphilitic, "no longer to be identified as different" (Gilman 1999, xxi), in this particular case by reconstructing a nose lost from the illness. Gilman shows that, with the emergence of ideologies of race and racial science, passing meant primarily racial passing, with patients turning their deviant "Jewish," "Irish," or "Black" noses into normative "Aryan," "English," or "white" ones (Gilman 1999, 23).

Labeling specific cosmetic surgery procedures ethnic, I argue, is problematic because it sets Caucasian physical features as the norm and labels looks that deviate from this norm "ethnic." Also, as the following account shows, it pays little attention to the complexities of local meanings of and motivations for surgery within particular social, urban, and cultural settings. As sexualized and prominent personal features, large breasts and noses are not problematic for women as racial or ethnic features per se, but they may become so in some cases and in particular social settings. Not least, female breasts and noses are scrutinized in a patriarchal society that seeks control over the sexual female body. Against this background, my ethnographic data suggest that surgery may also be a tool for women hoping to reduce "dominating stares" at their bodies by "normalizing" the latter (cf. Garland-Thomson 2009) in an attempt to regain control. In line with recent approaches to beauty and cosmetic surgery (Coleman and Figueroa 2010; Elias et al. 2016; Jarrín 2017), I argue for an understanding of these as affective processes embedded in particular biopolitical histories.

Finally, the discussion draws attention to the fuzzy line between health and aesthetics that both feature prominently in cosmetic surgeons' and their patients' accounts of breast and nose operations. Shifting between what is considered medical or therapeutic-functional and what is considered aesthetic, surgery patients may employ these labels strategically. Given the fact that *estetik* may have problematic connotations, especially in more conservative and lower social strata—as exemplified by the vignette from Kavacık quoted above—it is hardly surprising that the narrative focus often lies on surgery as a matter of health, rather than on aesthetics.

Racialization and Normalization in Turkish Cosmetic Surgery Practice

Normalization, studied so prominently by Michel Foucault (1990, 1995), involves disciplinary power and social control rather than direct force. It is a process enforced by various authorities, including medical authorities, based on the concept of the normal "as a principle of coercion" (Foucault 1995, 184) that eventually creates "docile bodies" self-monitoring their compliance with the normative order. As recent works that approach beauty through affect theory have shown, bodily normalization is not simply a disciplinary process, but an affective force directed at a particular body image rooted in history. As mentioned above, nose and breast-reduction surgeries are more frequent in Turkey than elsewhere, are generally called "ethnic plastic surgery" by cosmetic surgeons in Turkey, and are associated with particular bodily "defects." Ethnicity, in this cosmopolitan medical discourse, is commonly understood as a phenotypical and racialized feature that is more closely linked to earlier eugenic ideas than to cultural anthropological understandings that conceptualize ethnicity as a situated social practice (cf. Eriksen 2002). Accordingly, particular bodily features are scrutinized in relation not to national or ethnic identity, but to racialized bodily characteristics. These are embedded in a transnational aesthetic hierarchy that has its own local repercussions in Turkey.

In Turkey, this hierarchy is rooted in an Ottoman valuation of European over supposedly Arab or Middle Eastern looks. The early Turkish republic continued the Ottoman valorization of European looks within a wider fascination with eugenics. Thus, in the 1930s, a large-scale state-commissioned anthropological study concluded—in agreement with contemporary teachings in biological racism—that Turks formed a homogenous race with predominantly light skin and eyes and a straight nose (Maksudyan 2005). As Esra Özyürek has noted (2008, 219), in doing so it idealized the founder of the Turkish Republic, Mustafa Kemal Atatürk, as the perfect representation of this racial type. The racial vocabulary of "Turkishness," Cemil Aydin (2007) points out, has to be seen within the context of Turkey's nation-building process as a young republic seeking to replace and modernize a supposedly degenerate Ottoman elite, one that nevertheless already regarded itself as a part of European cosmopolitan society based on a strong desire for the aesthetics of modernity. Moreover, according to Murat Ergin (2008, 836), this was also "in part a response to European images of the sub-human" by seeking inclusion into the racialized category of the "White Man."

In contemporary Turkey, questions about body aesthetics often triggered general statements about "our race" (ırkımız in Turkish). During interviews, cosmetic surgeons commonly employed racial discourse in describing Turkish beauty and situated it in a transnational aesthetic hierarchy. In rather blunt fashion, Prof. Dr. Erol Kışlaoğlu, a cosmetic surgeon operating in Istanbul's private medical sector, told the national daily *Hürriyet*: "The Turks strive to look like the northern European races in terms of aesthetic appearance. This is because the form of the bodies and faces of the northern European races are generally beautiful" (quoted from *Hürriyet* 2009a).

Postulating a global aesthetic hierarchy in a generalizing and racialized way, Kışlaoğlu here relates the motivation for cosmetic surgery to a collective desire to mimic European looks. More commonly, however, cosmetic surgeons in Turkey claimed not to cure bodies of particularly prevalent ethnic or racialized features in order to create European looks, but rather to normalize, harmonize, or enhance bodies. This concurs with the cosmopolitan medical rhetoric linked to ethnic plastic surgery procedures that sees these as tools to enhance rather than obscure ethnic identity (Mann 2014).

In his work on cosmetic surgery in Brazil, Jarrín (2017, 28–53) speaks of the "eugenesis" of beauty, showing how eugenic thought "produced the backbone of the aesthetic hierarchy present to this day in Brazil" (Jarrín 2017, 30). Social institutions such as hospitals, schools, prisons, barracks, etc. became crucial in the process of creating ideal citizens and, indeed, of their normalization. Whereas national "mixedness," or *mestizaje*, is central to Brazil's self-portrayal as a beautiful nation, whiteness remains the unmarked ideal by which all bodies are measured. Within the cosmetic surgery practice described by Jarrín, this is played out as an anxiety about the "miscegenation" of Brazilian society and surgeons' emphasis on "harmonizing" bodily features (Jarrín 2017, 134). In similar ways, cosmetic surgeons in Turkey rely on long-standing aesthetic hierarchies and commonly speak of Turkish "mixedness" as both an aesthetic quality and a challenge in their daily cosmetic surgery practice. In the words of Prof. Dr. Onur Erol, a renowned cosmetic surgeon with his own clinic in central Istanbul,

> our race (ırkımız) has to be counted among the most beautiful races. Because we are mixed. Anatolia was so civilized that they mingled with other civilizations and created something beautiful. This also removed us from genetic diseases. The well-nourished and cultivated (iyi yetişmiş) segments of our people exhibit very beautiful features. (Quoted from Hürriyet 2009a)

Whereas here racial mixedness is seen as a positive aesthetic quality, it is also regarded as being distributed unevenly across the country, being especially prevalent among the upper social strata, the "well-nourished and cultivated." Even more common is the differentiation between the distinctive looks of particular regional "types" in Turkey. To quote Prof. Dr. Erol Kışlaoğlu again:

> [For example,] someone from the Black Sea is taller and of a lighter complexion, a Turk from central Anatolia may be shorter, stockier and of a darker complexion. When we take a look at the Mediterranean coast, the Mediterranean type looks pretty much the same everywhere. Aegean and Thracian people especially are migrants with a lighter complexion, light-colored eyes and tall in physique. (Quoted from Hürriyet 2009a)

Against the background of Turkish mixedness, cosmetic surgeons claim to play a crucial role in effecting bodily harmony and enhancing looks across the country. Like other bodily features, large female breasts and noses are seen as distributed unevenly across Turkey, being generally associated with rural looks and particular regions respectively. From this perspective, and as this chapter illustrates, the Istanbul-centered cosmetic surgery sector is indeed crucial for creating not just a more beautiful

Turkey, but also a more harmonious one, effecting urban belonging for those who are generally marginalized in the urban beauty economy.

Not least, cosmetic surgeons often regard bodily harmony as something measurable in a "scientific" way. In accordance with this idea, Prof. Dr. Ismail Kuran, president of the Turkish Society of Plastic-Reconstructive and Cosmetic Surgery in Turkey at the time of our interview, used an approach he termed the "mathematics of beauty" in his medical practice.[1] More concretely, he employed tables with standard measurements taken from medical textbooks and other scientific publications against which he then compared the measurements of his own patients, thus diagnosing and treating their bodily "defects." Kuran's understanding of bodily aesthetics relied on the idea of a universal, transcultural optimum. For him, in respect of its effective realization, it was irrelevant from whose bodies these measurements actually derived.

Like the women in Kavacık quoted at the beginning of this chapter, cosmetic surgeons in Turkey regarded the treatment ("enhancement") of bodies that defied hegemonic appearance norms as a right untouched by moral objections or religious bans. From this perspective, cosmetic surgery is crucial for the creation of normal and natural-looking bodies, especially when it comes to female breast-reduction and nose surgery.

Turning "Turkish" into "French" Noses

As outlined above, the idea of an aesthetic optimum is deeply racialized in cosmetic surgery, and particular types of noses attributed to particular populations are considered bodily defects in need of fixing. Within cosmopolitan cosmetic surgery discourse, the "Turkish" nose is generally subsumed under the category of the "Mediterranean" nose, described as follows in the high-ranking journal *Plastic Surgery Practice*:

> The typical Mediterranean nose (Greek, Italian, or Arabic) is similar [to the African-American nose] in that the tip has generous proportions (length and width), and is even hooked in appearance (the

---

1. Interview with Ismail Kuran, July 10, 2014. The following quotes by Kuran are also taken from this interview.

"tension nose"). The dorsum can be nonspecific or have a major bony pronouncement, a feature commonly referred to as the "dorsal hump." (Slupchynskyj 2005)

Istanbul-based cosmetic surgeons likewise mused about the particular aesthetics of Turkish noses within a global beauty economy. For example, Dr. Nuri Battal, a well-known cosmetic and plastic surgeon, explained in the *Hürriyet* daily newspaper: "The Turkish nose is of a very special form and format. It is typically hooked and big, with its tip looking downward. According to our current aesthetic understanding this type of nose is not considered as beautiful and appreciated in Western societies" (quoted from Erşan 2004).

Reflecting these valorizations of different types of noses within a transnational geography, interlocutors often half-jokingly stated their desire to change their Turkish or Greek noses into smaller French ones. Moreover, rather than being considered a national characteristic per se, big or hooked noses in Turkey are linked in particular with the Black Sea region and the Anatolian southeast. During an interview with *Hürriyet* in 2006, cosmetic surgeon Prof. Dr. Onur Erol talked about different types of deformed noses in need of correction in Turkey, differentiating between the "big and pointed noses" of the Black Sea population and the "big and fleshy noses" of those originating in the Turkish southeast (quoted from *Hürriyet* 2006a). Not least, large noses are considered male,[2] posing a particular problem for women of provincial origin in Istanbul. As the religious scholar Nureddin Yıldız put it, "women especially are obsessed with their noses . . . They write to me: 'My nose is too big!' Actually, in Turkey, in the Black Sea and eastern regions, women *do* have big noses. So when they migrate to big cities like Istanbul, they think they draw attention to themselves."[3]

2. For example, in an interview with the *Hürriyet* daily, cosmetic surgeon Nuri Battal warns men against getting noses that are too small or upturned (*kalkık*), since "a small nose makes the face feminine, that is, it gives a soft and female impression" (quoted from Erşan 2004).

3. Interview with Nureddin Yıldız, October 13, 2013.

Whereas Yıldız was known as a critic of cosmetic surgery, regarding it as a violation of bodily integrity and hence forbidden (*haram*) in Islam, in his rulings on the subject he did make exceptions to this rule, especially when a woman reported suffering from a large, "male-looking" nose.[4] According to Yıldız, in such cases, nose surgery is therapeutic, rather than merely aesthetic, and fully justified by Islamic law.

There is a history of nose operations in Turkey, with local surgeons taking pride in the fact that Istanbul was now considered a regional, if not a global center for this particular type of surgery. Among the numerous otolaryngologists—plastic reconstructive and cosmetic surgeons who routinely perform this type of surgery in Istanbul—Prof. Dr. Onur Erol was certainly among the most renowned, including internationally. Erol, affectively called the "father" of cosmetic and plastic surgery in Turkey by his colleagues, was a media star and had for several years served as the president of the International Rhinoplasty Society. In the late 1980s he invented the so-called Turkish Delight nose-surgery technique (cf. Erol 2000), popularized by his operations on numerous celebrities in Turkey. While media reports claimed that the technique was now fashionable worldwide (Sabah 2004), it produced an aesthetic outcome that in Turkey was no longer considered the fashion of the day, as the following accounts of Ruken's and Emine's nose operations illustrate.

Starting a New Chapter in Life with a New Nose

Whereas nose surgery in Turkey was long considered a privilege engaged in by the upper classes, in the early 2000s it became more easily acceptable, cheaper, and commoner among young urban adults, including those in lower social strata. During my research, it was considered a common choice among young women just after graduation or before getting married or entering the job market. One who had recently opted for nose surgery was Ruken, a 23-year-old lawyer introduced to me by her uncle, a friend of mine, shortly after she moved in with his family while flat-hunting in

---

4. For example, see Yıldız's rulings in the online forum of *Fetva Meclisi* (Fatwa Center, www.fetvameclisi.com).

Istanbul. About a year prior to our first meeting, she had graduated from university and taken up employment as a lawyer in Izmir, where her family had resettled from the eastern Anatolian region of Tunceli/Dersim during the Kurdish uprising and violent armed conflicts in the region during the 1990s. Shortly before starting to apply for jobs in Istanbul and eventually moving there, Ruken had undergone nose surgery to remove her "bump,"[5] as she put it. Arriving for our interview in a café in central Istanbul straight from a lecture given by the well-known philosopher and feminist-socialist writer Gülnur Acar-Savran, Ruken joked about the irony of talking to me about her cosmetic surgery right after listening to a lecture on feminism, something she clearly perceived as a contradiction in terms. She quickly moved on to tell me how important the operation had been for her, after many years of suffering a nose that made her feel "really ugly," even "handicapped."

Ruken had fantasized about nose surgery ever since childhood, but was forced to delay the operation until she was finally able to pay for it. It was her first major purchase from her income as a lawyer. Earning just over 1,000 Turkish lira per month (approximately US$500), Ruken saved hard for nine months to pay the 3,500 lira requested by the surgeon. Asking her parents for financial support had been out of the question because early on in the decision-making process, she had decided not to let them or anyone else from her inner social circle in on her surgery plans, for fear that they might dissuade her from it.

Like other cosmetic surgery patients, Ruken was especially concerned to acquire a natural-looking nose and engaged in much research along these lines in preparation of her operation. She did so mostly online, in the popular Turkish internet forum Women's Club (*Kadınlar Kulübü*).[6] Within the Women's Club forum, nose surgery was among the most hotly debated topics in the aesthetics section, with 192,268 entries out of a total of 488,412 in September 2014, ranking just behind the number of postings on body weight, diets, and hair problems. With the help of this virtual

5. Interview with Ruken, March 10, 2012. The following quotes by Ruken are also taken from this interview.

6. See http://kadinlarkulubu.com/portal/ (accessed March 18, 2021).

community, Ruken chose a surgeon who was renowned for his natural nose surgery designs. When this surgeon suggested that Ruken return with a picture of someone whose nose she liked, she was alarmed and her resulting query posted in the forum triggered a long debate on natural-looking designs. While some uploaded pictures of celebrities whose noses they liked for their naturalness—among them that of the Turkish model and actress Deniz Akkaya, rumored to have had her own nose modeled after the looks of American model Liv Tylor by celebrity surgeon Onur Erol—others warned that emulating another person's nose posed a great threat to natural looks. Among the forum discussants, the earlier aesthetic standard of the operated nose in Turkey, described by the president of the Chamber of Plastic Reconstructive and Aesthetic surgery in Turkey as a "small nose with an upturned tip," was considered exaggerated, artificial, and tasteless.

Ruken's surgery was performed in a private clinic in her hometown of Izmir, which, according to her online research, was notably cheaper than comparable clinics in Istanbul. With her new, smaller nose, she felt perfectly equipped to start "a new chapter in life," as she told me, and prepared to move to Istanbul. About ten months after the operation, with a new position at an Istanbul-based law firm and all signs of surgery gone, Ruken happily recounted how finally she felt "perfectly normal." Indeed, she expressed surprise at the fact that her initial euphoria about her long-desired new nose had quickly given way to a sense of "normal everyday life." Since the surgery had taken place, she had not returned even once to the online discussion forum, which had been so important for her during the decision-making process. Also, she did not tell her new colleagues or friends in Istanbul about the operation, still being somewhat ashamed about having engaged in cosmetic surgery. However, she knew that many of them had had the same type of surgery in recent months and mused that for young upwardly mobile women in Istanbul, a smaller nose or other cosmetic surgery was simply "part of the deal."

Becoming a Cosmetically Touched Woman

While Ruken's surgery narrative suggests what one might call a success story, I also encountered numerous stories of complications with and unsatisfactory outcomes to nose surgery. Among them was Emine's. A well-groomed and elegantly dressed freelance consultant in her mid-fifties from the Black Sea region, Emine underwent nose surgery in 2001. Like Ruken, Emine had suffered from the look of her nose from early childhood on. Her nose was "humped,"[7] though in retrospect she also admits it was "characteristic." She remembered that friends often remarked about her very photogenic face, a quality she apparently lost after the surgery. In any case, Emine fantasized about nose surgery for decades, until one day in her early forties, shortly after separating from her husband and moving to Istanbul, she finally made the decision to approach "the most popular [surgeon] of them all" to have her nose reshaped.

The surgery was performed in the prestigious private American Hospital located in central Istanbul and cost about US$5,000, an amount Emine could afford from her savings as a senior employee in a multinational pharmaceutical company. Her nose was operated on using the "Turkish Delight" technique developed by Erol, the celebrity surgeon mentioned above, in the late 1980s. The technique is described by Erol (2000, 2229) as a form of graft that uses "fine-textured cartilage mass . . . wrapped in one layer of Surgicel . . . moistened with an antibiotic . . . then molded into a cylindrical form and inserted under the dorsal nasal skin." Its flamboyant name derives from the fact that "[w]hen the mucosal stitching is complete, this graft can be externally moulded, like plasticine [or Turkish Delight], under the dorsal skin" (Erol 2000, 2229).

Among plastic and cosmetic surgeons in Turkey the Turkish Delight technique was controversial, and in 2014 the president of the Chamber for Plastic Reconstructive and Aesthetic surgery suggested that it served as an apt procedure for the "correction of the overdone nose," rather than "a good solution for a natural looking nose."[8] Erol himself told the *Hürriyet* daily newspaper that he had performed the technique in about 7,000 cases without complications (cf. Bildirici 2009). Emine, however,

---

7. Interview with Emine, January 15, 2014. The following quotes from Emine are also taken from this interview.

8. Interview with Ismail Kuran, July 10, 2014.

experienced complications about a year after the surgery, when the tip of her nose drooped and she was forced to return to the clinic for a corrective operation:

> It came as a huge shock to me. Because, if you haven't experienced it [nose surgery], you cannot imagine how painful it is! Of course, it was done under general anesthetic. But still, the first week after the operation was extremely painful. They break the bone and everything turns blue and becomes swollen. It is unimaginable. That's why, when he said I would need a second, corrective operation, I felt completely shocked. So then, instead of comforting me, the way he [the surgeon] behaved—I hated it! . . . he started picking on my face to find another—let's say "problem."

It took Emine almost three years to muster up the courage for a second operation, which she had performed by another surgeon, this time following a friend's recommendation. By the time I met her, Emine was satisfied with the look of her nose overall, though she lamented that she had turned "from someone with a characteristic nose into a regular cosmetically touched woman." Moreover, she continued to feel angry about the fact that she had paid a large sum of money to be treated by a famous professor, while she was almost certain that he had delegated the surgery to one of his medical residents. During our interview, she scolded herself for being blinded by the surgeon's fame. She explained that she had had no personal experience to rely on because in her social circle at the time, nose surgery was still a somewhat unusual choice that people did not usually talk about. In spite of the fact that there were only eleven years between Emine's and Ruken's operations, Emine indeed seemed to belong to an earlier generation of cosmetic surgery patients in Turkey. Thus, more recent nose surgery patients routinely relied on the internet and various personal recommendations for particular surgeons, techniques, etc. and proved well-informed of the costs and risks. Among them was Helin, who underwent nose surgery after at least six female members of her immediate family, including her mother, sister, and aunts, had already done so. While the nose surgery pioneers among them had experienced complications similar to those described by Emine, the more recent successes encouraged Helin likewise to have her nose "fixed." Even when the particular aesthetics of her nose were seen as problematic in her family and nose surgery had become fairly standard among its female members, she preferred to frame it in a discourse of health, rather than aesthetics. As the following shows, the definition of nose surgery as either functional-therapeutic or aesthetic formed a particular area for negotiation between doctors and patients.

Fixing the Breathing Problem

Within medical anthropological research, there exists a large body of literature on the doctor–patient relationship. In her review of this literature, Ellen Lazarus (1988) notes that this relationship has typically been characterized as problematic, with anthropological studies documenting patients' noncompliance and dissatisfaction with their treatment, as well as cultural misunderstandings and poor communication between doctors and their patients. As exemplified by the account of Emine's nose surgery above, the distribution of power and knowledge between female cosmetic surgery patients and predominantly male surgeons is uneven and may lead to unsatisfactory outcomes, though only rarely to legal measures, at least from the patient's side. In this section, I analyze a particular field of doctor-patient relations in nose surgery in Turkey, namely its interpretation as "functional-therapeutic," and therefore as a matter of health covered by the Turkish Social Insurance Foundation (SGK), or as "aesthetic." As pointed out by cosmetic surgeons operating in Istanbul's private sector, from the perspective of the welfare state, any operation they undertake is considered "aesthetic" and has to be paid for by the patients themselves. The following shows that cosmetic surgery patients who for various reasons are unable to undergo or are uncomfortable with cosmetic surgery commonly resort to a functional-therapeutic definition of the treatment, even when they actually desire aesthetic changes. While technically "fixing a breathing problem" by means of nose surgery is distinct from changing nasal aesthetics, cosmetic surgeons often contribute to the blurring of the boundary between health and beauty by suggesting that they also "remove the bump" when all the patient demanded was a functional-therapeutic treatment. This becomes clear in the following account of Helin, for whom a breathing problem served as the starting point for nose surgery:

> When I was twelve or thirteen I hit my nose on a rock. It wasn't that awful, but still, it grew bigger and the bone here [*points to her nasal bridge*], there was a hook, as they call it. And I had problems breathing. . . . The surgery was mostly about the breathing. I wanted to breath properly, because [before the surgery] I couldn't even sleep properly, and it made me feel tired all the time. So the doctor said: "Okay, at the same time, we can fix the bone. We will have to break it anyway. Would you like to have the whole thing changed?" And I said: "Sure, why not." So then he fixed it. . . . [9]

Like Ruken portrayed above, who mused about the irony of talking to me about her recent cosmetic surgery having just attended a lecture on feminism, Helin, a gender studies graduate and feminist activist, obviously felt an uneasy tension between her activism and her recent nose surgery. Later on in the interview, she returned to talking about this tension. She recounted how several friends had tried to talk her out of the surgery by telling her how "characteristic and nice" her nose was. To them, she replied that she also had breathing problems, "so I *need* to fix it! So if they break the bone anyway, I want them to make something nice." Health-related reasons enabled Helin to justify nose surgery to herself and to communicate that justification to her wider social circle. While in Helin's case the surgeon's suggestion that the aesthetic look of the nose be fixed at the same time aided her decision-making process, in other cases the suggestion that an aesthetic "fix" also be performed proved rather problematic. Given the powerful positions of doctors in their interactions with patients that are often reported by medical anthropologists (cf. Lazarus 1988), their suggestion that the nose's aesthetics also be fixed could come across in such an authoritative way that retrospectively patients felt they had been pushed into cosmetic surgery. A case in point was Filiz, an accountant in her early twenties, who had a nose operation two years prior to our

---

9. Interview with Helin, June 28, 2014. The following quotes from Helin are also taken from this interview.

interview. Filiz had been referred to her surgeon by her dentist, whom she went to see about a sinus infection that was affecting her gums:

> So he [the surgeon] checked it and . . . said: "We can clean it through your nose opening." In the first place I didn't want that, because I wasn't prepared to undergo such a surgery. My nose was also a bit hooked, and so he said, "We should fix that as well." . . . He was a friend of my cousin. He assured me that it would not be painful. He asked me to think about it, and I did, for a month. At home, I felt so undecided—"Should I do it or not?" I really didn't know.[10]

After her close friend found a prestigious job thanks to recent nose surgery, Filiz also felt encouraged to do it. However, she soon came to regret her decision and described her first reaction after removing the bandages from her remodeled nose as shock, and even as disgust. Two years later, she had somewhat come to terms with the changed look of her nose, though she confided that "the natural [nose] is the best. God created us in the best possible shape, I came to believe. Because with the operated nose, I can't mimic, I have no feelings. When the weather is cold, it doesn't feel cold, it never feels cold!"

In a rather mournful manner, Filiz's appreciation of her former, natural nose combines a faith-based morality with an affective longing for the thermal sensitivity that she reportedly lost. During the interview, it became clear that she continued to be puzzled about her decision to change the aesthetics of her nose, when all she had actually wanted was treatment for a toothache. Not least, she mourned the money the surgery had consumed: whereas treating her toothache would have been covered by her medical insurance, having her nose aesthetically "fixed" consumed her savings from an entire year of work. Like other patients who felt they had been tricked out of their money by cosmetic surgeons who had suggested adding aesthetic modifications to the treatment of medical problems, Filiz suspected her surgeon of being financially motivated.

10. Interview with Filiz, December 24, 2013. The following quotes from Filiz are also taken from this interview.

However, cosmetic surgeons also reported being tricked by patients who had approached them about a breathing problem when actually they wanted cosmetic interventions. Explained Prof. Dr. Kuran:

We shouldn't forget that for some of the younger generation, the eigh-teen- or twenty-year-olds, some of them *use* the breathing problem in order to persuade their parents to pay for the operation. I can see that very easily. Their history of a breathing problem is inconsistent, they are not certain when it started, and they don't make you believe it actually exists. And then, you don't see any indication of a breathing problem. Especially if they have a religious background, the breathing problem will give them a good reason for engaging in this kind of surgery. . . . So they think that if you fix the breathing problem, the aesthetics will automatically be better. I have to tell them, "It doesn't work like that!" You're entitled to better breathing [under public health insurance], but not to fixing your aesthetic problem.

In order to find out his patients' real motivations for surgery, Kuran routinely probed them by saying that if they desired merely to fix their breathing problem, they should resort to treatment in a public hospital, where this kind of treatment was free of charge. Most of his patients then admitted their aesthetic motivation, often urging him not to disclose it to (possibly accompanying) parents or husbands. According to Kuran, any such disclosure would jeopardize patients' ability to obtain funding for the surgery in the private medical sector from their parents or husbands and/or undermine their moral justification for engaging in such surgery at all. Indeed, in the Women's Club's online nose-surgery forum mentioned previously, foregrounding the health aspects in order to justify nose sur-gery was a strategy often recommended to convince reluctant parents or husbands of the need for such surgery. For example, in response to one user's question about how to convince her husband to support her plans for nose surgery—whether morally or financially remained unclear—another user replied: "Sister (*abla*), my nose used to be hooked, and I also suffered from health-related problems. I mean, it was hooked, but I had both [problems] treated at the same time, and due to my health problem, my husband couldn't refuse it. I'm not sure whether you have a health problem, but perhaps you can foreground it . . ."[11]

Apart from convincing reluctant husbands, defining the need for nose surgery as a matter of health rather than aesthetics also proved unproblematic from a religious perspective and served pious patients in justifying the procedure to themselves, as well as to religious authorities and their own social circles.

Cosmetic surgeons interviewed in the private medical sector in Istanbul generally accepted that they operated on patients regardless of whether they were motivated by health or cosmetic concerns, even though they admitted that misunderstanding a patient's main motivation for the surgery was risky in terms of patient satisfaction. From the perspective of cosmetic surgeons, however, a strict separation between health and aesthetics makes little sense. This also becomes clear from the notion of "aesthetic medicine," which is increasingly popular in cosmopolitan medical practice and generally includes a large variety of so-called rejuvenation and enhancement procedures (Edmonds and van der Geest 2009, 13).

To sum up, women's motivations for nose surgery are seldom straightforward, but include multiple deliberations. They are often narrated as based on an affective desire for normal rather than downright attractive looks, especially when engaged in by those considered provincial Others within a competitive urban labor market. In their post-surgery narratives, women may stress the element of individual choice in deciding to undertake these operations, or they may report feeling having been pushed into cosmetic surgery in a situation where this procedure is almost expected from young, upwardly mobile women. Once made known, surgery decisions need to be negotiated with close family members and friends, who more often than not are described as skeptical and dissuasive, especially in conservative social circles or when they are expected to pay for these operations. The account also illustrates immense changes in the availability of nose surgery, and indeed its normalization among particular groups

11. Reply 3 by "gizmoo" to posting by "daff," titled "help needed from those who have a husband!!!" [Eşleri olan arkadaşlar!!! yardım], November 17, 2009. Online: www .kadinlarkulubu.com (September 30, 2015).

of women. As the following shows, this is also true for female breast surgery, which in its different forms—breast reduction, lifting, and augmentation—is even more common in Turkey.

Reshaping Female Breasts

Human breasts are a symbol of femininity, and the popular imagination often seems to regard them as its measure. Thus, in her insightful book on *Staring*, Rosemarie Garland-Thomson writes that "[t]oo much breast means too much femininity; too little breast means not enough" (2009, 143). Given that women's breasts come in very different shapes and sizes, Garland-Thomson remarks upon the astonishing fact that, in the ubiquitous media images of them, they "look remarkably uniform" (Garland-Thomson 2009, 147). This too is the case for Turkey, where women use various techniques, including pushup brassieres, breast-shaping treatments in beauty salons, and cosmetic surgery, to change the size and shape of their breasts, and indeed, as the following account of Özge's breast-reduction surgery shows, to normalize them. Like elsewhere, in Turkey female breasts are symbolically charged, signifying sensuality, sexuality, fertility, and exuberance. A clear separation is made between the maternal and the erotic breast: accordingly, breastfeeding in public is not considered a violation of social norms, as long as the person breastfeeding is discreet and cautious not to expose too much skin. In contrast, erotic breasts are under no circumstances to be exposed in public, and news of a "topless crisis" made the headlines in summer 2014, when women were rumored to have taken off their bikini tops on a beach on the Turkish Mediterranean, even though this was a beach that granted access to women only.[12]

Large female breasts may be associated with either the erotic or the maternal breast, depending on a woman's age and social position. Especially when displayed by elderly, provincial women, they are associated with the maternal rather than the erotic breast and devalued as a common characteristic of the *köylü kadın*, the peasant woman. Like large noses, in the popular imagination such breasts are attributed to women from

12. For example, see *Hürriyet* 2014.

specific regions, especially southeastern Anatolia.[13] In the early 2000s, a global trend toward smaller breasts impacted on Turkey, where, according to the general secretary of the Chamber of Plastic Reconstructive and Aesthetic surgery, Ali Barutçu, the ideal breast size fell "from 85 to 80 [cm]," with the exception of performing artists, who continued "to prefer larger breasts" (quoted from *Hürriyet* 2002). The same report goes on to quote Barutçu saying that "[b]reast reduction surgery reduces stress in social life while it also improves the quality of women's everyday life and their success in working life." While such statements may not be self-explanatory, the following account of breast-reduction surgery illustrates the ways in which the size of women's breasts and their modification is linked to social stress, quality of life, and professional success in urban Turkey. Not least, it is linked to the management of gendered respectability and female sexuality in a particular social location.

Managing Respectable Femininity

Özge, a mathematics teacher at a private college and a cheerful woman in her mid-thirties with short black hair and a preference for casual dress (also mentioned in chapter 3), framed her breast-reduction surgery within a discourse of patriarchal oppression of the sexualized female body in Turkey. Early on in our interview, Özge distanced herself from "those women who easily have cosmetic surgery," stating that for her "cosmetic surgery had always been, well, something that popular culture *enforces* upon women."[14] Instead she emphasized the health aspect of her surgery, which resulted in the removal of two kilos of fat from her breasts, as her main motivation for undergoing the procedure. However, when I expected Özge to continue talking about backaches, an ailment women seeking breast-reduction surgery often reported suffering, she told me about the restriction of movement she experienced as the result of the "over-sexualization" of her pre-surgery body. In order to explain what she meant by this, she recounted the restrictive atmosphere of her coming of age as the daughter

13. See, for example, *Hürriyet* (2010b) and Arna (2009).
14. Interview with Özge, January 21, 2014. The following quotes by Özge are also taken from this interview.

of rural–urban migrants in a working-class neighborhood in Istanbul during the conservative post-military putsch era of the 1980s:

We were raised in the culture of the neighborhood [*mahalle*]. In those times, girls who had their period and whose breasts started growing, they couldn't play outside anymore. It was a society that forced you to grow up early. . . . If this [menstruation and the development of female breasts] happens too early, it is a disadvantage for the girl. I remember feeling ashamed [because of my breasts]. My friends were saying: "Are they really this big?" Such kind of things really troubled me. I had many problems during adolescence. I felt it [my body/my breast] was ugly. . . . I mean, as a kid, you want to play outside with your friends, but your physique has turned you into a woman from one day to the other. In this context, I experienced puberty too early—my breasts became big too early.

During high school, Özge remembered being constantly on a diet, trying to reduce the size of her breasts. Dieting, however, proved useless, she said, because, pointing to her breasts laughingly, "Everything I ate went there!" While Özge attempted to reduce the sexualized femininity of her body by losing weight, she felt she was becoming ever more attractive to men:

Girls are sexual objects in Turkey. For example, if your hips are big, it is not considered erotic. But if you are slim and your breasts are big, you're like "very sexy." . . . Like I said, you can have a big body and just be a fat person, but me, my body was thin, I was so thin. My size in clothes was 36, and my breast measurement was like 100 [cm], so these two things combined made me look "too sexy."

This resulted in ever more (self-chosen) confinement, because whenever she ventured out alone Özge felt men staring at her breasts, with some also leering at her and harassing her verbally. Accordingly, she tried to hide her breasts under layers of loose clothing.

It was only after breast-reduction surgery that Özge felt she was no longer being stared at and happily proclaimed that now, quoting her cosmetic surgeon, she had "standard size breasts." As soon as the bandages were removed, she went shopping for a new and indeed sexier set of clothes, including tight T-shirts and, for the first time in her life, a bikini.

Now that her body was "normal" and she felt she was in a position to control and regulate her publicly visible attractiveness better, men's stares no longer made her feel vulnerable. While her choice to undergo cosmetic surgery met with a divided response from her feminist friends, Özge felt that it had earned her respect among her female colleagues at the private college where she taught and where many female employees engaged in various forms of aesthetic body modification. Shortly before the surgery took place, Özge invited her close female friends to tell them about the ordeal with her breasts, as well as her plans to have them reduced. After decades of hiding her breasts even from her closest friends' eyes, that night she took off her shirt and brassiere to show them. Recounting this experience and the actual surgery that quickly followed, during our interview Özge spoke of a process of empowerment, consciously regaining a positive body image.

Like Ruken, portrayed above, Özge chose not to let her parents in on her decision to undergo surgery, shying away from discussing such an intimate topic with them. Whereas the Social Insurance Foundation (SGK) would have covered her surgery as a functional, rather than a cosmetic type of surgery, Özge chose to avoid the long queues at public hospitals and took out a loan to pay a private surgeon instead.

In contrast to Özge, who was single when she undertook breast surgery, many younger interlocutors intended to postpone their breast-reduction operations until after they got married and had had children, fearing that the surgery might impact on their ability to breastfeed or else harm their attractiveness for their sexual partners, who were generally assumed to prefer larger female breasts. This was the case with Sevda, the fashion-conscious daughter of a beauty salon owner in the conservative neighborhood of Fatih, who fantasized about breast-reduction surgery. Sevda's large breasts made her feel uncomfortable about her body, especially since she knew from female relatives who suffered from the same kind of problem that these tended to become even larger after giving birth and breastfeeding. While Sevda's maternal grandmother had undergone breast-reduction surgery several years earlier, other relatives shunned the procedure out of moral and religious conviction. Among them was her aunt, whose breasts Sevda had recently seen naked by accident, an encounter that continued to haunt her. For Sevda, her aunt's breasts made her look like "the typical old peasant woman (*köylü kadın*),"[15] namely those in her family's hometown in the Black Sea region, who had given birth and breastfed many children. Inheriting this look, Sevda confided, was among her greatest fears.

Talking to me about her breasts shortly before and again shortly after she got married, Sevda was still not prepared to undergo surgery. She knew that her husband actually "liked" her larger breasts and feared that reducing them might prove risky for their sexual relationship. As a good wife, she hoped to seek his consent in the near future, perhaps after giving birth and breastfeeding, which would provide her with the opportunity to frame the surgery as a form of postnatal reconstructive surgery that also had a health aspect to it, namely the reduction of backache. In postponing breast-reduction surgery, Sevda was juggling contrasting expectations of her as a young urban, modern, and sexually attractive woman. She clearly conceptualized her body as prenatal, that is, as a body yet to give birth and breastfeed, which would be in need of therapeutical measures afterward. These expectations and her related fears were tied to two distinctive connotations of larger female breasts in Turkey: on the one hand the erotic female breast as a strong symbol of sensuality and sexuality, generally seen as desirable by male sexual partners; and on the other hand the maternal breast, signifying fertility and exuberance but also, in the popular imagination, a characteristic of the devalued peasant woman. As indicated by common caricatures of the *köylü kadın*, as well as media coverage of the topic,[16] if not carried by an urban upper-class woman or a performing artist, large breasts risked linking its wearer with a lower social status and those regions most readily associated with peripheral rural life in Istanbul, namely the Black Sea or the Anatolian southeast.

15. Interview with Sevda, July 21, 2014. The following quotes by Sevda are also taken from this interview.

16. For example, in an article about breast-reduction surgery published in the *Hürriyet* daily, the focus of reporting on the topic is on southeastern Anatolia, where, the authors claim, the waiting period for breast-reduction operations is six months in the leading regional university hospital, and surgeons no longer give out appointments (*Hürriyet* 2010b).

In both cosmetic surgery patients' and surgeons' accounts, breast surgery is readily linked with bodily changes in the female life cycle, especially childbirth and menopause. As also outlined in the previous chapter on aging, these are seen as taking their toll on women's bodies, including their breasts. Apart from breast-reduction surgery, middle-aged women thus also engaged in breast-lifting surgery. This procedure promised women that it would restore and rejuvenate their looks to a state before aging and childbirth had caused bodily deformation. Among those who reported undergoing such a procedure was Esra, a middle-class İstanbullu woman from a family of early Republicans. Her breast-lifting procedure at the age of fifty-seven, as she laughingly put it during our interview, was her last attempt to save her marriage of thirty-five years. In contrast to Özge, who experienced "everyone's eyes" on her breasts as a form of sexual harassment, Esra remembered her youthful breasts as a source of pride for her. She explained that, thanks to her breasts, "I always had a Marilyn Monroe, sexy-woman kind of look. Everyone's eyes were on my breasts!"[17]

This changed when, after her second pregnancy and more dramatically after menopause, her breasts drooped. According to Esra, the loss of erotic attractiveness that this entailed proved fatal for her marriage, and her husband began to take an interest in other women. Once her care responsibilities declined and her children had left the parental home, Esra took out a loan to finance a tummy tuck and a breast lift in an attempt to keep her husband. Unable to save her marriage, the boost in sexual attractiveness that resulted from the surgery nevertheless "reenergized" her, as she put it. And indeed, when I got to know her through a family friend, she gave the impression of being an outgoing and popular youthful lady among her large circle of friends. Her breast surgery, it became clear throughout the interview, formed an important part in creating this image of herself.

These accounts illustrate that large breasts have different meanings for women in different social positions in Istanbul. Whereas for Özge

17. Interview with Esra, February 24, 2014. The following quotes from Esra are also taken from this interview.

large breasts were a source of shame, attracting the dominating stares of men, for Esra her large breasts were the source of a positive body image, almost of pride, as well as an erotic asset that she didn't want to lose. This reminds us that feminine respectability as a signifier of class is harder to attain by working- and lower middle-class women like Özge, whose bodies tend to be more readily sexualized as "fat, vulgar [and] disgusting" (Skeggs 2005, 965). Moreover, as exemplified by Özge's account of the neighborhood she grew up in, in more conservative and popular neighborhoods hegemonic norms of female sexuality and chastity tend to be more closely policed and enforced than in the liberal middle-class milieu Esra grew up in. While the sexual harassment of women, including dominating stares, verbal harassment, or leering in public spaces such as streets and public transportation, is a major problem for all women across Istanbul, wealthier women are often in a better position to protect themselves; for example, by avoiding public transportation. In the end, Özge and Esra both resorted to surgical interventions that helped them feel comfortable about their body images in relation to men without endangering the norms of feminine respectability or, perhaps more aptly in Esra's case, respectable femininity.

Whereas heterosexual female patients who opted for breast reduction or lifting treatments often attempted to regain breasts that complied with the norms of a youthful, non-drooping, and properly sized female breast in their respective social environments, those fantasizing about breast enlargement, the following shows, first and foremost desired to boost their feminine attractiveness.

Boosting Attractiveness by Breast Augmentation Surgery

Toward the end of field research I realized that, while three interlocutors had reported a desire for larger breasts, none of my interlocutors had admitted to actually having had breast augmentation surgery, even though this was one of the most common types of cosmetic surgery in Turkey (ISAPS 2019). Moreover, while friends and acquaintances put me in touch with a large number of their relatives, friends, neighbors, and colleagues for interviews about their aesthetic body modifications, none of these was a former breast augmentation surgery patient. In contrast to nose or breast-reduction surgery, which were generally considered "functional" rather than merely "aesthetic" operations and accordingly were more readily talked about, breast augmentation surgery was obviously not. Moreover, while other types of cosmetic surgery were related to the treatment of bodily "deformations," breast augmentation surgery was associated with female sexuality and attractiveness in a more straightforward way. Thus, the three interlocutors who talked to me about their desire for larger breasts also talked at length about their romantic and sexual desires and relationships, making a close connection between the two.

Among them was Gamze, a single woman in her early twenties, who once in a while helped out in her cousin's beauty salon. Whenever I met her there, Gamze was dressed in rather tight-fitting, sexy clothes, often also sporting long artificial eyelashes, hair extensions in platinum blonde, heavy makeup, and nail polish in a great variety of colors. Gamze desired larger breasts to improve her décolleté and boost her sexual attractiveness. She was a committed user of Facebook, where almost every day she posted pictures of herself in saucy poses and with deep necklines. With the help of these selfies, she explained, she hoped to stay in touch with the young man she had a crush on, who a few months earlier had moved to northern Iraq for business. She reasoned that the constant images of her on his account would remind him of what he had lost and eventually make him return to marry her. Living in a strictly regimented parental home in the conservative neighborhood of Başakşehir, Gamze was obviously bored and tired of being the *ev kızı* (house girl), the unmarried daughter, still dependent on her parents. Boosting her attractiveness by way of investing in her breasts seemed like a safe passage out, toward a marriage that, in contrast to her parents' arranged marriage, would be based on erotic fulfilment and romantic love.

İlkay's consideration of breast augmentation surgery likewise began with marriage deliberations, albeit her mother's rather than her own. Thus, she recounted how recently, shopping for a dress for a cousin's marriage, her mother had made a suggestion: "Every dress was fitting around here [points to her hips] but not here [points to her breasts, indicating that they were too small for the dresses she tried on]. So she said: 'If you want to get a breast enlargement, you should do it!' and I said something like 'OK, I'll think about it.'"[18]

While during her cousin's wedding İlkay resorted to wearing a pushup brassiere, her mother's suggestion of breast surgery stuck in her head. She consulted a cosmetic surgeon, who indeed encouraged her to undergo such surgery. When talking to me shortly thereafter, it became clear that the main thing that held her back was that it had been her mother who had suggested surgery. Thus, İlkay was convinced that the comment in preparation for her *younger* cousin's marriage was tied to her mother's anxiety about İlkay not getting married in spite of her advanced age (she was twenty-nine at the time). Living the comfortable life of someone who was able to afford a flat of her own in a wealthy center city district, İlkay enjoyed the life of an uncommitted young woman. Nevertheless, her mother's comment about her body's sexual and aesthetic deficiency, as she saw it, continued to trouble her.

Finally, there is the account of Tuğba, a recent divorcée. In contrast to the majority of women who, in cosmetic surgeons' estimates, were in their (early) twenties and unmarried when they underwent breast augmentation surgery, Tuğba was in her late thirties when she first started thinking about it. Similar to what was reported by Dicle in the previous chapter, Tuğba's breasts had changed after giving birth and breastfeeding. In contrast to Dicle, however, Tuğba did not simply want to have her breasts restored, but rather "boosted" to add to her feminine attractiveness and be in a better position to compete in Istanbul's sexual market among its upper middle-class young professionals. Thus, after years of a rather dull marriage, since her recent divorce Tuğba was enjoying a reawakening of her sexuality, going out on weekends, flirting, and having affairs. She was not ready to give up on her newly discovered liberty anytime soon and mused that "in a few years," when aging hit harder, breast augmentation surgery would fit perfectly into the new, sexually liberated image of herself as an independent woman.

18. Interview with İlkay, November 8, 2013.

Within the Women's Club online forum, debates on breast augmentation surgery likewise circled around sexual relationships and female attractiveness, with larger breasts commonly being seen as boosting both. Male sexual partners were assumed always to desire fresh and youthful breasts, with larger breasts signifying beauty and sexiness. Common questions included whether husbands enjoyed the outcome of the surgery and whether women's sexual lives really improved after surgery. A common anxiety among its female users during the decision-making process was that sexual partners would view enlarged breasts as fake. Women generally advised each other on not letting anyone in on the surgery, including their sexual partners or fiancés.

To sum up, changing the size of their breasts was never an easy choice for women, and it was generally hidden from or else had to be negotiated with relatives and/or sexual partners. Within more conservative or, as in Özge's case, feminist circles, decisions about breast-reduction surgery were generally framed within a discourse of bodily normalization and health, rather than aesthetics. Women with parents like Özge's and Sevda's, who had been part of the large influx of rural-urban migrants to Istanbul in the 1960s and 1970s, seemed to be especially haunted by the symbolic connection between larger female breasts and rural cloddishness. However, as exemplified by Sevda's hesitation to undergo surgery and Özge's and Esra's accounts of men's stares at their pre-surgery and youthful breasts respectively, they were well aware of the normative link between larger female breasts, sexual attractiveness, and gendered roles, carefully weighing their surgery decisions against it. To Özge, her choice to have surgery giving her more standard-size breasts seemed an almost subversive act against the ever more sexualized, hyperfeminine bodily ideals that for many years had made her the object of dominating male stares and consequently restrictions on her movements. Finally, reshaping breasts is embedded in the social and professional environments of socially aspiring or sexually liberated women, who clearly know how to take care of themselves and actively participate in the urban beauty economy. In spite of the high costs, pain, and risks involved, the reshaping or restoring of breasts seen as abnormal or unattractive is a powerful way of managing one's adherence to gendered appearance norms oscillating between feminine respectability and respectable femininity.

Conclusion

Given the construal of large female breasts and noses as particularly prevalent and problematic in urban Turkey, the treatment of these bodily "deformations," in medical language, was generally narrated as based on a desire for, and indeed a right to, a normal rather than a merely beautiful look. As Edmonds and van der Geest note (2009, 15), notions of health and beauty are interlinked, forming a special relationship of interdependence. On the one hand, beauty practices such as nose and breast surgery imply health risks; on the other hand, beauty may also be understood as a matter of health, if broadly defined, by covering aspects of mental and social well-being as well. While the cosmetic surgery patients portrayed in this chapter varied in their pre-surgery pain and suffering, they all underwent surgery to cure or heal their bodies from mental and/or social forms of dis-ease. From this perspective, the strict boundary between beauty and health that is commonly drawn by insurance companies or Muslim legal scholars makes little sense. Instead, cosmetic surgery, especially nose and breast surgery, may allow women within a patriarchal society that scrutinizes the female body to reshape and, in some cases, normalize their body images and thus produce bodily well-being.

Within the urban beauty geography of Istanbul, the large influx of domestic migrants from the Black Sea and southeastern Anatolia has led to a particular form of social distinction by long-term urban residents. Female breasts and noses, as well as their surgical modification, are imbued with specific meanings in this particular location, with large breasts, for example, connoting both erotic femininity and rural backwardness, depending on who has them and at what point in the life course. Tanıl Bora (2010) analyzes the stereotypes that the urban and secular elite, the so-called White Turks, hold of those who do not qualify as modern city-dwellers in their eyes as a form of "racism that has an emphasis on class, relating social differences of people [poverty, that is] with cultural and

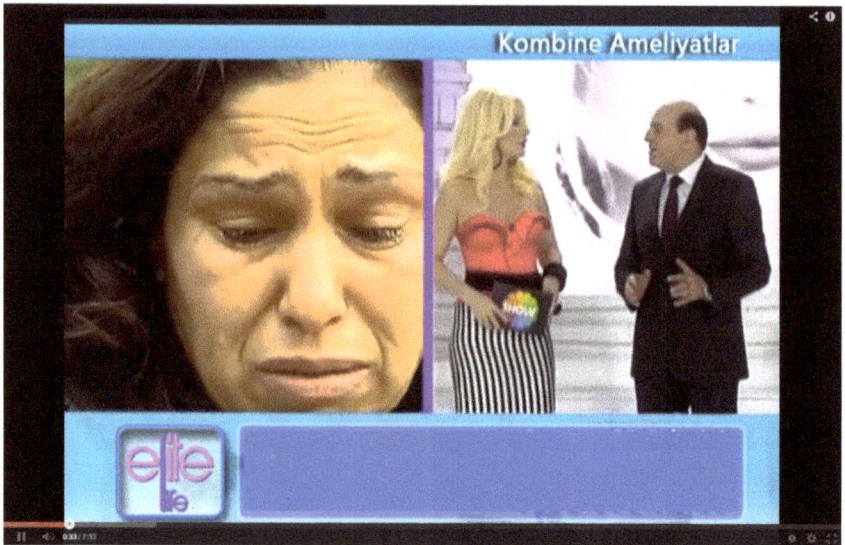

6. Screen shot from a private TV "makeover" show: women's surgery motivations are often narrated as based on affective desires for "normal" rather than downright attractive looks. (Claudia Liebelt)

even physical characteristics." Immigrants to the city or those living in more marginal neighborhoods are scrutinized visually for not belonging fully and may thus place a particular emphasis on reshaping their bodies in order to conform to certain gendered ideals concerning their appearance. For them, invasive beauty service work proves especially tricky because both their bodies *and* their aesthetic body modifications may give away their more peripheral regional backgrounds, especially if the latter produce "unnatural" results.

Whereas early Republicans were eager to emphasize that Turks formed a homogenous race with predominantly light skin and a straight nose, in contemporary aesthetic discourses a heterogeneous image and ideal of national "mixedness" is emerging. Similar to what Edmonds (2007) discusses with reference to cosmetic surgery in Brazil, rather than creating room for maneuver for women by making it possible for them to conform to one of many different models of gendered appearance, the national ideal of "mixedness" places additional pressures on women to conform to the demands of femininity by enhancing or at least normalizing their bodies through surgery. Depending on women's position within the urban geography, the demands of femininity are tied to those of respectability in varying degrees, with working- and lower middle-class women being more readily scrutinized for their assumed lack of respectability. As this chapter illustrates, this is clearly played out in their decisions on their personal body images and surgery decisions.

6

Becoming *Prezentabl*

In the scholarly literature, the boom in the global beauty industry and the popularization of cosmetic surgery and beauty services in recent decades have often been linked to the growth of the personal service sector. More specifically, they have been linked to the feminization of labor that occurred in the form of a global increase in the proportion of women in paid work. In *The Beauty Myth* (2002 [1991]) Naomi Wolf argues that, while American women gained power and access to the labor market in the 1960s and 1970s as an outcome of feminist struggles, in the 1980s their professional success became increasingly tied to good looks and a standardized female appearance. According to Wolf, the mass media and beauty industry both produced and profited from women's insecurities about their bodies. Hence women who were increasingly dissatisfied with their appearance and seen as unfit for a competitive labor market invested in beautification in order to reach often unattainable norms and remain professionally competitive. Wolf coined the term the "third shift" (Wolf, 2002 [1991], 25f.), consisting of beauty work that women have to complete after returning home from paid work, their first shift, and fulfilling domestic duties, their second shift.

From a different perspective, a number of economic and psychological publications indeed proclaimed the positive impact of good looks on earnings and labor-force participation, especially for women.[1] Based on small-

---

1. Among these studies, Nancy Etcoff's *Survival of the Prettiest* (2000) is one of the better known. Etcoff traces the evolutionary function of human beauty as a form of biological adaptation and a key for women's success especially. In another example, the economists Hamermesh and Biddle (1994) claim to be able to measure the impact of looks

scale quantitative research designs, the universal claim of these studies, namely to be able to measure beauty, as well as its causal relationship with professional success, needs to be questioned. Nevertheless, an emerging anthropological literature also points to the fact that investments in bodily beauty are seen as crucial to professional success by younger women and men in various locations worldwide, including Brazil (Edmonds 2007, 2010), Venezuela (Ochoa 2014), and China (Wen 2013). For example, Alex Edmonds (2010) describes how cosmetic surgery and the beauty industry promise upward mobility and the fulfilment of dreams for women especially. He notes that cosmetic surgery has become almost a prerequisite for finding a job in Rio de Janeiro's highly competitive service sector. Along similar lines, Wen Hua (2013) analyzes the "beauty capital" accumulated by young Chinese women by undergoing cosmetic surgery as vital in the competitive labor market in Beijing. In Venezuela, where feminine beauty now forms a part of the political economy, Marcia Ochoa (2014, 194) sees aesthetic body modifications as "to a certain degree expected" from young, upwardly mobile women.

A number of questions arise from the assumption of increased beautification efforts as a form of professional investment: can beauty, as a form of bodily capital, be understood as a tool of professional empowerment for women individually, as a kind of social elevator? Or rather, are women trapped in the lower ranks of the service and other sectors, while being tricked out of their time and money by the "beauty myth," which promises a career to those hampered by structural and gendered inequalities? In what ways is the relationship between good looks and professional success a global phenomenon, and how is it played out differently in diverse local settings? And finally, how do women perceive the relationship between professional success and beauty, and what gendered appearance norms do

---

on earnings. They conclude that "[p]lain people earn less than average-looking people, who earn less than the good-looking" (Hamermesh and Biddle 1994, 1174) and speak of a "plainness penalty" and a "beauty premium" of 5 to 10 percent. While they see similar effects at play for men and women, they argue that "[u]nattractive women have lower labor-force participation rates and marry men with less human capital" (Hamermesh and Biddle 1994, 1174).

they conform to, negotiate, and challenge in professional environments on a day-to-day basis?

Taking these questions as its starting point, this chapter seeks to contribute to the debate on beauty and gendered norms of appearance by drawing on research on female employees in Istanbul. It focuses on the perspectives and practices of women employed in the city's expanding and feminizing service sector, that is, in professional, managerial, or administrative work performed mainly in offices (the so-called white-collar sector), as well as in service-oriented work that involves interactions with customers, entertainment, and sales (the so-called pink-collar sector). As will become clear, in Turkey, where participation rates for women in the labor force are comparatively low due to patriarchal norms that discourage women from formal employment, especially in the case of married mothers, the term *çalışan kadın* (working woman), as opposed to that of the housewife (*ev hanımı*) has strong identificatory connotations. In the popular imagination there exists a strong normative link between the urban beauty sector and women's participation in the labor force, with the working woman being someone who, almost by definition, invests in her outer appearance by consuming a wide range of cosmetic practices. This link was even more pronounced in earlier decades, when, according to one elderly hairdresser, beauty salons catered almost exclusively to the professional female elite. "Today," Hilmiyye Hanım, a hairdresser in Istanbul since the 1950s, said of one of the major changes in her sector over the past five decades, "even *housewives* arrive to have their hair styled, with their children in tow."[2]

While attractiveness and beauty may give women an edge in a highly competitive urban job market, this chapter shows that in order to succeed professionally women do not seek beauty per se, but rather a look commonly described as *prezentabl* (from the French *présentable*). After a short section on the changing urban labor market, in the following I describe how my interlocutors, working women of various ages in Istanbul, gain and maintain presentability as part of their everyday routine. Drawing

---

2. Interview with Hilmiyye, April 24, 2014.

on participant observation during a week of research in the hair salon of an international banking headquarters in Maslak, Istanbul's business district, I offer a description of women's beauty routines as part of their work routine. Finally, this chapter presents and discusses several cases of beauty discrimination suffered by female employees who did not comply with or else challenged gendered appearance norms in their workplaces. The chapter also underlines the fact that efforts in respect to beautification and normative looks are a crucial domain for women in their professional lives. Beauty work, I argue, is highly significant not only due to its aesthetic outcomes, but also for the affective and sensual changes it brings about in professional women's presentations of self.

The Role of Appearance in a Changing Urban Labor Market

In an influential volume on Istanbul, Çağlar Keyder (1999) describes the city's transformation into a global and globalizing city following the neoliberal doctrine of economic opening-up in the 1980s. One of the most significant aspects of this transformation according to Keyder was the deindustrialization of the urban economy and the growth of the personal service sector to substitute for the loss of employment in manufacturing. New employment opportunities were created in the fields of marketing, accounting and management, telecommunications, banking and finance, transport, insurance, computers and data processing, legal services, auditing, consulting, advertising, design, and engineering. In contrast to an earlier prevalence of men in most sectors of the formal Turkish labor market, many of these new job opportunities now sought out female employees. This signaled a major shift in the urban labor market "from manufacturing to services, from male to female, from brawn to cultural capital, and from local to global" (Keyder 2005, 129).

Given the fact that until well into the 1990s urban shopkeepers and their sales personnel, secretaries, and office workers, and even hairdressers and waiters in cafés and restaurants, were almost exclusively male, the large number of young women who suddenly started appearing as the employees in Istanbul's newly built shopping centers, large retail complexes, hotels, and restaurants was remarkable indeed. In addition, a new generation of female entrepreneurs opened up businesses such as new-style cafés, fitness and dieting centers, and hair and beauty salons, employing and catering to a growing number of women. In spite of these changes, researchers describe the ongoing low participation of women in the urban labor force, as well as in Turkey more generally. For example, in the 2020 Global Gender Gap Report published by the World Economic Forum (2019), Turkey ranks 130th out of 153 countries, mainly due to its low average numbers of women's economic participation and opportunity. Accordingly, only 37.5 percent of women participate in the labor force, as compared to 78.1 percent of men. Moreover, women suffered from higher rates of unemployment, were five times more likely than men to engage in unpaid work, and were three times more likely to engage in part-time rather than full-time work. It is interesting to note that, in spite of the feminization of the urban labor market in recent decades, female labor-market participation in Turkey declined from over 70 percent in the 1950s to 32.7 percent in the mid-1980s (Özbay 1995).[3]

In her study of paid domestic work performed by women from the lower strata of society in middle-class households in Ankara, Gül Ozyegin (2001) describes how patriarchal control of women's labor contributes to the scarcity of such workers. She describes a situation in which husbands control and indeed prohibit their wives from participating in domestic service or any other form of employment by arguing that "women's employment equals prostitution" (quoted from Ozyegin 2001, 53). Other studies have shown that the large influx of working peasant women into urban centers in the 1970s and 1980s often resulted in their "housewifization," with some estimating women's employment in the formal and informal urban labor market as low as 5.5 percent (Ozyegin 2001, 41). Not least, in these lower social strata participation in the urban labor force was mostly restricted to young, unmarried women, who typically left their jobs once they got married.

3. This is often explained by the effects of the rural exodus during the 1960s and 1970s in Turkey: thus, women who engaged in unpaid family labor in agriculture were officially considered workers in the 1950s but went unregistered by official statistics once they went abroad or to the city, where they typically engaged in informal employment in the urban textile and retail markets or domestic work (cf. Özbay 1995).

Far from being a phenomenon of the lower social strata, however, a study of the reproduction of class in Istanbul by Rutz and Bakan (2009) shows that women's low participation in the labor market also holds true for the urban middle classes. Many urban middle-class women likewise give up employment once they marry and give birth. Thus, Rutz and Bakan note the crucial role of mothers in reproducing class status in Istanbul, mainly by caring for and tutoring children, arguing that "middle class families want their daughters to be educated and to have careers, [but these] should not come at the expense of having families" (2009, 60). Against the background of a highly competitive urban labor market with long commutes and working hours, insufficient childcare, and a desolate state school sector, the combination of professional success and motherhood appears simply out of reach for many middle-class women. Not least, familistic norms and women's orientation toward households and families rather than professional careers are strongly encouraged by the ruling AKP government, which openly encourages women to give birth to three children or more (Güneş-Ayata and Doğangün 2017, 619). Patriarchal norms that stress the male role of the breadwinner and the female role of the homemaker are thus not the preserve of the lower social strata, but persist in the urban middle classes as well. Within these classes, Rutz and Bakan remark (2009, 60), "having a [female] spouse at home for the family" is a highly cherished privilege of male managers, businessmen, engineers, and academics.

In spite of these structural and normative obstacles, women are well represented in management and, at 43 percent of all employees in Istanbul's banks and insurance companies in the mid-1990s, the percentage of women in the urban service sector is high even compared to industrialized western economies (Kabasakal et al. 2004, 282). Perhaps as a result of their privileged status, women who do make a career in Turkey and continue employment after giving birth tend to profess a strong identity as "working women" (*çalışan kadınlar*). As a vanguard within the highly globalized service sector, much is expected from them, not least in terms of their outer appearance.

While under the Turkish constitution (1982) the discrimination of individuals along the lines of language, race, color, sex, political opinion, belief, religion, or disability is explicitly prohibited, studies of recruitment practices point in a different direction. Zeynep Aycan (2006), who studied human resource management practices in Turkey, notes that, in the context of rising unemployment, large companies receive "thousands of job applications every day," but rarely apply structured recruitment policies. In her view, recruitment in Turkey suffers from a "pervasive problem of favoritism and nepotism," (Aycan 2006, 26) with job interviews often being "heavily influenced by the interviewer's subjective evaluation and personal intuition" (Aycan 2006, 20). She concludes that gender equality remains one of the main problematic areas of human resource management in Turkey (Aycan 2006, 27), with so-called "soft skills" or connections, rather than merit, often being decisive when it comes to hiring female employees. Indeed, women who made it into and in this highly competitive white-collar sector commonly attribute their success to personal characteristics such as "high self-confidence, achievement orientation and determination" (Aycan 2004, 472). Moreover, attractiveness, youth, or good looks are commonly seen as adding value to the worker, especially in frontline service jobs, in which she is a kind of poster child for the company (see also Williams and Connell 2010, 357–60).

Thus, the relevance of beauty for recruitment and professional success is varied across different segments of the service sector. It is of particular significance within the pink-collar sector, especially entertainment and sales, which rely on interactions with customers. One interviewee, Dicle, a singer and performer in her early forties, described the significance of good looks in the entertainment sector by drawing on her own personal experiences:

> Poorly groomed women remain in the background in our business. If one of them takes care of herself well enough and is a little bit pretty, if she has light-colored eyes, for example, she will stand out. Or, if she doesn't have [light] colored eyes, but the way she looks is impressive, you think she's attractive, then she will stand out. So instead of working with Ayşe and Fatma [common female names in Turkey], these women work with the stars. Women have to take care of themselves these days. For example, if there are three women in a voiceover studio, and one

of them is sexier and more attractive than the others, she will get more pages [to work on and by implication, better pay]. It's as simple as that.[4]

The firm belief that good looks and beauty are prerequisites for professional success and that they result in better pay for women—according to Dicle even in the voiceover studio, where the worker's looks should have no effect on her output whatsoever—was generally held by interviewees and resonated with media discourses. The president of the Istanbul Chamber of Beauticians, Manicurists, and Tattoo Artists, Ayşe Aydın, told me that "working women are more well-groomed (*bakımlı*) [than housewives]. That's due to their social environment. They are part of public life, and they have to pay attention to their looks. At home, you can hang out with your hair undone and in sweatpants, but at work, that's simply impossible!"[5]

Even more emphatically, in 2004 Ayşe Arman, a well-known columnist and interviewer for the daily *Hürriyet*, began an interview with a cosmetic surgeon with what was clearly intended as a rhetorical question: "In our age, the interest in good looks is socially accepted. That's why it is so popular. Just think of two persons of equal education and characteristics, one of them smart-looking and beautiful, the other one ugly and dishevelled. Whom would you choose?" (Arman 2004)

While both Arman and Aydın stress the importance of good looks for professional women rather than men, men have also been reported as investing in their bodies as a conscious career move in Turkey. Thus, in 2004, the daily *Hürriyet* published a report on aesthetic surgery titled "My Pretty Boss" (Yenal 2004). In it, the acting president of the Chamber for Plastic and Aesthetic-Reconstructive Surgery, Prof. Dr. Mesut Özcan, estimated that 25 percent of the total number of surgeries per annum in Turkey were performed on a person in a leading position. While female leaders, whom Özcan estimated to form eighty percent of his patients, typically consumed Botox injections, liposuction, silicone implants, and various liftings for reasons of professional competitiveness, male bosses

---

4. Interview with Dicle, February 19, 2014.

5. Interview with Ayşe Aydın, April 22, 2014.

commonly had abdominoplasty and eyelid surgery, as well as hair transplants to cover bald spots. According to Özcan these operations were chosen "to increase their self-confidence and support their entry into the job market" (quoted from Yenal 2004). Toward the end of the report, a surgeon from the Plastic and Aesthetic Surgery Department in Acıbadem Bakırköy Hospital was quoted as saying that "the first impression is especially important in business life and is high up on the priority list [of our patients]. To be saved from (bodily) deformations increases self-esteem in both work and social life. This reflects on the professional success of a person" (Yenal 2004).

Beauty, attractiveness, and increased self-esteem may indeed boost professional success. However, it is not necessarily beauty or attractiveness per se, but (also) a sector-specific look most commonly described as *prezentabl*, which is expected of both men and women in managerial and administrative professions performed in offices. This is also reflected in the language of job advertisements.

A glance through job advertisements for positions gendered female in Istanbul's service sector in 2016 produced a number of appearance-related attributes for the description of desired candidates. While *prezentabl* is the standard term, other terms and expressions frequently listed included "well-groomed" (*bakımlı*) or "attentive to outer appearance" (*dış görünümüne özen gösteren*). For example, the ideal candidate to fill the position of a secretary in an international logistics firm located in Esenler, Istanbul, was described as "cheerful," "presentable," "attentive to outer appearance," and "well-groomed;" moreover, she possessed "speaking etiquette" and "representative skills." Like many positions directed at female candidates, this one was restricted to younger women between twenty-two and thirty years old.[6] As the account below shows, in recent years, and in parallel to the urban beauty boom, the normative ideal of female looks in one's professional life has slightly shifted toward a more sexualized and beauty-intensive kind of look than the term *prezentabl* might imply. The following

---

6. The original advertisement reads "Güler yüzlü, presantable, diksiyonu düzgün, dış görünüme önem veren bakımlı ve temsil yeteneği gelişmiş" (cf. www.kariyer.net, accessed July 27, 2016).

section shows how the normative ideals implicit in these descriptions are played out in the everyday grooming practices and extraordinary cosmetic surgery decisions of different female employees in Istanbul.

Beauty for Employment

At noon one Tuesday in December 2013, my research assistant Selen and I are waiting for a prospective interviewee, Filiz, an accountant in the stock management department of one of central Istanbul's large international companies. Referred to us by another interlocutor as a cosmetic surgery patient, over the phone Filiz asks to meet us at the food court of the exquisite Kanyon shopping mall in central Istanbul, where she usually takes her lunch. Selen and I arrive shortly before noon to settle in what looks like a quiet corner of the restaurant Filiz recommended. After a few minutes the scenery changes dramatically, as hundreds of employees from nearby offices stream into the food court and within seconds fill up every corner. The uniform appearance of the employees is remarkable, with the men dressed in dark suits, light shirts, and ties, and most of the predominantly young and slim women sporting long hair and female suits or light-colored blouses and skirts ending just beneath the knees, also wearing high heels or ballerina shoes. Filiz arrives with the crowd. She is a tall and slim woman with long blonde hair in her early twenties, dressed in a cream-colored trench coat over a white blouse and a dark blue skirt. She is carefully made up with lipstick and mascara, her fingernails polished in bright red. When, after a first round of introductions and the ordering of sandwiches for lunch, I share my observation about the uniform appearance of the employees, Filiz laughingly tells us:

> Actually, there is no dress code at our company, but we do dress classically, like in the other offices. Apart from this, they don't expect much from us. I don't do much anyway; sometimes I even leave for work without wearing makeup. Styling up is something for the marketing and public relations departments (*laughs*)! If you are a customer consultant, you'd better style up. Your job requires it.[7]

---

7. Interview with Filiz, December 24, 2013. The following quotations from Filiz are also taken from this interview.

During our interview, Filiz repeats the claim of not "doing much" about her looks, an assessment that seems to contradict her carefully made-up appearance. On the other hand, given the fact that Filiz usually leaves her parents' home in the suburban district of Bakırköy at 7:30 in the morning for work and returns there around 8 p.m. after a bus ride home that can easily take up to two hours, her personal assessment that there simply is "no time for beauty" makes perfect sense to me. But what about the cosmetic surgery? I ask her. It was nose surgery, undertaken for medical rather than aesthetic reasons, Filiz explains (see also chapter 5). Removing the hook of her nose while having her infected sinuses cleaned up was the surgeon's suggestion, she tells us. So why did she agree to his suggestion, I go on to ask. After pausing for a while, Filiz recounts that her close friend underwent nose surgery just before she went job-hunting, and the smaller nose actually helped her find a job. To our surprise, she goes on to explain: "I mean, people always tell you that when you want to earn money you should have it [the nose surgery] done. This is not about beauty, but about self-confidence!"

Like Filiz, many professional women we interviewed were reluctant to relate personal beauty investments directly to their professional success. However, they did believe that these investments produced a boost in self-esteem that was badly needed in their professional environment. Filiz explained her initial reluctance to talk to us about beauty as follows:

> I think beauty is not the most important thing—intellect is more important. People at work always ask me why I hide my beauty. . . . I mean, I graduated from two universities. So if people talk to me about my looks rather than about my knowledge, I feel like this is a degrading thing for me. Intellect should be more important than looks!

Here, the ambivalence of beautification for Filiz in relation to her professional life, as well as more generally, stands out clearly: as the first in her family to graduate from university—from two universities, as she emphasizes—she naturally takes pride in her intellectual achievements. Also implied in her statement is a powerful critique that dismisses the practice of judging women by their appearance as a form of objectification and personal degradation—an experience that Filiz, a young woman at the very beginning of her professional career, can obviously relate to. Finally, the statement points to the immense pressure with regard to feminine beauty ideals that Filiz and many other interlocutors reported feeling at their workplaces, with colleagues encouraging them to show rather than hide their beauty and comparing the beauty services they consumed to "make more" of themselves with each other. At that point in our interview, Filiz's lunch break was almost over. Taking a bite from her sandwich while also glancing at her watch, she continued:

> You know, in Istanbul, people are, like, in a constant contest. Not only in terms of beauty, but also in terms of professional success. The two are anyway related. We live so fast here. Every minute is full. When I was abroad [in the Netherlands, as part of a student exchange for one semester], I felt I could breathe. I had leisure time. But here your time is limited and people have to allot their time: apart from the working hours, there is the time you need for bodily upkeep. You actually have to save time for beauty. For example, on the weekends, if I spend four to five hours at the hair salon and I only have two days off per week, this means that I spend a quarter of my free time at the hair salon! And this is for what is obligatory only. Because my hair started to turn white and I can't go to work like that. Not because this is the rule, but because I won't feel good unless I dye it. It's like an obligation!

At this point, it became clear that, while Filiz rhetorically downplayed the importance of good looks and beautification for her professional career, and in spite of her insightful criticisms, she put immense effort into complying with the appearance norms of her professional environment. This included a considerable amount of time and—given the fact that her nose operation was a strategic, career-related choice—pain and financial resources to do "what was obligatory." While at the beginning of our interview Filiz described work-related beauty work as boosting professional women's self-confidence, at a later point she added another layer of explanation, namely that of a highly competitive urban environment where bodily upkeep, not to speak of a bodily upgrade, were clearly part of the game for women. Moreover, like many other women we talked to or interviewed, Filiz had clearly internalized a particular bodily discipline; in a Foucauldian kind of bodily "care of the self," she complied with appearance norms not because they were codified as a rule, but because she didn't feel good about herself if she violated them.

Several months after the interview with Filiz we interviewed Ayten, an accountant in the management of an international firm based in Kartal on the Anatolian side of Metro Istanbul, again during her lunch break. While waiting in the lobby of the company's glass tower, Selen and I noted that the employees passing by looked strikingly similar to those who had rushed past us in the Kanyon mall during our meeting with Filiz. Ayten appeared dressed in high heels, tights, a black miniskirt, and a tight white shirt with a low neckline. She was a petite woman in her mid-forties with long blonde hair, wearing gold jewelry and a golden watch as well as heavy makeup, including pink lipstick and orangey nail polish on her long and carefully manicured nails. In contrast to Filiz, who criticized the role beauty norms played in the professional lives of women, Ayten was rather assertive of the role of styling up for (working) women:

> A woman, no matter where, even at home, should always be clean [*temiz*] and stylish [*bakımlı*], well-dressed, in shape [*düzgün*], wear nice shoes, etc.; in short, be stylish. That's what I try to be at least, no matter what others expect from me. When you're a working woman, you need time to style up every morning before leaving the house. You're entering a social world of meetings, so it's simply a must![8]

Indeed, every morning before leaving for work, Ayten claimed she spent at least one hour getting dressed and styled up for work. Like Filiz, she attended a regular hair salon every two weeks to have done "whatever is necessary," including shaping eyebrows, removing body hair, manicures, pedicures, styling, and coloring her hair. Once in a while she had facials and other kinds of beauty treatment. Ayten took great care not to gain weight and laughingly admitted that she was usually on a diet. She was fond of makeup and spent at least 100 TRY (approximately US$50)

---

8. Interview with Ayten, May 5, 2014. The following quotations from Ayten are also taken from this interview.

per month on cosmetics and personal care articles. Among her female colleagues, some of whom were also her close friends, aesthetics, diets, and the latest fashion were common topics of conversation. Most of them had undergone cosmetic surgery. When, more than a year prior to our interview, Ayten decided to remove the hook of her nose, she relied on her colleagues' recommendations in finding a cosmetic surgeon. By the time we interviewed her, Ayten dreamed of having facial fillers, a treatment currently popular among her female colleagues that her cosmetic surgeon claimed would make her face look softer. While Ayten felt this would clearly give her an edge within her highly competitive work environment, she was financially restricted, still paying back the loan she had taken out to cover her nose operation.

In spite of the time and cost involved in her beautification efforts, Ayten, much in contrast to Filiz, experienced beauty work as part of her positive identity as a working woman. Like Filiz, Ayten was the first in her family to graduate from college and the first female family member to continue employment after marrying and giving birth. She had grown up in a lower middle-class household where her father was a clerk in a shipping company, while her mother took care of the household and children. She proudly recounted that ever since graduating from college more than twenty years ago she had never experienced a day of unemployment, working full-time except for a few weeks after giving birth to her son. As a divorced single mother who divided her time between work and family, beauty work for Ayten felt like the only time she truly had for herself.

Differently though they positioned themselves with regard to the role of beauty in women's professional careers, Filiz's and Ayten's routines of bodily grooming were rather similar to each other and to those of many of the other female service-sector employees interviewed for this study. When I asked Hiranur, a beauty therapist and former salon-owner, about the basic things a working woman should do, she provided the following list ordered by priority: "clothes, hair, and makeup, depending on the circumstances."[9] As emphasized in the accounts of Ayten, Filiz, and many

---

9. Interview with Hiranur, February 20, 2014.

others, time for attending to dress, hair, and makeup was indeed crucial before leaving for work in the mornings. The fact that the amount of makeup depended on the woman's specific professional environment, as noted by Hiranur, is an important factor to mention. Thus, highly visible, colorful makeup was considered almost obligatory in some sectors, especially marketing and public relations, as observed by Filiz above, whereas in others it was regarded inappropriate and exaggerated. For example, this was the case for the medical sector, as Ayşegül, a nurse in her early twenties, explained:

> For me as a nurse, it's important to look clean [*temiz*] and nice [*hoş*]; people take comfort in a nice-looking nurse. We are *not* supposed to wear exaggerated makeup. So we try not to wear *bright* nail polish or eye shadow, for example, because we work in the health sector, and it would be inappropriate to look as if you're on the way to a wedding or clubbing. . . . I often put on light nail polish or makeup, but *not* in an exaggerated way.[10]

Knowing the appropriate amount and style of makeup and beauty work is an important skill that working women are expected to master. Whether the implicit appearance norm included light or bright makeup, making up could easily consume much of women's precious time before leaving for work, and several interviewees reported that they had had permanent makeup tattooed on their eyelids and lips in order to save time in the mornings.

Finally, hair is of crucial importance in the process of becoming *prezentabl*, and indeed one female executive manager provided the following definition of *prezentabl*: "it means your hair not going crazy." Since many women employed in the service sector like Filiz or Ayten opted for long, rather than short hair—following the dominant norm for younger women—the task of preventing hair from going crazy could indeed be a major one. As the following section shows, it is one that is served by an increasing number of hair salons located *within* the companies these women work in.

10. Interview with Ayşegül, February 20, 2014.

Manufacturing the Bank Standard

During one week in June 2014, I was granted access to do research in the hair salon of one of the large international banking headquarters in Maslak, Istanbul's business district, also known as the "Turkish Manhattan." Maslak, a glass city built in the 1990s, is the home of the Turkish stock market, its international investment banks, insurance companies, five-star international business hotels, and similar institutions. Its high-rise buildings can be seen from practically everywhere in the city. The small hair salon where I did research was located in a corner of the underground parking lot of one of them, right next to the company's fitness salon. Both establishments catered exclusively to the bank's employees and offered their services at reduced prices. Owned by a larger chain that also held franchises for other salons elsewhere in Maslak, it was subleased by Orhan, a hairdresser in his late twenties. Orhan worked in the salon alongside two younger male colleagues and a female manicurist, who, however, was on sick leave during my research.

The salon workers' main job, Orhan jokingly remarked during our first meeting in the bank's cafeteria, was not to do "fancy things" with women's hair, but to manufacture "the bank standard."[11] This meant that hair had to be washed and styled in order to look in shape (*düzgün*), that is, without one errant strand of hair, unintended waves, or gray bits showing. Since time management was of crucial importance in this salon, with customers often simply requesting "something fast," the most frequently performed treatment was to blow-dry hair so as to make it look straight and shiny—a *fön*, in Turkish.

The daily work routine in the salon went as follows. Around 7:30 in the morning Orhan and his colleagues opened the salon's tinted glass doors, then switched on the lights and the salon's stereo. From 8 o'clock until about 9:30 a.m. was the salon's first rush hour; within these ninety minutes or so, each morning about fifteen to twenty-five exclusively female customers arrived, one quickly after the other, in order to have their hair styled and sometimes washed. During the morning rush hour

---

11. Interview with Orhan, June 16, 2014.

all three hairdressers worked nonstop in order to serve as many customers as possible before they had to leave for their offices. In order to save time, many customers arrived at the salon with their cosmetic cases and applied makeup while waiting to be served, leaning over the hairdressing chairs to get a good look at the large mirrors. Many of them preferred to arrive at the bank's headquarters well before their shift began, not only to style up for work, but also to avoid the traffic congestion that routinely affects Maslak just before 9 o'clock, when thousands of white-collar workers rush into its high-rise buildings to begin their working day.

After 9:30 or so the salon turned quiet, giving the hairdressers some time to clean up and rest. At about 11:30 a.m., the first lunch-break customers arrived, again to have their hair washed and styled, but also for more time-consuming treatments such as cutting, coloring, or highlighting their hair. Early afternoons in the salon were quiet again. More customers came in the late afternoons or early evening after their shifts had ended in order to style up for after-work dates or meetings. Occasionally, a customer arrived with an after-work appointment. Most, however, seemed to have another regular beauty salon for more time-consuming treatments, as well as for services not on offer at Orhan's such as body hair removal or hair extensions.

Some customers arrived at the salon irregularly; for example, on days when they had important business meetings, or fulfilled representative functions outside the building. Others relied regularly on its services, typically twice or three times a week in the mornings before work. Among them, many were from the human resources and marketing departments; these, so Elin, a human resource manager in her late twenties and regular salon customer told us, were expected "to simply look perfect." Elin herself came to the salon three times a week to demand a blow-dry for straightening her long blondish hair. When we first met her at the salon, she was dressed in high heels and a short skirt, heavily made up with bright nail polish on her carefully manicured nails, certainly making an effort to "look perfect." Other regular clients from the human resources department looked somewhat less fancy than her, illustrating how styling up for work was also influenced by personal tastes and fashion preferences.

Another regular was a leading manager in her late forties, who usually arrived packed with papers that she read while waiting to be served. This employee made a direct connection between her visits to the company salon and her recent promotion as her department's team leader. The regular salon visits made her look "more professional" all through the week. This, as well as the boost to her self-esteem, she was convinced, had done the trick within her male-dominated work environment. From chatting to the women waiting in line to be served at Orhan's salon, it became clear that they took the relationship between good looks and professional success for granted. Moreover, like the interviewees quoted above, if not "perfect," they emphasized the need to look *bakımlı*, stylish, or *prezentabl*, rather than beautiful (*güzel*). Several customers quoted the saying that "there are no ugly women, just careless ones," thus associating their beautification efforts with their more generally disciplined and moral endeavors at work.

In *Queen for a Day*, Ochoa (2014) describes the relationship between the male stylist and the female contestant in a Venezuelan Miss Beauty pageant as "essential in producing the stage persona, what is often called a *mujerona*" (Ochoa 2014, 227). By exercising his beauty expertise and talking her up, the stylist contributes significantly to creating the *mujerona*, a sexualized being, ready not only to look stunning but also to perform impressively on the *pasarela* or catwalk (Ochoa 2014, 228). The interaction between Orhan, the handsome and carefully styled hairdresser, and his female salon customers, who were typically older and way higher up in the hierarchy of the bank, bore startling similarities to Ochoa's observation: by styling them up, giving them compliments, and sometimes flirting jokingly with his customers, Orhan in fact did much more than simply manufacture the bank standard. Rather, he prepared them for a tough day in the bank's male-dominated, formal, and hierarchical pecking order. After they had had their hair done at the salon, the bank's female employees left not only looking "perfect" for work, but also seemed to feel much better about themselves, ready to handle whatever came along in their working day.

This became especially clear from Orhan's interaction with Seher, a long-term bank manager and regular customer in her early forties. Having learned about our research while settling down in the hair-dressing chair to get a blow-dry for straightening her hair one Monday at noon, Seher laughingly shouted across the salon toward us: "You know, the truth is, I come here because I'm in love with [Orhan]!" Approaching her chair from behind, putting his hands on her shoulders and looking her straight in the eye through the mirror in front of her, Orhan smilingly replied, "Oh darling, I love you too! So what should I do to your hair now?" While blow-drying Seher's long hair, Orhan continued chatting with her casually, about the weather and, this being a Monday, her weekend, complimenting her on her dress, and addressing her as "darling" (*canım*) all throughout the conversation. Upon leaving the salon, Seher once again looked into the mirror, touching her straightened hair appreciatively and exclaimed: "Oh, I just love you, [Orhan]!" After paying and kissing Orhan goodbye on the cheek, she shouldered her exclusive handbag and turned to the door, saying "*Haydı bakalım!*" (Let's get on with it!). Like many women who arrived at the salon tired from too little sleep and the long commute through Istanbul's heavy traffic in the morning, their hair and faces undone, Seher left the salon obviously feeling great about herself, her high heels clicking authoritatively on the ground of the underground parking lot toward the lift on her way up to her office, well prepared for another day in Maslak's competitive corporate life.

Disturbing Gendered Appearance Norms in Professional Contexts

In her bestselling monograph *The Beauty Myth*, mentioned at the beginning of this chapter, Naomi Wolf sets out to make the case against an ideology of feminine beauty that generates insecurity and makes women "feel 'worth less'" (2002, 18). Indeed, she describes the beauty myth as a form of conspiracy created by the commercial beauty sector in the 1980s "as a way to legitimize employment discrimination against women" (Wolf 2002, 21). Recollecting several court cases filed by women against their appearance-related discrimination at work, she concludes that "[a] woman can be fired for not looking right, but looking right remains open to interpretation" (2002, 33). This section focuses on women's struggles to fulfil, challenge, or change professional gendered beauty norms. Beauty norms may vary slightly in different professional sectors, but not fulfilling them has grave consequences in all of them. Moreover, the gendered aesthetics of looking appropriate for work may change. In recent years hegemonic ideals of beauty have been challenged by an emphasis on hyperfemininity and sexual attractiveness on the one hand and socioeconomic and political changes toward more pious norms of femininity in Turkey on the other. In order to illustrate this, I draw on interviews with three interlocutors who chose to leave salaried work due to the pressures that resulted from gendered appearance norms at their workplaces, focusing in particular on the story of Neda. I also examine two cases of appearance-related labor conflicts at Turkey's national flag carrier, Turkish Airlines (Türk Hava Yolları, THY), widely discussed in Turkish public debates in 2010 and 2013 respectively.

Neda was a talented writer who, during her short academic career, struggled against what she perceived as "the tyranny of feminine looks in academia."[12] When we first met, she appeared as a self-conscious, cheerful, energetic person with light blue eyes and complexion, her short hair dyed a bright red. The meeting took place in a neighborhood café in Moda on the Anatolian side of Istanbul, where we both lived at the time; it had been arranged by a mutual acquaintance who was still employed in academia. Neda arrived for the interview in colorful cotton pants and a T-shirt, wearing flat cotton slippers. Shortly into the interview, when I asked about the role of beautification and styling up in her professional life, she answered:

> I mean, I just came from work. So you probably expect a person who is coming from work to be wearing a skirt, or fabric pants and an elegant shirt, with her hair brushed and all that. I mean, "beauty" [*güzellik*] is commonly understood as something like this, like wearing high heels etc. But I am wearing slippers with cats [printed on them], and my clothes are not in such a good condition. I mean, the concept of beauty is a norm that people decide on. You have to follow that norm in order

---

12. Interview with Neda, June 12, 2014. The following quotations from Neda are also taken from this interview.

to be beautiful. Your hair must be brushed. It is a convention. . . . But my intention was never to be beautiful. I always wanted to be *myself*, like, *different*. I was like this when I was young, even during puberty. When all my friends started to get blow-dries, I was stubborn and stopped brushing my hair.

Partly due to her desire to be "different" and "herself" rather than follow conventional gendered beauty norms, Neda had recently given up a prestigious position in the department of political science at a high-ranking state university, where she had also completed her PhD. Instead, she had rented office space close to where she lived and was currently writing a TV series script as a freelancer, obviously enjoying the freedom this entailed in terms of her outer appearance. In our interview, she remembered the constant appearance-related pressure she was subject to at university because she did not conform to the expectations of a Turkish civil servant in terms of looks.[13] She described how it had been her female rather than her male colleagues in the department who had constantly advised her to "make more" of herself; that is, put on makeup or let her hair grow longer, and more generally dress up "in a more feminine way." They commonly framed their advice within a discourse of sisterly or motherly care, emphasizing the need to take care of herself if she planned to pursue an academic career.

When once Neda came to her office with her hair dyed red, one of them, a renowned feminist, remarked: "Wow, you're a woman after all!"— ironically praising Neda for taking an interest in her looks, while also making it clear that the color she had chosen was terribly wrong. Later that day, the head of the department admonished her by saying: "You're a teacher, so go and dye your hair a proper color!" He had reprimanded her before for not covering up the tattoo she wore on her upper arm, the image of a small cartoon character that Neda had created in one of her short stories. While Neda was prepared for the head's reactions, she was outraged by those of her colleague: how could she possibly consider herself

---

13. Academic staff at state universities are commonly employed as civil servants in Turkey.

a feminist if a person's outer appearance led her to doubt that person's proclaimed gender identity?

Another blow came after Neda's defense of her PhD thesis, for which she had chosen to dress in one of her favorite dresses, printed with colorful flowers. Following the defense, her supervisor took her aside to tell her that she would have made a better impression and possibly received a higher mark if only she had dressed more appropriately. When Neda looked surprised, she specified that her dress had been too colorful for the occasion and that something "more grayish" or at least "monochrome" would have been a better choice. Agitated that once more it was her looks rather than her intellectual capacities that were being judged critically, Neda took the decision to leave academia. In our conversation, she commented on what she perceived was "a weird contradiction" among Turkish academics: priding themselves in speaking up critically when it came to politics, while simultaneously being overly formal and conventional when it came to the way they presented themselves. How could she possibly teach her students critical or queer theory if she herself did not even feel free to wear her hair the way she liked?

Neda's account exemplifies the extent to which not only superiors, but also colleagues commonly comment on, police, and sanction each other's looks in terms of their appropriateness and gender-conformity. Moreover, it makes obvious the intricacies and detailed knowledge required to look appropriate for work. Insisting on her own style (and her nonconformity), sometimes consciously and sometimes unconsciously—as in the case of the flowery dress—Neda disturbed the gendered norms that were considered appropriate in her professional context. In her case, looking appropriate meant first sticking to the written and unwritten dress and grooming codes proper for a civil servant or teacher, namely someone who served as a role model to students; and secondly, it meant adding what interlocutors commonly referred to as "a little extra," namely feminine accessories such as makeup, jewelry, or the high heels Neda mentioned (and abhorred). Neda, who offered a critique of heteronormativity in her teachings and insisted on being different as part of her feminist identity, saw no possibility of reconciling these expectations with the way she liked to dress and style herself. In her attempt to defy the assumptions of the "beauty myth" as an individual—and in contrast to many of my interlocutors described above, who employed beautification to increase their professional self-esteem—Neda obviously drew her self-esteem from other sources.

Another interlocutor who had left academia due to what she described as appearance-related problems was Jale, a woman in her early sixties (see also chapter 4). Jale had been a lecturer in the fine arts department of a prestigious state university in Istanbul back in the 1970s. As a young woman with long, naturally blonde hair and light-colored eyes who was fond of makeup and fashion, Jale had conformed closely to the standard ideals of feminine beauty. However, at university her looks likewise created problems, as she put it, when the male head of department started making advances to her and publicly favoring her. Jale felt harassed, but saw no way to react against him. Rather than support her, her colleagues accused her of using her good looks to advance her career. The atmosphere at her workplace became so unbearable that Jale made the decision to leave her position and, as a consequence, give up her academic career.

The experiences of Neda and Jale show the fine line women have to walk between being criticized for not styling up enough or adding "a little extra" and being judged for looking too feminine and, as a consequence, too sexy and seductive. Indeed, sexual harassment of women at work is comparatively high in Turkey, where, according to a study conducted by Wasti and Cortina (2002, quoted from Aycan 2006, 14), a staggering eighteen percent of female employees have experienced such harassment at their workplace.

In this context, it is interesting to note the shift that one interlocutor, Emine, called "the sexualization of working women" in recent decades in Turkey.[14] Emine, a pharmacist and freelance consultant who was employed in a leading pharmaceutical company for many years, was in her early fifties when we first met to talk about her multiple cosmetic operations. Much in contrast to the advertising or banking sectors, which had been "show-off" sectors from the beginning, the pharmaceutical and

---

14. Interview with Emine, January 15, 2014. The following quotations from Emine are also taken from this interview.

medical sectors in Turkey, according to Emine, had favored a classic look up until the early 2000s. This look required women to appear neat and well-groomed, but to refrain from heavy makeup or more generally a colorful or flamboyant outer appearance. When, in 2007, Emine returned to Istanbul after living and working abroad for several years, she noted a generational shift among the employees in her company that had brought with it a visible shift in female employees' aesthetics:

> All of a sudden, there were all these young employees who were dressed as if they were going to a disco, or to the beach. Not formal at all! Instead, they wore miniskirts, a lot of naked skin during summer, shiny makeup, their hairstyles changing all the time. It surprised me a lot, because in the past, in my generation, in the pharmaceutical industries being presentable was very important. But by "presentable" we meant a kind of business standard. Now I can see that the business standard is changing to a kind of "fancy casual." They consciously work at looking ever more attractive. When I was a young employee, we would not have dared to style up like this!

Emine's irritation about her changed working environment stands out clearly in this quote. While for Emine looking presentable for work had meant downplaying female attractiveness and looking classy, the look favored by younger female employees stresses instead female attractiveness and playfulness by way of dress, makeup, and hair. Emine locates the appropriateness of these kinds of looks in more sexualized social environments such as the beach or the disco, rather than in professional contexts. The beauty work-intensive new style of everchanging hairdos, bright makeup, and an increasingly erotic way of dressing up created feelings of alienation and exclusion for Emine that ultimately led her to leave the company to become a freelance consultant.

The complex relationship between gendered appearance norms in professional contexts and female employees' compliance with and challenges to these norms becomes apparent when looking at two labor conflicts at Turkish Airlines (THY), the privatized former state airlines. In mid-2010, THY released twenty-eight flight attendants from duty, among them thirteen women with weight problems, stating that it would reinstate

them into full service if they managed to lose weight sufficiently to conform to the company's weight regulations within six months.[15] Moreover,
the company publicly prided itself on offering contracts with "dieticians,
sport salons, and aesthetic surgery centres" (quoted from Tuduk 2010) at
reduced prices for these workers. The media reported that accordingly
female flight attendants "rushed in numbers" to fitness and beauty salons
and clinics to lose weight and have cosmetic operations, including liposuction and face-lift surgery, out of fear of losing their jobs (Tuduk 2010).
Asked for his opinion on this measure, Betül Mardin, the director of a
public relations agency, was quoted stating:

> I used to train flight attendants for many years. Each male and female
> flight attendant is a showcase. It is not enough to have ideal measure-
> ments; their hands and faces should be clear, their hair well-groomed.
> When they tell you "Have a safe flight," you should tell yourself "How
> lovely." . . . They are a showcase for Turkey. Therefore, those serving in
> this sector should take great care of the subject [of appearance]. (Quoted
> from *Güncel Turizm* 2010)

Turkish Airlines is, of course, not the only company to have grooming
regulations in Turkey, and indeed most large companies, as well as airlines
worldwide, have comparable guidelines that claim to exert control over
workers' physical appearance, often including detailed prescriptions in relation to workers' body weight, height, styles of dress, and makeup. As noted
by Arlie Russell Hochschild (2003 [1983]) in her groundbreaking analysis
of "emotional labor" based on an empirical study of American flight attendants, from the perspective of airline companies, this control is backed by
the reference to "professionalism." Accordingly, "[t]he flight attendant who
most nearly meets the appearance code ideal is therefore 'the most professional'" (2003, 103). Hochschild lists a number of individual or collective
protests by flight attendants since the 1970s that "have quietly lodged a

---

15. Cf. Tuduk (2010). Turkish Airlines' body-weight regulations for women were
quoted elsewhere as being at least 20 kg below or up to 2 kg above a person's body height
minus 100 cm.

counterclaim to control over their own bodily appearance" (Hochschild 2003, 126). While some of these protests indeed brought about changes, however subtle, in gendered norms, individual forms of noncompliance typically have grave consequences, a fact that is also underlined by THY releasing flight attendants for being overweight. For example, in 2013 the Turkish media reported on a female flight attendant who had been sacked in 2010 after she was unable to reduce her body weight from 108 to 64 kilograms within six months, as demanded by the company. She had taken the case to court and it was eventually referred to the Supreme Court, which stated that the dismissal was valid if the worker's diet had not been affected by medical issues (*Hürriyet Daily News* 2013).

A few weeks later Turkish Airlines was in the headlines again, this time internationally, for what quickly came to be known as the "lipstick ban." In early May 2013 the company had issued guidelines specifying plain makeup in pastel colors and banning flight attendants from wearing certain shades of lipstick and nail polish, such as bright red and darker colors, claiming that "the use of lipstick and nail polish in these colors by our cabin crew impairs visual integrity" (quoted from Yackley 2013). The case quickly went viral, and countless critics took to the social media to voice their outrage. Yonca Tokbaş, a columnist with the Kemalist daily *Hürriyet*, framed the practice of wearing red lipstick within her family's history of "Republican Women Wearing Red Lipstick." Seeing the values that these women represented as being under attack, Tokbaş (2013) encouraged women to send in photos of themselves with red lipstick to start a "Red Lipstick Movement."

Within this debate, the THY administration became complicit in the attempts of the pro-Islamic government to redefine the role of women as mothers and housekeepers and aligned itself with it in what the media commonly labeled a "culture war" between liberal secularism and authoritarian Islamism. In a much-noticed column for the *Milliyet* daily, Mehveş Evin (2013) wrote:

> We will not be surprised if soon they ban high heels, eyeliners and the appearance of "one strand of hair uncovered." The actual problem is that they have defined flamboyance by red lipstick and dark-colored nail

polish. What lies beneath this is . . . the efforts of the THY administration to re-design "womanhood." A woman who wears red lipstick and nail polish, in their eyes, is "loose" or "unsuitable." This is the essence of the issue, but of course they cannot say it openly.

Evin was one of several secularists who took on the role of defending women's liberal right to wear makeup by painting the grim picture of an Islamizing Turkish Republic where women, including flight attendants on the national flag carrier, would not be allowed to style up and would be required to wear pious dress for work. Reveling in the topic of red lipstick, typically illustrated with an image of a pair of slightly parted female lips painted bright red, the international media widely reported on the "Turkish lipstick ban" along similar lines. Reports and comments continued to be published even after THY backed down on the regulation on May 9, claiming that the company had "no problem" with lipstick and that the order "was made by over-zealous junior managers who did not consult senior bosses about the initiative" (quoted from Faulconbridge 2013). Moreover, media coverage of the company continued to focus on the question of cosmetics even after thousands of Turkish Airlines employees went on strike on May 15, 2013, in a labor dispute over pay and the reinstatement of workers who had been sacked the previous year. The fact that their ongoing strike received little attention compared to the "lipstick ban" caused several hundred mostly young female flight attendants to protest publicly in early June 2013 (*Hürriyet Daily News* 2013). It became clear that for the activists the public debate over the use of lipstick reflected not just secularist fears of an Islamizing republic, but a male gaze on the sexualized body of the female flight attendant.

The THY "lipstick ban" was one of several cases in 2013 which attracted high levels of media attention in which the embodied practices of female employees were linked to larger questions of gendered norms and appropriate behavior for professional women. Another prominent case was the sacking of a private TV channel moderator in October 2013, presumably for her low neckline (*Hürriyet* 2013). During interviews, self-defined secular interlocutors repeatedly referred to these cases as a clear sign of creeping Islamization. For some of these women, the presentation of a self-conscious and attractive, rather than a standard, conservative femininity, including at work, took on strong political and identificatory implications. For them and like-minded observers, the beauty-intensive looks of the female private service workers in Istanbul's center city business world became an epitome of a self-determined liberal femininity within the increasingly polarized political climate that was emerging under the rule of the pro-Islamic conservative AK party government.

Conclusion

This chapter has described the immense importance of an appropriate physical appearance for female employees within a changing urban labor market. Gendered appearance norms are subject to change in urban Turkey, from the elegant looks of a vanguard of professional women in the 1960s and 1970s to the *prezentabl* business standard of the more recent past and its current beauty-intensive sexualization. Female employees, like their colleagues and superiors, play an active part in controlling adherence to gendered appearance norms, as well as challenging them. Whereas intense beauty work and time-consuming grooming routines for professional reasons may boost self-esteem and foster the careers of some female employees, for others they are simply out of reach, produce unintended results, or else do not go well with their own preferred appearance. Beauty therapists and cosmetic surgeons who routinely claim to correct aesthetic deformations and increase self-esteem contribute to creating the sexualized stage personae that can "handle stuff" in a highly competitive and gendered urban service sector. Not least, there are the sensual outcomes and experiences of the beauty salon, with its scents and sounds and cheerful chatter, that form an active part in this endeavor. In places like the company salon described above, beauty is manufactured within social relationships, resulting in more than shiny hair and perfectly painted nails or lips.

Beauty work is thus significant for working women due not only to its visible outcomes, but also to the affective changes it brings about. Within the ruling religio-conservative gender climate that prefers to keep them at home rather than see them rise within the hierarchies of the service sector,

7. Manufacturing the "bank standard:" Hair had to look in shape, without one errant strand, unintended wave, or gray bit showing. (Claudia Liebelt)

especially after marriage, investments in outer appearance may help women to feel in command of themselves and, perhaps, of others around them. It is in this sense that beauty for employment may be regarded as, if not a social elevator, then at least as a form of empowerment on an individual basis, though with few effects on the structural adversities that women face in the labor market, or society at large.

Finally, given that an increasing number of young, urban middle-class women choose to wear pious forms of dress and sport the Islamic veil, their nonappearance within the professional spaces described in this chapter is indeed remarkable. While pious women are no longer excluded from higher education, they continue to be excluded from what Berna Turam has called the "secular spaces" (2013, 410) of central Istanbul. For Istanbul's hitherto dominant secular elites, these spaces are associated with "a sense of spatial belonging, intimate familiarity, and territorial entitlement" (Turam 2015, 8). Pious women's exclusion from the central business district of Maslak, for example, functions not least through the definition of what is considered a *prezentabl* professional appearance and what is not. As we have seen in respect to the public debate on THY's so-called lipstick ban, the fear is great among the secular elite that these appearance norms are being subjected to change in the direction of more pious and conservative images of femininity, a theme that the following chapter explores in greater detail. And indeed, if we understand beauty not as an essential quality that determines professional, marital, or even evolutionary success, as proposed by some scholars cited at the beginning of this chapter, but as a situated social practice, what it means to look beautiful, attractive and, indeed, presentable for work continues to be subject to change.

7

Feminine Self-Fashioning in Times of Change

The early twenty-first century saw the rise of a new Islamic middle class in Turkey, backed by the electoral successes of the Islamic political movement since the 1980s and, more recently, the consolidation of power by the ruling AKP. Middle-class women publicly wearing pious forms of dress have become ever more prominent in the social and political life of urban Turkey, with the piously dressed wives of leading AKP politicians figuring as the embodiments of a new type of pious yet fashionable middle-class femininity. For the secular urban public, since 2011 the emergence and immediate success of conservative women's magazines such as *Âlâ*, *Hesna*, *Aysha*, and *Noura* on the Turkish market have drawn attention to the existence of a significant faction of the middle class that is both pious and fashion-conscious.[1] While *Âlâ*'s editor-in-chief, Ebru Büyükdağ, was quoted saying "we like the same things: we like to look good, we like style, we like to eat good food" (quoted from Letsch 2011), emphasizing the commonalities between her readers and those of conventional women's magazines, the secular public grew alarmed, taking the publication of *Âlâ* and similar women's magazines as yet another sign of Turkey's creeping Islamization. The engagement of upwardly mobile pious women in fashion and beauty disturbs the usual assumptions of the secularist elite that they are of lower class, backward, or lacking in taste. Within the religio-conservative gender climate established during the AKP rule, pious forms

---

1. For example, the circulation of *Âlâ*, the first conservative women's magazine in Turkey, quadrupled to 40,000 only four months after its first appearance in June 2011.

236

of femininity have come to challenge hitherto dominant ideals of femininity, namely of the Republican female citizen as urban, middle class, Western and, most importantly, secular.

At least since Turkey's authoritarian turn after the reelection of the AKP in 2011, the "secular–Islamic divide," which may have little explanatory value as an analytical term with regard to Turkey at large, evolved into a strong mobilizing force in everyday life. As Deniz Kandiyoti puts it, in recent years it assumed the quality of a "national obsession" (2012, 514). Far from being merely an abstract notion or argument, against the background of the political, cultural, and economic marginalization of the secular elite the defense of secular lifestyles, spaces, and aesthetics has become a deeply embodied, classed, gendered, and affect-laden disposition in contemporary Istanbul. In this final chapter, I focus on the supposedly mundane acts of embodied self-fashioning in everyday life beyond dress among different segments of the middle class. In *Politics of Piety*, Saba Mahmood (2004) showed that the embodied ethical formation by Egyptian women in the revivalist mosque movement is not reducible to political tactics or strategies. Nor are they reducible to *ethical* practices, as the following will show. Moreover, like forms of religiosity, Fadil and Fernando pointedly write, "secularity too includes a range of ethical, social, physical, and sexual dispositions, hence the need to apprehend the secular via its sensorial, aesthetic, and embodied dispositions and not only its political ones" (2015, 64). While I agree with this, the following will show that, within a highly charged atmosphere, and in times of significant changes within the political system, even seemingly mundane forms of an embodied self-care are traversed by webs of power and may take on political meanings. Hence, during research the fashioning of the "secular" and "Islamic" feminine urban body respectively through aesthetic body modification, beauty practices, and public performance was readily understood as an act of immediate concern shared by many middle-class women, regardless of whether they identified themselves as secular or as consciously Muslim.

In what follows, I provide a brief outline of the role of secularism in Republican Turkey, presenting it as an embodied disposition in a particular historical line of tradition, namely that of the "Republican woman" as a normative gendered ideal. Secondly, I analyze pious forms of self-fashioning as attempts to develop both a new, Islam-based middle-class femininity and an increasingly beauty-intensive "care of the self" (Foucault 1984, 45) engaged in by consciously Muslim women. Finally, a section on contemporary tattooing practices among middle-class women shows that, while tattoos are not secular per se, in the context of social polarization and shifting forms of femininity they signify subversive bodily messages of alternative ways of being and living.

Turkish Secularism and the Republican Women of Istanbul

Amid the repeated electoral victories of the conservative ruling party and its subsequent aim to restructure the political system, "the secular" in Turkey has acquired many rapidly changing meanings and does not indicate a homogenous social group, especially in socioeconomic terms. While some scholars argue that claims of Turkish national belonging were never entirely divorced from being Muslim and Sunni (Kandiyoti 2012, 516), for many decades "secularism" was clearly a state project and an identificatory reference for its hegemonic elite. It was first introduced with the 1928 amendment to the newly founded republic's constitution of 1924 by removing the declaration that the "religion of the State is Islam." In its 1937 constitution, the Turkish republic was officially declared secular or more precisely *laik*, derived from the French word and principle of *laïcité*. In fact, *laiklik* became one of the six principles of the state ideology of Kemalism implemented by the founder of the Republic of Turkey, Mustafa Kemal Atatürk, prescribing the state's position as one of active neutrality rather than one of a strict separation between the state and religion. Religious symbols and institutions such as religious orders, schools, Islamic clothes, and the fez (male headwear during the Ottoman period) were discarded or banned. The Roman calendar was adopted alongside the Roman alphabet, and the day of rest moved from the Muslim Friday to Sunday.

In contrast to José Casanova's conceptualization of modern secularism as a "transcultural" phenomenon, Jenny White (2013) has emphasized that in Turkey, practices of both religion and secularity "are highly culturally specific" (White 2013, 4). In Turkey, she sees a particular culture of secularism at play that exemplifies "struggles over blasphemy of the sacred" (White 2013, 4). The early cadres attempted to replace Islam with a civil religion which, as Esra Özyürek (2006) and Yael Navaro-Yashin (2002) argue in their insightful ethnographies on the topic, centered around the figure of Mustafa Kemal as the founding father of the republic. Navaro-Yashin in particular analyzed the way in which the Turkish state in the 1980s and 1990s employed a rhetoric of nationalist secularism that cast religion as counter-progressive, while at the same time engaging in the self-declared secular "cult" of Kemalism. The politics of secular Kemalism, according to Navaro-Yashin, were tied to a particular form of authoritarian statism that in the Turkish nineties was "coeval with violence" (2002, 202), against Kurds and Cypriots, for example, and certainly helped the Islamic movement to achieve electoral victories on almost all levels of the state, ultimately transforming the relationship between the state, secularism, and Kemalism.

Writing of the early 2000s, when the Islamic movement managed to form a government but had not yet taken over the state apparatus, Esra Özyürek (2004, 2006) observed that the state ideology of Kemalism, and with it secularism, began to move from the public into the private spheres. Subsequently, secular symbols, such as Atatürk posters or buttons, began to be displayed as part of a personal emotional attachment to the principles of the early Republic. In the widespread rhetorical return to early Republican values described by Özyürek, the modern and beauty-conscious self-fashioning of early Republican women figured strongly. In the promotion of a modern and secular feminine ideal—for example, by holding beauty contests—early Republicans attempted to project themselves as part of the Western world in clear distinction from the recently abolished Ottoman Caliphate (cf. Sirman 2005). Many of my self-identified secular, middle-aged to elderly research participants readily identified with this feminine ideal, and when asked what beautification meant to them, began talking about their Republican mothers or grandmothers. One example was Esra, a retired teacher and Kemalist activist in her early sixties whom I also talked to about her multiple cosmetic surgeries:

> My mother was born in 1923. They were the women of the Republic, the Republican women of Istanbul. They were very special. They used to go to coiffeurs, especially for haircuts and hair care. Perhaps not as often

as I do, but nevertheless, they went. However, as far as makeup is concerned, my father was very conservative, a man of his time. That's why my mother used lipstick for special occasions only. It took her three to four minutes to put it on, because her understanding of makeup was: putting on lipstick. Her hands and feet were well-groomed, and she used to go to the salon for this. She was a biology teacher, an educated [and] well-groomed person for her generation. . . . She would probably regard my understanding of taking care of myself as wasteful. . . . However, when I look at the pictures from back then, they were always better dressed than we are today, and they had more elaborate hair styles than we do.

Like Esra, secular middle-class women of a particular generation compared their own, rather extensive beauty practices to those of their mothers, who, in their descriptions in the plural of "Republican women," or of the generic "beautiful woman," were clearly a yardstick for their own self-fashioning as educated and modern middle-class women taking care of themselves. For my interlocutors, these women embodied the vanguard of a secular modernity in Turkey that followed Western and European precedents and looks. They also served as role models as modern women at a time when this implied novel and possibly risky bodily practices, such as unveiling or having one's hair touched and cut by nonrelated men such as hairdressers—not to speak of the application of nail polish or lipstick, which required a social redefinition of what was considered respectable and shameful respectively for middle-class women at the time. By taking into account her husband's concerns about makeup in the case of Esra's mother, the Republican woman respected gendered norms and hierarchies and held her respectable middle-class femininity in high esteem. With their ascribed rigor and discipline, these women functioned as shining examples of the ongoing obligation of middle-class women to take care of themselves (*kendine bakmak*).

For those who could claim them as their ancestresses, the emblematic Republican women of Istanbul created a genealogy of urban belonging in beauty. Amid anxieties over losing one's quasi-inherited cultural hegemonic status, the narrative of standing in a line of modern and European female urbanists taking care of themselves served as a form of social distinction from those who were "still" unwilling or unable to afford the bodily self-fashioning this implied. In comparison to secular middle-class women like Esra, who looked back on two or three generations of women consuming modern (and costly) beauty services in the city, most female residents of current-day Istanbul were clearly newcomers to the urban world of beauty. Among them, upwardly mobile pious women are particularly scrutinized for what is assumed to be their novel participation in the urban beauty economy.

Pious Self-Fashioning

As the most visible symbol of new Islamic (elite) lifestyles and feminine subjectivities, much has been written on the role of the headscarf and other pious sartorial styles in Turkey.[2] For example, in an article on new fashionable veiling styles, Sandıkçı and Ger (2009) argue that, in the early 2000s, veiling moved from being a stigmatizing and marginal cultural practice to a popular and somewhat more ordinary consumption choice for urban middle-class women. This process has been put into effect by a growing number of young urban middle-class women adopting the new, more vigilant veiling style of Tesettür during the 1980s, as well as by its resulting appropriation, commercialization, and pluralization by an emerging Islamic beauty and fashion market. For the secular elite, the Tesettür style, which in contrast to earlier, more casual forms of veiling fully covers the hair, neck, and shoulders and is typically combined with a long and loose-fitting overcoat, came to symbolize a political threat from the Islamization of society. As such it was politically condemned, and from the late 1990s the authorities discovered a fresh determination to implement the headscarf ban in public institutions, especially at universities. Amid stigmatization and exclusion from higher education and employment opportunities within an authoritarian society based on the principles of state laicism, for consciously Muslim women, self-fashioning became more than a religious choice; it became an identity project.

2. See, for example, Çınar 2005; Gökarıksel 2009, 2012; Gökarıksel and Secor 2009, 2010; Navaro-Yashin 2002, 78–113; Secor 2001; Turam 2013; White 2002, 29–55, 212–41.

Pious self-fashioning in contemporary Turkey, I argue, consists of more than just donning the veil and pious dress: it has come to imply an engagement with beauty practices and aesthetic body modification despite the fact that some of these treatments are problematic from a religious perspective. This has also been noted by the secular public in Turkey: during the early 2000s, a large number of articles in the secular media dealt with the consumption of aesthetic services and cosmetic surgery among the so-called "covered" (*kapalı*), the *tesettürlü*, those in Tesettür, or the *türbanlı*, those who wear a particular style of veiling reminiscent of a turban. From some of these articles, stereotypes of these women as backward and uneducated become obvious. For example, in one article in the *Hürriyet* daily, a cosmetic surgeon explains the popularity of abdominoplasty (so-called tummy tucks) among the *türbanlı* by saying that "women who are opposed to giving birth only once, who do not keep a healthy diet and don't do any exercise are prone to drooping" (quoted from *Hürriyet* 2005). By implication, veiled women are seen as being in need of abdominoplasty due to their ignorance of or ideological opposition to family planning, and also as irresponsible with regard to their own health and well-being. In another report, also in *Hürriyet*, on why "Headscarved Women Also Engage in Cosmetic Surgery," the secular journalist Ayşe Arman (2009) writes:

> Yes, the covered ... She's also a woman ... There's no difference between us, she's also ageing, married to a husband who seeks to escape, afraid that someone else might enter [their relationship]. . . . She works hard to beautify and stay in control ... But before, she is forced to get a *fetva* [permission] from the *hoca* [Islamic cleric]. . . . As soon as she gets it: Cosmetic surgery!

While here pious women are acknowledged to engage in beauty services and cosmetic surgery due to the fact that they are women, they are also portrayed as doing so in a rash and irresponsible manner. Moreover, their decision to undergo cosmetic surgery is seen as dependent on male authority, namely the *hoca*'s permission, rather than on their own deliberations and ethical scruples. In the same report, a female cosmetic surgeon is quoted as saying: "You wouldn't believe how many covered patients

I have [for Botox treatments]. They take incredibly good care of themselves!" Against the background of the common assumption that taking care of oneself is tied to secular middle-class femininity, the affect that this statement bespeaks is clearly one of surprise. Indeed, the large number of articles during the early 2000s that made news out of the observation that pious women too engage in the consumption of beauty services, including cosmetic surgery, speaks of the widespread incredulity that this was even possible.

Some of my self-defined secular interviewees denied outright the fact that a pious lifestyle was easily combinable with urbane style and fashion, making an implicit class distinction between "regular" covered women and "exceptional" ones. For example, one cosmetic surgeon whom I interviewed in his office across the street from the prestigious American hospital in the secular upscale neighborhood of Nişantaşı, where he operated on his patients, explained that, when thinking about pious women's attitudes toward body aesthetics,

> Don't look at the president's wife or other [conservative] politicians' [covered] wives. These dress very colorfully etc. I think this is a perversion. A *regular* covered woman is not brave enough to show herself as a lady. So makeup etc.—they cannot do it! They suffer from social pressure and cannot show their femininity.[3]

From this point of view, a pious Muslim femininity is a contradiction in terms. Moreover, a moral argument about the "perverseness" of pious women who are into beauty and fashion is mixed up with the common secularist assumption that women engage in pious lifestyles because they are forced to do so within the patriarchal social milieus they are presumably situated in. As the following account will show, veiled women's self-fashioning as feminine indeed relies not just on a social redefinition of what is considered feminine, but on pious women's interpretations and negotiations of what is permissible and respectable from an overall Muslim perspective, as well as within particular social settings. Not least, pious

3. Interview with Prof. Dr. Gürhan Özcan, March 11, 2014.

women's consumption of beauty services and cosmetic surgery needs to be understood against the background of a far-reaching debate on the topic among Muslim scholars and within Islamic circles.

Muslim scholars and commentators commonly emphasize inner beauty in contrast to outer appearance and frequently quote the well-known saying that beauty and ugliness lie in the eye of the beholder. In Sunni Islam and the Hanafi school of thought and jurisdiction, which are dominant in Turkey, changing one's features as created by God and, following a particular hadith, shaping one's eyebrows and tattooing are prohibited (*haram*), an interdiction that has been confirmed by a number of religious commissions and individual clerics.[4] Time and again the Turkish High Commission on Religious Affairs and other religious experts are quoted in the media as issuing warnings that aesthetic body modification is a sin (*günah*) for both men and women. Among the most outspoken critics of the recent beauty boom I encountered during research was Ahmet Mahmut Ünlü, also known as Cübbeli Ahmet Hoca, an eccentric preacher of the conservative Ismailağa mosque in Istanbul, who in 2013 was quoted saying that cosmetic surgery was "the devil's work" (quoted from *Radikal* 2013).

Among some religious factions and individuals, such statements create an atmosphere of zealous contempt for the beauty sector that occasionally triggers acts of outrage and violence, such as those suffered by Sibel Hanim when she opened a beauty salon in the conservative district of Fatih, allegedly committed by followers of the same Ismailağa mosque (see chapter 1).[5] However, even the most staunchly conservative religious experts are prepared to consider exceptions to the prohibition of aesthetic body modification; for example, if the treatment is predominantly

4. For example, the Religious Commission Committee in Konya prohibited cosmetic surgery in 2000 (*Hürriyet* 2000a); the grand mufti of Istanbul, Ahmet Okutan, in 2005 (Ferah 2005); and the mufti of Edirne, Ömer Taşcıoglu, in 2009 (*Hürriyet* 2009b).

5. Another incident was reported in the media in 2016, when a man injured four people in the Black Sea town of Trabzon by opening fire on a market booth advertising laser epilation in a local beauty clinic, claiming that the treatment was "against our religion" (quoted from *Cumhuriyet* 2016a).

a matter of health or is intended to correct bodily abnormalities. As in other situations of Islamic decision-making, the final decision is with the believer, who is forced to scrutinize his or her intention (*niyet*) to undergo a particular beauty treatment or surgery.

In a situation in which neither social conventions nor religious rulings are fully worked out, young pious women were found to draw heavily on the Internet, especially online forums such as the Women's Club (*Kadınlar Kulübü*, in Turkish) or Fatwa Center (*Fetva Meclisi*), to inquire about and discuss the permissibility of aesthetic body modification and beauty practices. In 2013, three years after he had set up the Fatwa Center, I had a long conversation with Nureddin Yıldız on the relationship between Islam and feminine beauty in the headquarters of his religious *waqf* (foundation) in the conservative neighborhood of Bayrampaşa. Yıldız, a religious teacher commonly known as Nureddin Hoca among his tens of thousands of followers on social media, spent at least an hour a day answering the queries posted by users of his online forum. While only a fraction of these queries concerned beauty treatments and body aesthetics (about ten percent in late 2013), Yıldız described the anonymous format of the forum as especially suited to asking questions on beauty and femininity, claiming that "Turkish society is censored on that matter . . . I mean, a Muslim woman cannot openly ask about aesthetics."[6]

Of the Fatwa Center queries on body aesthetics in 2013, most concerned the permissibility of body hair removal—including of pubic hair and eyebrows, and by laser depilation (33 percent)—as well as cosmetic surgery (22 percent). Other users wondered about the permissibility of hair extensions, permanent makeup (as a form of tattooing), nail polish, and attending beauty salons more generally. Like other religious scholars, Yıldız was concerned about cosmetic surgery changing God's creation and warned against the use of forbidden substances such as lard oil or alcohol in cosmetics, or of foreign human matter, as in hair extensions. However, much like other religious commentators quoted in the conservative

---

6. Interview with Nureddin Yıldız, October 22, 2013. The following quotes by Yıldız are also taken from this interview.

media, he encouraged women to invest in an attractive outer appearance within the confines of a heterosexual marriage:

> It is completely legitimate for married women to spend money on beauty in order to look good [for their husbands]. Moreover, it is not accepted if the woman does *not* strive to look good for her husband. The only conflicting point in our religion and with the modernist interpretation [of Islam] is that women share their beauty not only with their husbands, but also with outsiders. A woman can go to the coiffeur, have hair care, skin care—everything. But it should be for her husband only. . . . Beauty shared with people other than her husband is regarded as a breach of religion. It is considered like a betrayal of the husband. . . . Woman should be beautiful, and if she's not, if she doesn't meet the expectations of her husband, this can be problematic for him, and it can make him search for another woman. . . . Our religion encourages things to be beautiful in all kinds of ways, and it requires us to keep the family intact.

From Yıldız's perspective, beauty is an obligation for the married woman, with those not legitimately or commonly regarded as sexually reproductive seen as standing outside of the realm of beauty altogether. Recognizing the sensual and erotic aspects of beauty, for Yıldız feminine beauty is a prerequisite for the success of heterosexual marriage. By implication, a marriage is condemned to fail if the wife withholds her beauty from her husband or shares it with others. Thus, a wife (woman) should meet her husband's expectations with regard to her appearance, giving him a considerable definitory power over the looks and meaning of beauty. Here female beauty is perceived as highly sexual, triggering male sexual desire virtually automatically. By carefully managing her appearance, the socially sanctioned sexual female is responsible both for satisfying her husband and for keeping her family intact. It should be emphasized that, while Islamic rulings on beauty practices may not always (or even commonly) be followed, the arguments put forward by religious experts like Yıldız draw on (and confirm) widely shared cultural conceptions, such as the sexual connotations of female beauty that are seen as requiring social regulation. Their arguments are widely reported and discussed in the Turkish public sphere against the background of heated controversies around issues of sexuality, femininity, and cultural identity, and they also have impacts on treatment decisions, regardless of whether prospective beauty salon customers and cosmetic surgery patients consider themselves pious or not. Not least, within the religio-conservative gender climate established by the AKP in recent years, voices such as Yıldız's have gained ground and are slowly moving from the social margins toward its center.

Toward an Islam-Based Femininity: Sibel Üresin

During my research, I found that one of the best-known proponents of an Islam-based femininity was Sibel Üresin, a private coach and family counselor to various municipalities governed by the AKP. Following her public defense of polygamy, legally abolished in Turkey in 1926 but reemerging as an urban phenomenon among the pious middle classes in the early 2000s, during a private TV talk show in 2012, Üresin became a frequent guest of such programs. She was an avid supporter of the then Prime Minister and AK party leader Recep Tayyip Erdoğan and indeed was commonly perceived to be the public face of the new type of femininity that the regime intended to create.

In these talk shows Üresin's pious yet fashionable way of dressing, her light complexion, and her invisible makeup formed a spectacular contrast to the appearance of the other female guests and presenters. Among the presenters who regularly invited Üresin was Seda Sayan, an avowed cosmetic surgery aficionada and a conspicuously made-up blonde who typically appeared on her shows in revealing dresses that exposed her deeply tanned skin. Whereas Üresin's conservative outlook on gender politics clearly shocked the liberal secular public, among conservative circles her unapologetic position and her composed and sovereign posture on TV quickly made her into a female role model. In the conservative middle-class neighborhood of Başakşehir, where I conducted research in two beauty salons, she was a sought-after family counselor.

In November 2013 we arranged for an interview in her office in Başakşehir on the second floor of a local trade center to discuss her conception of Islam-based femininity. Üresin arrived for the interview carefully made-up in a stylish long gown combined with an elegant silk headscarf in a monochrome, greenish color. A petite woman in her late thirties, she appeared wary at first, but visibly relaxed after she read my preformulated guideline questions, which focused on her concept of feminine beauty rather than on more openly political issues, as she had perhaps suspected. Sitting on baroque sofas in her reception room below a bookshelf that contained works by the thirteenth-century Islamic scholar and Sufi mystic Jalal ad-Din Muhammad Rumi, we were served tea by her secretary wearing fashionable Tesettür. Üresin recounted that she attended high school in the working-class neighborhood of Pendik, a formerly rural area on the outskirts of the Asian side of Istanbul. She moved to the newly created district of Başakşehir soon after it was established because it was a highly symbolic settlement for "conservative people"[7] heavily invested in by the then Prime Minister Erdoğan. She explained that most of her clients were conservative, "closed" (kapalı) women who came with particular theological or spiritual questions or due to marital problems. Those seeking advice on beauty often arrived with questions on the permissibility of particular treatments, such as artificial hair or nails, tattooing, or cosmetic surgery.

Üresin's Islam-based concept of feminine beauty was part of a larger cosmology of bodily well-being and healing based on the teachings of the medieval Islamic scholar Ibn Sina (Avicenna, 980–1037), whose *Book of Healing* and *Canon of Medicine* she mentioned during the interview. Among the treatments recommended by Ibn Sina that she also recommended to her patients were cupping (hacamat) treatments and particular dietary recommendations, such as herbal teas and homecooked meals, rather than stressful fast food eaten out. She also often advised against the use of cosmetics and makeup, claiming that "woman is beautiful when she is clear [ak], in my opinion. . . . a clear and well-groomed skin looks more beautiful than a skin covered with makeup. Very clean teeth, eyes that look beautiful . . . these things are more important than anything else in my opinion."

Üresin's own investments in beauty and bodily well-being included regular spa and gym visits, massages, and facial treatments. She attended

---

7. Interview with Sibel Üresin, November 21, 2013. The following quotes by Üresin are also taken from this interview.

a regular hairdresser every three weeks to have her hair dyed and styled. On the topic of cosmetic surgery and tattooing, Üresin advocated rather conservative views in favor of a ban (to be applied selectively), stating that "according to religion . . . you cannot change the shape of your nose, for example. . . . Also, you shouldn't change your breast, except for pleasing your husband, and if he gives his permission." She claimed never to have had cosmetic surgery herself and was opposed to it not just for religious reasons, but also, like many conservative women in this neighborhood, because of the artificial look it created. For a long time during the interview she talked about the objectification of women and the commercialization of femininity in Western mass media and advertisements. While she felt that Turkish women who self-defined as secular and Muslim-conservative respectively shared many problems when it came to their body image, typically lacking self-confidence, she also spoke of the need to correct the common misrepresentation of pious women in the secular public:

> Wearing a headscarf doesn't cover the beauty of a woman. Actually, I think that wearing a headscarf adds an air of niceness and naivete [naivlik]. Even if you cover a beautiful woman with a chador [çarşaf], she is still beautiful. You can understand this from her every move, even from her eyes. It is not an absolute necessity to open up every part of yourself in order to show that you are beautiful! . . . [To the contrary] I feel that women with headscarves attach more importance to body care and beauty than women without a headscarf. From underwear to the roll-on they use . . . I mean, they really attach importance to hair etc. They go to the gym a lot, for example. Public opinion doesn't usually recognize that.

In defiance of secular public opinion that rests on the assumption that pious women are backward, rural, and unattractive, Sibel Üresin helped to promote a novel form of femininity that relied on a significant amount of Islam-based consumption and self-scrutiny with regard to outer appearance on the one hand while strengthening rather than questioning women's role in society as subservient and dependent on the other. As a family counselor she actively contributed to what Kandiyoti (2016, 106–8) has called "the marriage of neo-liberalism and (neo-)conservative familism" within the ideology and practice of the ruling AKP.

To sum up, for Muslim scholars and conscious believers like Sibel Üresin, the creation of feminine beauty, especially in the form of more permanent aesthetic body modification, is highly ambiguous. While on the one hand it potentially changes God's creation and creates a mass-mediated "Western" artificiality, on the other hand it also creates female sexual attractiveness that is regarded as vital within the heterosexual marital contract and a must for the modern pious woman. Due to the fact that female sexuality and attractiveness are also potentially destructive of the heteronormative social order, they are seen as requiring containment within legitimate social relationships by disciplined selves. The following shows how pious women armed with information and messages obtained from the internet, from trusted teachers and counselors like Sibel Üresin, or indeed from the sources of their faith, adapt Islamic norms creatively to negotiate the boundaries of social and ethical permissiveness and bodily well-being in a way that can be reconciled with their aesthetic desires.

Young Muslimas in Style

Around the time the first issue of *Âlâ*, the conservative women's magazine, was published in Turkey, new terms were coined to describe young, upwardly mobile, pious fashionistas, who became increasingly visible not only in *Âlâ*'s glossy pages, but more generally in the urban public space. Among these terms was *süslümanlar*, a newly created combination of *müslümanlar*, "Muslims," and *süslenmek*, "to style oneself up," supposedly first used as a self-description by a group of pious female university students.[8] When I first came across this term, the person I most readily associated it with was Sevda, the daughter of Sibel, whose beauty salon in Fatih was one of my regular research sites. Sevda was in her early twenties when we first met and had recently finished an apprenticeship with an Istanbul-based fashion designer. She helped out in her mother's women-only salon, where she usually applied makeup, operated the hair removal equipment, and taught belly-dance classes to her mother's customers. Sevda first started to veil when her menstruation began and in contrast to her mother, who a

8. I thank Sertaç Sehlikoğlu for pointing this out.

few years earlier had adopted the more vigilant veiling style of the *çarşaf*, described her own style as Tesettür.

Sevda, a tall and energetic young woman with a light complexion and long black hair, paid great attention to even the smallest details of her looks and outer appearance and spent much time informing herself of the latest styles and fashions. During slack hours in the salon, she could often be found watching YouTube tutorials on the application of makeup and new hair or veiling styles and never failed to watch the latest international fashion shows. As someone who was Tesettür, Sevda found it difficult to admire the looks of Turkish celebrities, who she claimed were mostly upper-class and only beautiful because of their cosmetic surgery. Instead, she was a great fan of Jennifer Lopez (because of her hair), Britney Spears (because of her body shape), and Beyoncé (because of her complexion). When coming to the salon, Sevda carefully combined fashionable waisted coats with silky headscarves in pastel colors, rarely leaving the house without makeup. After taking her headscarf off at the salon, she often had a blow-dry or else pinned up her hair carefully, sometimes assisted by the two female hairdressers her mother employed. She had facial treatments on a regular basis and was often the first to try out a new technique that the salon was introducing. This had been the case with the IPL machine to remove body hair, a technology she was personally so convinced of that she trained herself to operate it, subsequently treating a large number of her female friends.

For Sevda and her circle of friends, some of whom I met as regular customers of her mother's salon, there was clearly no contradiction between being Tesettür and styling up. As she explained,

> All this [being Tesettür] means, as far as I understand it, is that outside you're not supposed to draw attention to yourself. As a woman you can wear the latest fashion and style up—there's no problem at all—but when you go outside, people shouldn't turn their heads to look at you. That's the one thing that's important. That's my understanding of Tesettür, as a form of protection for the woman. But if you imagine that I was wearing something *very* fashionable in a bright color or even in red, those passing by me on the street would be turning their heads. This is something we discussed quite a lot. But among my friends, fashion and

styling is something we are all fine with, and we talk about it a lot. It's like "This is the fashion, so let's go for it!" (*laughs*). But still, (*more pensively*) there's this *mani* [hindrance].[9]

Rather than being simply a negative aspect, for Sevda the "hindrance" implied in combining Tesettür with beauty practices also represented a clear boundary, a comforting kind of stability and protection outside the confines of her intimate social sphere, the *mahrem*. It implied a considerable amount of self-scrutiny and discipline, and from what I observed on numerous occasions it meant that Sevda rarely left the house without soliciting her mother's or friends' advice on her looks. New beauty treatments, such as the use of hair or eyelash extensions (both of which Sevda used for special occasions such as weddings and engagement or henna parties), were discussed with regard to their permissibility with them or with Islamic teachers whom her mother consulted during her regular Qur'an reading classes that the Fatih municipality provided for women. Not least, the ultimate goal of not making "people turn their heads" relied on a substantial amount of daily experience in moving about public spaces in different kinds of pious outfits.

As hinted at in the quote above, among Sevda and her friends particular kinds and colors of makeup were perceived as especially problematic and visible. Like other young women wearing Tesettür, Sevda favored invisible rather than visibly heavy makeup (see also Ünal 2018). This meant avoiding bright colors such as pink, orange, or the highly sexualized color red and applying more "natural" colors, such as beige or rosé, for lipstick or eye shadow instead. For Sevda invisible makeup also meant using a light foundation in the tone of her skin and not exaggerating with the black eyeliner and kajal she usually applied to her eyes. Her usual makeup thus made her look fresh and professional for work, she explained, but did not compromise her "guard" by making her look overly attractive: "The way I apply makeup, people don't turn around to look at me."

9. Interview with Sevda, July 21, 2014. The following quotes by Sevda are also taken from this interview.

Like other pious women I met in beauty salons and clinics, Sevda emphasized that, when she engaged in beauty practices that were debatable from a theological point of view, she did so in a minimal and disciplined rather than exaggerated way, always careful in her description of the treatment. As in the beauty salons frequented by pious Muslim women of South Asian origin in northern Britain studied by Hester Clarke (2018), in the salon in Fatih where Sevda worked and had most of her own beauty treatments eyebrows were not commonly "shaped," but merely "cleaned." Pubic hair removal—which implies the problematic exposure of one's tabooed "private parts" (*avret bölgesi*) to unrelated beauty workers—was justified as a therapeutic rather than an aesthetic treatment and was seen as taking place in a protected, intimate space that did not compromise one's respectability (cf. Liebelt 2016). While with a few exceptions most of the beauty treatments Sevda and her friends engaged in were congruent with those that more secular Istanbulites of the same age and social position engaged in, these were nevertheless scrutinized more carefully in their effects and motivating force by pious women. They often had to be negotiated within restrictive social environments and, at least until recently, with a secularist public.

In our recurring conversations, Sevda talked at length about the discrimination she faced as a veiled fashionista because in Turkey, she explained, beauty and fashion are not generally seen as compatible with a visibly Muslim lifestyle. Due to restrictions imposed by the laic state, Sevda had not been able to attend university because she refused to remove her veil to take the university entrance exams. Instead, having graduated from a theological *İmam Hatip* school with excellent grades and completed a year-long course at a private tutoring school (*dershane*) in preparation for the exam, she had hoped for a political change or any other solution until the very day of her exam. On the morning of the exam her mother suggested that she wear a wig (likewise forbidden, but only rarely detected by the security personnel guarding the entrance to the exam), but Sevda decided against such a "compromise," claiming that "I will never open up my head by force." In order to circumvent the headscarf ban, she eventually studied at the University of Sarajevo in Bosnia for a few semesters, but returned without completing her degree "due to home-sickness." Instead she completed a course in fashion design at a private college in Istanbul in combination with an apprenticeship with a fashion designer. She recounted how her teachers at the college "always clashed with me, because—how can I put it?—I think, simply because I'm Tes-ettür." One of them in particular teased her repeatedly, for example, by saying that she wouldn't be able to wear any of the daring designs she produced in the class. Likewise, at her workplace, her female master often used Sevda's designs, but in contrast to how she treated her other appren-tices (who did not cover their heads) hardly ever acknowledged her talent. Whenever Sevda attended fashion shows, she experienced being stared at by uncovered visitors who clearly formed the majority at these shows and had to put up with foreigners' nosy questions ("Are you really into this kind of fashion? Why?").

Thus, while Sevda clearly belonged to a new, pious segment of the mid-dle classes that was able to send their children to private university prepa-ration classes or abroad to study, her professional career was impeded not just by restrictive state laicism, but also by the usual assumptions, not to say class-based arrogance, of a secular public that did not easily accept her participation in the fashion and beauty economy. By the time our con-versation took place in 2014, the headscarf ban in universities had been lifted, and some of Sevda's female friends had decided to take their exams finally. For Sevda, however, the change in regulations came too late. By now, she had already postponed her dream of becoming a fashion designer and instead focused on her imminent wedding, clearly seeing no way of combining married life with the life of a student.

Upon her engagement, Sevda's makeup and fashion choices became more restricted due to her fiancé Ali's concerns—and also, as she sus-pected during a conversation we had shortly before her wedding, due to his jealousy, which she took as a positive sign of his love and protective commitment to her. First of all, Sevda was careful to seek his consent over the way she looked and felt that this was clearly expected from her as a prospective wife. For example, Ali asked her to refrain from using lip-stick and nail polish, a request she readily complied with. She also tried to adjust her wardrobe to his liking, though this was a subject of ongoing negotiation between the young couple. For example, Sevda recounted a shopping spree she had with Ali in preparation for their first holiday in which he persuaded her to exchange a white blouse she had chosen for a darker one. They ultimately settled on blue, but when back home Sevda opened the shopping bag and found a black blouse in it, she suspected that Ali had had it exchanged behind her back. Without confronting him, Sevda exchanged it back to blue and hoped he got the message.

Sevda thus diligently managed her outward appearance and aesthetic desires in the context of both religious and social constraints. While she was ready to stretch the boundaries of religious permissibility when it came to engaging in beauty practices, she took great care not to violate the norms of gender behavior and female chastity that were strongly enforced in her social environment. Another example of this was the strict monitoring of Sevda and Ali's meetings by family members up until their wedding, which took place within a year of them first having been introduced to each other during a friend's wedding, in order not to compromise Sevda's reputation as a virgin.

Sevda's beauty and fashion investments reached a climax before her engagement, pre-wedding henna night (*kına gecesi*), and marriage parties, all lavishly celebrated in quick succession in large banqueting halls in Fatih with more than a hundred visitors each. Pictures of the carefully made-up Sevda in a peach-colored dress and matching *türban* lavishly adorned with embroidered pearls on the day of her engagement, taken by a professional photographer in Istanbul's Emirgan Park, were proudly presented to the regular customers of her mother's beauty salon and subsequently were also used as an advertisement for the salon in social media. For her pre-wedding shopping, Sevda traveled to the Ukraine with her mother, bringing back with her a variety of cosmetics and a number of new evening gowns and dresses, four of which she wore on her henna night alone.

Before each of these celebrations, Sevda spent hours in her mother's beauty salon alongside her female friends to get styled up for the occasion (see chapter 3). In particular, the women-only henna night celebration just before her wedding was an opportunity for them to get dolled up. In contrast to some of her friends, who had agreed to gender-mixed parties and consequently covered themselves up, Sevda had insisted on a female-only event that would allow herself and her guests to get styled up and dress up in the latest fashion without having to worry about their "guard." Carried away by the festive mood of the event, she almost agreed to the hairdresser's somewhat joking request to refrain from covering her (extended) hair on the way to the banqueting hall in order not to ruin her carefully styled locks. When her loosely applied headscarf slipped out of position on her way out, Sevda laughingly remarked that anyway, this wasn't her real hair showing.

Finally, each of these celebrations showed that, in contrast to secular middle-class stereotypes of conservative working-class neighborhoods such as Fatih being populated by homogenously pious and veiled women, there was a great variety in style and appearance among the female guests. Some of the younger and even a few of the older women on Sevda's family's side, including her maternal grandmother, did not cover their hair at all. Others sported a variety of veiling styles, among them the black *çarşaf*, more common on the groom's side; Tesettür, often in combination with more or less invisible makeup; and, worn by some of the more elderly women on both sides, the rural headscarf. Among the fifteen or so carefully made-up women from Sevda's closest circle who left the salon to head for the banqueting hall on the evening of her henna night were her mother covered in an exceptionally protective black cloak; her friend and neighbor in white high heels and matching miniskirt, who had had her long bleached hair styled into romantic curls; her grandmother and several younger cousins and sisters-in-law, who were likewise uncovered, but carefully styled; two aunts from her home region on the Black Sea coast in colorful cotton headscarves, commonly worn by elderly village women; and several other friends and relatives in a variety of Tesettür styles, all clearly beauty- and fashion-conscious.

In her study of pious Turkish-Muslim women in the Netherlands, Arzu Ünal (2018) describes a shift within conservative circles from "hiding one's beauty" to carefully managing it. This certainly holds true for Sevda and many of the other young, stylish, and fashion-conscious women I met as the clients of her mother's beauty salon in the conservative neighborhood of Fatih. Moreover, while, shortly before marriage, younger consciously Muslim women are often more into fashion and styling up than their mothers or older female relatives, the shift from "hiding" to "managing" one's beauty is not simply a generational one. As exemplified by the diversity of feminine looks among Sevda's maternal relatives, as in more secular middle-class families, the consumption of beauty services across the generations was far from linear, being tied to personal preferences and changing norms of femininity and moral sensibilities throughout women's life course, as well as within the wider political climate of the day. While the young *süslümanlar* I met in Sevda's mother's beauty salon and her circle of friends certainly tried to comply with the norms of an Islam-based femininity proposed by Sibel Üresin and others, they were clearly also influenced by pop-cultural norms of femininity, a fact they shared with many women their age. Unwilling to relinquish accessories such as artificial eyelashes or hair extensions even when these were controversial from a religious perspective, they clearly considered themselves to be part of the urban world of beauty. This, as the following section will show, was not readily accepted, especially in neighborhoods marked as secular by their residents.

Intruders into the World of Beauty

As observed by Turam (2015), in recent years Istanbul, which has long been a segregated city clearly divided into secular and conservative neighborhoods by its residents, has become more mixed. Accordingly, members of the new Islamic middle classes are increasingly intruding into spaces and neighborhoods of conspicuous consumption hitherto defined as secular, such as Nişantaşı, Etiler, or Kadıköy, mentioned repeatedly throughout this book. When musing about recent changes in the city, self-defined secular interlocutors often related their encounters with women in pious dress in the urban spaces they clearly defined as their own. Among them was Asya, an upper middle-class woman in her late sixties:

> even the closed ones [i.e., veiled women] invest in beauty these days. . . . I can see them when I visit my doctor [a dermatologist] during the day—*ours* seem to arrive in the evening after work, I suppose. These days, they walk around with makeup and all—I was surprised! The other day I was walking in the street [in Nişantaşı]

and they [a group of veiled women] had their car parked by a butler, entering a boutique. So apparently they went shopping there. I
know this place, it's quite expensive, so I was surprised!

CL: So before, veiled women were not into fashion and body
aesthetics?

ASYA: No, not at all. But these are the newly rich, I guess . . . [10]

What is interesting here is the clearcut distinction between veiled women
as "them" and those Asya describes as her own kind (ours). Asya's repeated
surprise at the beauty investments of pious women can only be explained
through her realization that the women she saw must have been exceptionally rich, though certainly "newly" rich. As such, she perceived them
as spatial intruders and as foreign to her own urban territory, upmarket
Nişantaşı.

Secular middle-class women are ready to defend the spaces they
consider their own against such intruders, most visibly embodied by
headscarved women. As described by Turam (2015, 30) for a particular
neighborhood in Nişantaşı, this creates an atmosphere of "microlevel
urban contestations" that in some cases leads to verbal or even physical
harassment. In spring 2014 I was able to observe one such confrontation
when, for the first time ever, a young woman in the conservative veiling
style of Tesettür visited the mid-morning Pilates class that I regularly
attended in a women-only fitness and beauty club in the secular middle-
class neighborhood of Moda. Apart from me, there were ten to fifteen
other women from the neighborhood and adjacent area, some married
housewives in their thirties and forties, some retired women in their fifties
and sixties. Relationships between the women were close (*samimi*), with
participants chatting and drinking tea after class and sometimes moving
on to the hair salon or spa in the same building or to eat lunch together in
the neighborhood. All participants invested a great deal of effort in their
looks, fancied colored or highlighted hair, used nail polish, and had often
had cosmetic surgery. They certainly recognized themselves and others in
the neighborhood as women who took good care of themselves.

10. Interview with Asya, January 29, 2014.

At first my classmates did not notice that the newcomer was covered because she had arrived late and entered the gym in trendy sportswear, with her long, highlighted hair pinned up in a bun that made her look not much different from the other participants in the course. However, back in the changing room after the class the small talk that had begun between the women ended abruptly when the newcomer put on her long overcoat and covered her hair, provoking an awkward silence and uncomfortable stares. The woman did not return to the club, and as far as I could tell the incident was soon forgotten among its members. However, two days later I conducted an interview with one of these members, Nehir, a retired teacher in her mid-sixties. The interview circled around Nehir's beauty practices—including a face-lift, cheek implants, and blepharoplasty—as well as her life as the daughter of an army officer and a beautiful Republican woman. Toward the end of the interview, seemingly unconnected to what we had just been talking about, Nehir blurted out:

> But you know, those religious [*dinci*] women, they have no idea about looking beautiful, unfortunately. They don't know how to take care of themselves, also in terms of birth control. Also, they don't have any chance to wear modern clothes, and because of religion they wear ugly clothes, you know. They look ugly, I mean, they make themselves look ugly unfortunately.
>
> CL: You mean, because they are covering themselves?
>
> NH: Yes, yes. It's not natural—the way they dress and the way they behave, it's not natural, it goes against their own instincts. [They do that] because of social pressure, they wear [clothes] like that. But I think that a woman, wherever she lives, whoever she is, God gave her the instinct that she must look clean, beautiful, and attractive, even a little bit sexy. A woman has these feelings. Any woman who doesn't behave like this is under pressure. Because it is against nature [*tabiata karşı*]. I mean, God created woman to be beautiful! But when you are under these clothes, you don't look beautiful.

Nehir's emotional outburst about the *dinci* (religious)—a term that, in contrast to "Muslim" or "pious," has a rather pejorative meaning and serves to distance the secular speaker from the person thus identified—mixed frustrations about the politics of the day with resentments on a deeper level. In a quite typical way, beauty here is not only associated with cleanliness and modern looks, but it also becomes a marker for a quasi-natural and instinctive femininity based on attractiveness and a self-controlled ability and knowledge of how to take care of oneself. By violating the natural order of things with their sartorial choices, pious women not only make themselves "ugly" but are ideologically fixated. This stood in stark contrast to Nehir's own "natural" belief in God, and in feminine womanhood for that matter. As *dinciler,* the pious Others were not supposed to look fashionable, modern, or attractive. If they did, like the woman who had recently entered our Pilates class and had obviously been able to pass as a club-mate until she put on her headscarf—this was clearly proof of their being hypocritical or, in Nehir's assessment, unnatural.

Another account of intrusion into a particularly important urban space of beauty, namely the Istanbul fashion week, was narrated by Demet, a female fashion photographer in her early thirties:

> Last year I was at the Istanbul fashion week as a photographer for a Turkish blog, and there were so many headscarved girls! They came backstage and wanted to see the designs in detail, the models, etc. . . . Actually, I don't know how they combine the designs they see there [with their way of dressing]. I'm not sure because there's no way they can wear them. But they really followed the fashion week from beginning to end, and they even came backstage!
>
> CL: You mean, they were professionals?
>
> DE: They were clearly professionals. But still I don't think they are very tasteful. Turkey is so in between. Like, some people have a sophisticated style, the kind of Turkish *Vogue* style. And the others, they are more into the Islamic style. You know, in Islam you don't have to be very attractive for men. But how can it be that you have tons of beauty magazines for covered women, and some of the models are quite attractive?[11]

11. Interview with Demet, December 18, 2013. The following quotes by Demet are also taken from this interview.

Demet's obviously ongoing reflections about her encounters with professional women with headscarves during the Istanbul fashion week summarizes in condensed form some of the secularist assumptions about the new Islamic middle class: first that they are not supposed to be attractive; secondly that although they do not belong in the urban world of beauty and fashion, they are increasingly encountered there; and thirdly that in following an Islamic definition of beauty they are perceived as lacking in taste and sophistication. Upon inquiry, Demet explained that the Islamic look meant she was superficially chaste, whereas in reality it was based on an Arab-style exaggeration with makeup and jewelry, which she summed up as having the effect of "bling, bling." In spatial terms this kind of look was removed from the secular city center and located in the *varoş*, the former urban squatter areas on the outskirts of the city that in some instances had been transformed into gated communities and planned settlements for the Islamic bourgeoisie. The secular middle-class notion of the *varoş* was thus tied to assumptions about the look of its residents, the so-called Black Turks, who were seen as "black" not so much with regard to their complexion but rather their supposed lack of cultural refinement (Demiralp 2012).

The conceptualization of pious middle-class women intruding into the urban world of beauty is somewhat contradictory in that these are seen both as marginal outsiders to the city and as the new hegemonic elite of the current conservative pro-Islamic regime. However, secular women's stories of intrusion into "their own" spaces of fashion and beauty reflect their anxiety at losing not only their culturally hegemonic status, but also certain rights and liberties which they saw as directly threatened by the AKP regime. This included reproductive rights, such as access to abortion and birth control, which were repeatedly mentioned in this regard. The pious middle-class women they increasingly encountered in the center city spaces they considered their own thus became symbols of the religio-conservative gender climate encroaching into their own daily lifeworlds. Irrespective of their political outlook, for them these spatial intruders embodied the new feminine ideal that the government was obviously striving to create. Against this background, women's bodies and practices became a battleground for secular and Islamic ideologies (Gökarıksel

2012, 15) amid changing norms of respectable middle-class femininity. In the following, this is outlined further by looking at middle-class women's increasingly popular tattooing practices, which, in the political climate of the day, have assumed the status of a subversive bodily act.

Feminine Subjectivities Inked into the Skin

Against the background of a real and imagined loss of power by the Kemalist, urban elite in the late 1990s and early 2000s, urban restructuring and the rise of a new pious middle class, Esra Özyürek (2004) observes that being secular and Kemalist became a question of identity carried into the intimate spaces of daily life. While Özyürek writes of Atatürk busts in living rooms and buttons pinned to coats and bags, amid the political polarization in progress during research for this book, the fashioning of secular bodies operated on a much deeper level and included not just nail polish and lipstick (as described in the previous chapter), but indeed, Atatürk signatures inked into the skin. As elsewhere in Europe (cf. De-Mello 2000), the practice of tattooing used to be popular among sailors and other working-class men in Istanbul, later becoming restricted to particular subcultural groups such as prison inmates, soccer fans, or motorcycle gangs. In the last decade, following a global trend, tattoos have become increasingly popular among middle-class women. Whereas an older tradition of female tattoos exists in southeastern Anatolia, the recent urban trend is entirely disconnected from it, being informed instead by international Western tattooing styles such as the American traditional or old school, neotraditional, and new school styles.

During research, I found that tattoos signified both a particular kind of middle-class femininity and a challenge to it. Tattoos have become visible on women's bodies in hitherto unthinkable spaces and places, including—often in the form of butterflies or flowers—in the headquarters of a bank, where I conducted research in the company-owned hair salon. They also appeared on the necks, arms, and shoulders of the many female anti-government protesters in the public streets and squares throughout 2013 and 2014, with some tattoos depicting the iconography of the Gezi Park protests. Finally, in the form of Atatürk signatures they might be seen on the forearms of female civil servants in municipal offices.

Far from being a secular practice in itself, tattooing and its motifs, I argue, function as cultural bodily messages of changing norms of respectable femininity in urban Turkey. As in women's tattooing practices in North America, studied by Atkinson (2002) during the 1990s, Turkish women employ tattoos as "communicative signifiers" of different kinds of femininity. As Atkinson notes (2002, 220), tattoos are adopted by North American women "because radically marked bodies tend to subvert hegemonic ideologies about femininity, especially images of the weak, sexually objectified, or otherwise submissive woman." However, in contrast to homogenizing feminist accounts that view women's tattooing practices as a form of political resistance against misogynist ideologies, Atkinson (2002, 220) finds that female tattoo collectors may both consent to *and* negotiate hegemonic constructions of femininity with their tattoos.

The eleven women whom I interviewed about their tattoos for this study varied significantly in their motivations for getting tattoos, as well as in the motifs they chose. They were between twenty-six and forty-six years old (thirty-three years old on average) and had all acquired tattoos in the decade before the interview took place, most of them after 2010. From what I learned and observed, this is representative of the novelty of middle-class women's acquisition of tattoos. With the exception of a twenty-three-year-old student who had acquired her first tattoo when she was just fourteen years old, the other interviewees had been at least in their twenties when they acquired their first tattoos. None of them wore pious dress, but otherwise they seemed to share little in terms of social status, professional background, political preference, or place of residence in Istanbul. Whereas one of them, Hande, was a married housewife and mother of two in the working-class district of Kavacık on the outskirts of Istanbul, others were professional white-collar workers in the city center. They included Ebru, a human relations manager employed in a large international company, and Zehra, an architect and tattoo model well-known on the urban tattooing scene. They all liked the aesthetics of tattoos and felt that their tattoos added to their feminine attractiveness.

Apart from their aesthetics, tattoos were also chosen for the political message they conveyed within the conservative pro-Islamic political climate in Turkey. Thus, each interviewee was aware of the fact that tattoos were considered un-Islamic, with frequent statements from the Turkish Directorate of Religious Affairs (*Diyanet İşleri Başkanliği*, or in short, Diyanet) and leading politicians of the ruling conservative party against this form of body modification being widely reported in the media. By getting tattooed, some intended to convey a visible sign of resistance to the ruling regime and its interference in their respective lifestyles and everyday lives. Nevertheless, before getting inked, some had given the religious arguments against the practice some thought. This was the case with Salma, an artist in her mid-forties, who in the six years prior to our interview had collected a number of tattoos on her body:

> Of course, before getting them I did some research—about it being prohibited from a religious standpoint because it prevents *abdest* [ablution], that it's forbidden for us, etc. . . . In my opinion, it doesn't interfere with the *abdest*. I heard that even nail polish doesn't render ablution invalid. . . . It didn't *really* affect my decision. But it's good to know. Like, when my friend's son wanted to get a tattoo, my friend told him about the ban. But I told him: "*Abdest* is valid even with a tattoo, so don't worry."[12]

Whereas the pious women I met as customers in beauty salons in Fatih and Başakşehir often stated that they disliked the aesthetics of tattoos, they argued along similar lines in justifying their own decisions to have permanent makeup treatments. These treatments relied on a similar, though less permanent inking technique, with the ink being inserted into a more superficial layer of the skin. Neriman, a beauty therapist who often applied permanent makeup to consciously Muslim women in a beauty salon in Fatih, explained that the ban on tattooing issued by the Diyanet was

> not justified in my opinion because what is the reason for them to ban it? They say it prevents the water from being absorbed by the skin. Neither permanent makeup nor tattoos prevents the skin from absorbing water. . . . That's why I think that, from a truly Muslim perspective, they

12. Interview with Salma, June 12, 2014. The following quotes by Salma are also taken from this interview.

should say: "It's forbidden because it permanently changes the essence of the body,"—and this is indeed a sin [*günah*]. It changes the essence of your soul, and this is why it should be considered a sin.[13]

Among consciously Muslim women in this salon, the "repulsive" aesthetic of tattoos was indeed more readily accepted as an argument against this practice than the official directive based on religious grounds. Regardless of the directive, as Helin, another tattooed interlocutor pointed out, tattoos on female bodies indicated a particular (political) positioning at this moment of time:

> I think that having a tattoo is already by itself—it's a political act, because you're modifying your body, no matter why or for what. And for some beliefs the body is sacred, you cannot touch it. For example, in Islam. . . . You're modifying whatever is natural, so if you take this,—if I do that, it means it is kind of political, even if I'm not aware of it. . . . Having a tattoo on my body, I don't know, in the current moment, it means taking a stand for sure![14]

Helin's argument that she was reclaiming her body, a body that may have been abused or else subjected to social control and violence, has been analyzed as a common gendered motivation for tattooing by women (Atkinson and Young 2001). Moreover, as Helin points out, the public presentation of tattoos in the religio-conservative climate of the day was understood as a deliberate violation of the feminine norms propagated by the AKP. They marked female bodies as resistant and liberal, which, against the background of ever more normalized acts of violence committed against "unruly" women (Kandiyoti 2016), has reportedly led to a number of attacks on women sporting tattoos.

Although Helin considered her decision to be tattooed to be political, her motifs—a triple spiral, a bird, an anchor, a flower, and a star decorating her back, arms, and elbow—did not convey any explicit political messages, as she herself pointed out. As noted by Zehra, a professional

13. Interview with Neriman, June 10, 2014.

14. Interview with Helin, June 28, 2014. The following quotes from Helin are also taken from this interview.

tattoo artist who at the age of thirty was quite possibly the most heavily tattooed woman in Turkey (as her favorite tattoo artist pointed out in an interview), Istanbulite women's tattoo motifs were clearly gendered, with women preferring flowers, butterflies, mandalas, or the faces of angels or babies, rather than more masculine motifs:

> While men can have anything, like knives, fists and stuff, women, when they choose a motif, they mostly choose something they think is "sexy." . . . I think that's wrong. Because tattoos—they are like a strong statement. "No pain, no gain." Even if you're a woman, if you do tattoos, you show that you're tough. But not in Turkey. They want to be sexy, or sweet . . .

Zehra's own body certainly spoke of her toughness and courage in that it was covered with a number of motifs not generally considered feminine, including some on parts of her body that were painful to ink: a roaring tiger on her knee, a gun in a holster on her leg, a snake on her left arm, and several skulls. Inspired by the tattoos on the bodies of elderly women she saw in a Portuguese port city where she completed a year as an Erasmus student, Zehra returned to Istanbul to become a tattoo collector and, eventually, a certified tattoo artist herself. By opening up her own large tattooing studio on the prominent Beach Boulevard of the upper middle-class neighborhood of Caddebostan on the Anatolian side of Istanbul, Zehra had clearly contributed to tattooing becoming an ever more widespread bodily practice among middle-class women in this part of the city.

Women also often chose tattooing as a sign of commitment, for example, by having the names of their children or a deceased parent tattooed on to their arms. While tattoo artists generally looked down on this kind of tattooing ("lettering") because it gave them very little leeway in terms of creativity and was considered a mere fashion statement, I found it was the most common female tattoo choice during my recurrent visits to two tattoo studios on the Asian side of Istanbul. A particular kind of lettering that displayed the Kemalist commitment of its wearer was the inking of an Atatürk signature, offered for free by many Istanbul tattoo artists on November 10, Atatürk Memorial Day and a public holiday that commemorated the anniversary of his death in 1938. Among those to wear an Atatürk signature was Figen, a twenty-nine-year-old white-collar employee whom I met as a neighbor in the secular middle-class neighborhood of Moda.

Figen started telling her story by recounting that, just like Atatürk, she was born to Turkish parents in Thessaloniki and emigrated to Turkey with them at the age of four. On Atatürk Memorial Day in 2009, she was in a taxi on her way to work in the central business district of Maslak when she got into an argument with the Kurdish driver just before the ringing of the siren that announces the exact time of Atatürk's death every year at 9:05 a.m. When the siren sounds, most vehicles and people in Istanbul stop for one minute in remembrance. Figen had asked the driver to turn off the Arabesk dance music he was listening to at full volume, and when he talked back to her instead of reducing the volume, they started to argue. Eventually, Figen was so outraged that she left the taxi, perceiving the driver's reaction as a calculated affront to the Republican values of the Turkish nation. The same day she made the decision to display her love for Atatürk publicly by acquiring a tattoo of his signature. By then, the signature was already a common sight in the urban space, especially as a sticker on cars. Figen chose her left arm for the tattoo because, she explained, it was closer to her heart, underlining the theme of her love for Atatürk.

Telling me about this instance more than four years after it occurred, Figen was still visibly upset with the driver and how he could have played "such music" shortly before the commemoration of her beloved national hero. Probably unsure whether I, as a foreigner, knew about Arabesk music, she moved her hips in an exaggerated belly-dance movement by way of illustration. Her mocking remarks about Arabesk—a popular music genre that forms the background to an "entire anti-culture" (Stokes 1992, 1) by marginalized rural-urban migrants from south-east Anatolia, which the Kemalist state attempted to control and even ban due to its seemingly uncultivated character—as well as the marking of the driver as "Kurdish," indicated her underlying class-based, perhaps even racialized resentments. This was underlined by the fact that to an extent she excluded the driver from the national collective she so strongly identified with, underlining her own understanding of belonging to the nation as a republican Kemalist. To dispel my unvoiced concerns, she quickly moved on to tell me that she had no problems with Kurds whatsoever and that during the antigovernment Gezi Park protests she had stood "next to them" in an unforgettable experience of solidarity. For Figen, one year after these protests, the tattooed signature on her arm spoke of her unshaken patriotism and resistant subjectivity in times of creeping Islamization and a changing gender order, which she also saw being materialized in the driver talking back to her. Figen paid an ongoing price for her tattoo; for example, by being rejected for a number of positions due to the highly visible political symbol on her underarm.

Other female tattoo collectors likewise reported being stigmatized because of their tattoos, especially within more conservative social milieus. Helin, who started collecting tattoos in 2007 when tattoos on female bodies were still uncommon, described how she initially attempted to hide them but eventually became more daring, encouraged by the increasing visibility of tattoos on female bodies in the city. By the time she talked to me about her tattoos in 2014, she had become used to people staring at her tattooed arms in public, especially when they were crammed together on public transport. She differentiated between different kinds of stares and starers, saying:

> Older people, they're more direct, they don't even hide that they're looking at it [the tattoo]. . . . But older people, at least they don't usually say anything. Instead younger men, they take them as an excuse to start a conversation. . . . The tattoos make people pay attention to my body and [before revealing them] I never realized that people were actually looking at my body. I mean, it's my arm, but it could be anything! And they don't really seem to mind looking. Looking at the face is usually fine in Turkey, also in Hungary [where Helin studied]. But looking at the body or at particular body parts, it's *not* really—I mean, some people might call this a form of sexual harassment. Because it's this very long kind of a gaze (*laughs and imitates it by looking at me intensely*). I never know if they appreciate [the tattoos], or if it arouses them . . .

This indicates that, in the popular imagination in Turkey, tattoos clearly affect the respectability of the female wearer, with tattooed women becoming women that some men feel entitled to approach verbally in public, a serious breach of etiquette. Moreover, in the cultural context of Turkey, where the possibility of injury by vision has a particularly long history, a penetrating gaze may easily be considered as impacting on those being gazed at in an almost tangible way. Hardly surprisingly, Helin perceived the affective stares on her body, whether motivated by curiosity, sexual, or aesthetic attraction or repulsion, as a breach of her intimate sphere on the verge of sexual harassment.

In particular, women were subject to strong reactions from within their closer social environment, most importantly parents and children, when they had been tattooed. Female tattoo wearers tended to hide larger designs from their parents or else took care not to offend them by displaying them publicly in their presence. In fact, while "protest against parents" is listed as one of the main motivational categories for contemporary tattooing and piercing practices by Wohlrab, Stahl, and Kappeler (2007), I never came across this reason as a motivational force for women in Istanbul, who tended to get their tattoos when they were well past their teenage years and had already moved out of the parental home. Some female tattoo-wearers stated that they would not have dared to collect tattoos while their mother was still alive. Among them was Zehra, quoted above and the daughter of a high-ranking military man from Izmir, who recounted her father's "murmuring growl" when he first saw her tattoos. In consequence, Zehra made an effort to cover up her increasing number of tattoos whenever she visited home, saying:

> For example, I don't like going to the beach with them [i.e., her relatives], I just wear my pants. Because, think of it: people who know them will see me, and they will surely gossip about it. Also, whenever I'm in a smaller place I cover my tattoos, because otherwise people will stare at me. Even if I walk with my father, they will stare, looking at my butt, my legs. I don't like that. So whenever I visit them I cover up, and everybody is happy.

For Zehra, covering up her tattoos in more provincial settings or when accompanied by her father and extended relatives in her hometown was a form both of protection and of paying respect. This was based on the fact that her father's reputation would surely be compromised not simply by her uncommon look, but also by the fact that people would feel invited to stare unashamedly at her body in his presence. Within the cultural codes of her hometown, this would reflect back on her own respectability, as well as on that of her male protector, her father. Whereas gendered norms of conduct and cultural codes of respectability certainly cut across the usual divisions between the traditional and the modern, the liberal and the conservative, the secular and the Islamic in present-day Turkey, not for nothing did mixed social spaces such as public transport or the beach figure high in female tattoo-wearers' accounts of the stigmatization, harassment, and public shaming they feared.

By revealing their tattoos (or piercings) in public, women thus made themselves vulnerable to being publicly stared at and thus sexually shamed, as well as risking compromising those who were considered responsible for them within the patriarchal order. For Hande, a married housewife and mother in her late thirties in the conservative working-class district of Kavacık on the outskirts of Istanbul, this meant taking into consideration her mother-in-law, who lived in the same house and watched over her whenever her husband was away on one of his many travels. She suffered from her mother-in-law's constant vitriolic comments about her tattoos and nose piercing, as well as her refusal to leave the house with Hande if the latter's tattoos were visible. Within the neighborhood, Hande reasoned, she was the only married woman with tattoos and a nose piercing; most of her female neighbors her age were "not looking attractive, not taking care of themselves."[15] Within this tightly knit neighborhood they were simply "not daring enough," she said, or else submitted to the restrictive gender norms enforced by their fathers, husbands, and mothers-in-law. Whereas Hande proudly recounted the fact that among her children's friends at school she was much admired for sporting such a "cool" and "modern" look, in contrast to their own mothers, her own daughter proved more critical. As I was talking to Hande over cups of tea one afternoon while her teenage daughter was seemingly preoccupied with watching a Hollywood

---

15. Interview with Hande, June 11, 2014. The following quotes by Hande are also taken from this interview.

blockbuster in another corner of the living room, at one point during the interview the latter burst out shouting that her mother prevented her from even putting on makeup, while she herself styled up "like a teenager."

Indeed, teenage children were often described as the most critical of their mothers' decision to have tattoos or piercings. Among them was Salma's son, who according to Salma wanted her to "sit at home" after she had filed for a divorce from his father:

> To him, I'm old. Perhaps, because I'm not the typical mother, having tattoos, making myself attractive, he behaves as if he is protesting. That's how friends explained it to me. Because I'm a liberal mother who wants to live freely and still do things with my life. . . . At one point, they [her children] will live their own lives and I will have to live my own life: I'm struggling to make them understand this!

For Salma, the daughter of a military officer and a staunch Kemalist, collecting tattoos was a form of female emancipation and of reinvestment in her bodily attractiveness at a time of marital and life crisis that eventually led to her divorce. Aesthetic body modification, which in her case also included cosmetic surgery, Botox injections, and permanent makeup, formed part of her newly found identity as a free and liberal woman who was reclaiming control over her own life and body, in contrast to the social expectation that she should give up her sexual identity after divorce. The motifs of her tattoos, among them a butterfly (for freedom) and a phoenix (for rebirth), marked great personal crises, namely her mother's death in a car accident and her recent divorce. They proved to be a means of handling personal experiences and developed significant agentive capacities on her body:

> I took the decision [for the phoenix tattoo] while we [Salma and her husband] were in the process of separating; we had not yet talked about a divorce. Then, after I already got it [the tattoo], when one day I looked at it: it made me realize that what I really wanted was a fresh beginning, a kind of rise from the ashes (laughs)! So the next day I filed for a divorce.

To sum up, the motifs and the act of tattooing send out strong bodily messages that simultaneously subscribe to and challenge hegemonic femininity within an increasingly conservative gender order. They challenge femininity in that they subvert images of women as submissive and passive by marking the social body with a technique that in nonurban settings especially is still commonly associated with lower-class masculinity. However, as tattooing is considered a primarily aesthetic form of body modification, female tattoo collectors are often intending to add to the feminine attractiveness of their bodies rather than violate it or make it masculine. Not least, in present-day Istanbul tattoos are sending out subversive political messages at a time when women's rights, including women's bodily autonomy, are increasingly under attack. Within this polarized political climate, younger middle-class women's tattooing practices have become markers and reminders of women's insistence on the ownership of their own sexual bodies, making them prone to attacks, but also providing them with the strength to fight them.

Conclusion

Coined by Greenblatt in an analysis of sixteenth-century artists, the notion of self-fashioning implies "a characteristic mode of address to the world" that has the power "to impose a shape upon oneself [as] an aspect of the more general power to control identity—that of others at least as often as one's own" (1980, 1). Similar to what Greenblatt describes, in Turkey's polarized political climate, embodied self-fashioning for middle-class women involves "some experience of threat, some effacement or undermining, some loss of self" (Greenblatt 1980, 9). For the self-identified secular women portrayed in this chapter, this threat is typically described as Islamization and includes a sense of the loss of cultural and economic hegemony. Consciously and visibly Muslim women, on the other hand, struggle with the ongoing hegemony of the secular elite in the fields of beauty and fashion, supported by common stereotypes of them as unmodern and backward elements of a laic state structure, which, however, the current conservative government is in the process of transforming. Pious women of different generations, this chapter has shown, are creative in reconciling imaginings of themselves against the background of changing notions of appropriate feminine appearance and behavior within the Turkish public. Within the conservative, pro-Islamic climate of the

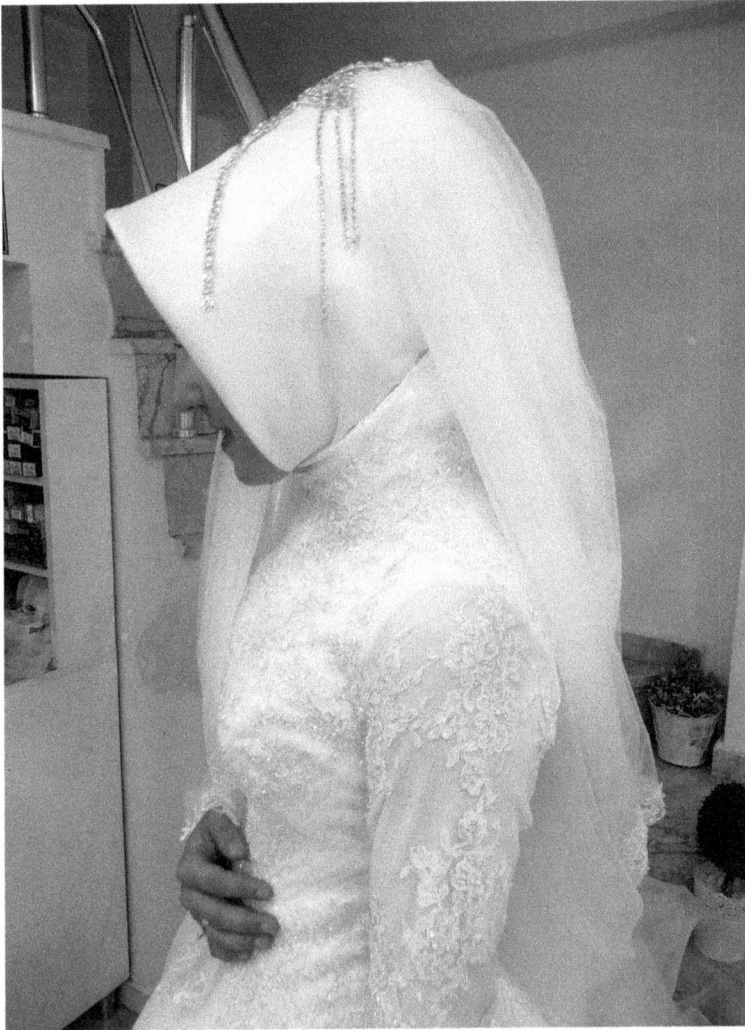

8. For consciously Muslim brides, many salons in Fatih routinely offer the arrangement and lavish adornment of headscarves with pearls and other decorative elements (*türban tasarım*). (Claudia Liebelt)

ruling AKP they are venturing into hitherto secular domains and terrains increasingly self-consciously.

It should be noted that when pious women engage in beauty-intensive forms of self-care that are similar to those of secular middle-class women, this does not necessarily lead to a more inclusive perspective on what it means to be a proper woman in contemporary Istanbul. Within a polarized political climate, and amid secular anxieties over losing ground in one's own intimate social spaces, stereotypical views of the pious Other as ultimately unmodern, Arabesque, or tasteless are confirmed in a somewhat contradictory manner. Rather than being "a place to start" overcoming the Islamic–secular division of society, as suggested by the editor-in-chief of the conservative women magazine *Âlâ* quoted at the beginning of this chapter, the self-fashioning of feminine middle-class selves presents itself as a battlefield between various factions of the middle classes, generations of women, and political opponents.

While pious women continue to face multiple exclusions within the urban hotspots of fashion and beauty, lifestyles, dispositions, and spaces considered secular have come under increasingly violent attacks themselves.[16] Arrests on the grounds of "secular propaganda" (*laiklik propagandası*), which in 2017 prompted the main Kemalist opposition party to create the hashtag "Secularism is not a crime," have fueled the sentiment of many self-described secularists that secularism is under threat in Turkey. Finally, it would be a mistake to describe my interlocutors' self-fashioning as merely defensive or reactive: in their everyday workings and political dispositions, which are often made visible by symbolically charged forms of beautification such as Tesettür style or tattooing, they may be exclusive, combative, or forceful in making their ontological claims to knowledge and truth.

---

16. See, for example *Birgün* (2017) and *BIA Haber* (2017).

Conclusion

When I arrived in Istanbul for a year of fieldwork during the last gasp of what came to be known as the Gezi Park protests in 2013, questions of beauty and femininity seemed far removed from people's concerns. Comments by colleagues and friends on my research topic often reflected the common understanding of feminine beauty as somewhat ephemeral, superfluous, and politically irrelevant, especially in times of political crisis. In contrast, this book has argued that the study of embodied beauty offers unique insights into the gender dynamics and the politics of social and political reproduction in present-day Turkey and beyond. Most of the research for this book took place during what has been called the second phase of the AKP regime (Ataç et al. 2018, Özkazanç 2020), between 2011 and 2015. Ever since, an escalation of violence in the Kurdish southeast, the political crisis after the breakup of the political alliance between the AKP and the Islamic Gülen movement, and the establishment of a presidential regime have exacerbated the process of political polarization described in this book, fueling an increasingly authoritarian and populist ultranationalism.

Like the emergence of an intimate public sphere after the neoconservative revolution in the United States described by Lauren Berlant (1997), amid the recent conservative-authoritarian turn in Turkey, matters of feminine appearance, sexuality, and morality have all become hotly debated public issues. They are embedded in a neoconservative politics of gender in present-day Turkey, which Deniz Kandiyoti (2016, 105) forcefully argues is "*intrinsic* rather than *incidental*" to the characterization of the AKP ruling ideology, forming part of a larger project of remodeling gendered citizenship. Thus, in contrast to an earlier state version of feminism "from above" that sought inclusion on the basis of the equality of men and women, the AKP's ideology conceptualizes women as different from and dependent on men by virtue of their *fıtrat*; that is, their "biological and divinely ordained nature" (Kandiyoti 2016, 104). As Kandiyoti notes, apart from the curtailment of women's rights and the normalization of violence against women that this policy entails, the AKP regime relies on a populist climate of the resentment of "ordinary" Sunni Muslim Turks against an allegedly westernized, "infidel" urban elite.

In the field of beauty, this is played out in the populist notion of Turkish feminine beauty being linked to moral integrity, cleanliness, and conformity to gendered roles, as opposed to the supposedly Western-style elite approach to beauty that confuses it with conspicuous consumption and "artificial" looks. It is something of an irony that, by adopting neoliberal policies such as the privatization of health and the media, the AKP has contributed to the flourishing of invasive cosmetic procedures—commonly seen as resulting in "artificial" looks—which may not be in line with its gender ideology. Moreover, we have seen how mundane acts of self-fashioning, especially if they relate to secular or Islamic bodily practices respectively, such as sporting a headscarf, using lipstick, or publicly exposing one's tattoos, have taken on political meanings and become tokens of urban nonbelonging, and by extension political disloyalty, in a visceral sense.

From the *fıtrat* perspective on gender, women engage in feminine appearance work and beautification by acting upon their natural desires and selves. Istanbulite women's desires for beauty, however, are a social relation that is not static, but rather in flux. They transcend the lines of social and political polarization and are transnational in scope, embedded in urban and transnational beautyscapes that are traversed by traveling knowledge, mediated body images, networks, and products. Most notably, amid Istanbul's inclusion in the globalizing sector of beauty, access to aesthetic body modification and beauty products and services is no longer restricted to the secular urban elite but has become more easily accessible to and acceptable for broader segments of the population. During the 1990s and early 2000s, aesthetic treatments that have long been regarded as inappropriate, even shameful, due to their links with female sexuality and attractiveness, became ever more popular, normalized, and chic, including in working-class neighborhoods or on the outskirts of the city. What has changed in this process is not the importance urban middle-class women place on feminine appearance, but the normalized role and, indeed, the increasingly mandatory nature of body-centered services and aesthetic body modification in the creation of proper female selves in the city. For those seeking employment in the growing and feminized service sector, investment in one's outer appearance is both a prerequisite and a form of aesthetic investment.

This study has illustrated dramatic changes in the urban world of beauty during the past few decades, which are not specific to Istanbul but can also be found in other emerging centers of an increasingly global beauty market. Like elsewhere, in Istanbul beauty work is increasingly relegated to professional beauty service workers and engaged in by ever younger women, as well as by a growing number of older women, who conceptualize their bodies as "prenatal" and "postmenopausal" respectively. While in earlier decades the beauty sector was closely linked to the participation of women in the urban service sector, this link has become somewhat less automatic. To reiterate, these changes are not peculiar to urban Turkey: one could say that in a neoliberal consumer society in which the separation between one's work and private life has become less clearcut and stable, *everyone* is expected to invest in one's outer appearance as part of one's dual role as a potential worker and consumer-citizen. Moreover, in an age of surveillance medicine within an increasingly privatized medical sector, new cohorts of aging women—in urban Turkey, but most likely also on a global scale—no longer accept their "fate," as my interlocutors put it, but instead have internalized a conceptualization of aging as an aesthetic-medical risk to be actively treated. Clearly, the intense attempts at body maintenance and aging well among the middle-class women described in this book are a response to the growing economy of beauty, as well as to the heightened expectations of and pressures on women within a neoconservative gender climate.

Earlier conceptualizations of aging, however, are not simply disappearing: indeed, heteronormative middle-class women are still valued for their social achievements as the main caregivers in private households of children, grandchildren, and aging parents, at least rhetorically, and within a familistic political regime. Within conservative segments of the population, the ongoing consumption of beauty treatments and services, particularly more invasive ones, by women beyond menopause is seen as the preserve of urban, upper middle-class, and secular women. For provincial women or those from lower social strata, invasive procedures may be difficult to come by, not only due to their high costs but also because their consumption needs to be negotiated with their close kin, especially their parents or husbands. Investments in beautification and self-care that exceed the standard routines of bodily grooming are seen as potentially vain and narcissistic.

Nevertheless, women belonging to an emerging pious middle-class are venturing into the urban world of beauty in increasingly self-conscious ways. While young pious women engage in beauty practices that are often congruent with those that Istanbulites their age, but of a more secular outlook, engage in, they often see the need to scrutinize their motivating force and the resulting effects more carefully. Their increasingly visible investments in beauty are tied to a claim for inclusion in a competitive urban terrain and to their recognition as properly modern and urban. Their intrusion into the exclusive spaces of beauty consumption, such as boutiques, fitness centers, beauty salons, and clinics in so-called secular, upmarket city-center neighborhoods, produces narratives of distinction by those who consider themselves a constitutive part of this urban terrain.

Citizenship, Aihwa Ong (1996, 737) has argued, is a "process of self-making and being-made." In this study, I have chosen an ethnographic approach that has highlighted questions of subjectification, affectivity, and sensuality in order to improve understanding of the process of becoming a proper female citizen in urban Turkey. As elsewhere, feminine beauty is an embodied and situated social practice in Istanbul, not an essential and easily measurable natural quality that determines success. It relies on a process of bodily cultivation that is played out differently in various parts of the city and is subject to local as well as transnational structuring forces within a growing economy of beauty services and products. This study demonstrates that the making of middle-class femininity in urban Turkey requires sustained effort and an ongoing cultivation of the self in a deeply relational process, including one that takes place between those gendered male and those gendered female. While husbands, sons, and fathers, as well as female kin, male and female colleagues, friends, and neighbors, loomed large in women's narratives of why they engaged in or refrained from particular beauty practices, in this study I have focused on women's interactions with their most immediate judges of beauty in commercial settings, namely beauty therapists and cosmetic surgeons. Due to the intimate nature of the interaction and the specialized expertise of cosmetic surgeons and beauty therapists, the latter wield considerable influence over their clients' and patients' beauty decisions and imaginations of themselves. Beauty service work is significant not only due to its visible aesthetic outcomes, but also for the affective and sensual changes it brings about in women and their imagined female selves.

As a process of sensorial and embodied subjectification, the making of feminine citizens in urban beauty salons and clinics during the AKP rule offers an interesting case for political subject formation. In the "new" Turkey proclaimed by its ruling elite (Yilmaz 2017), female beauty therapists in particular are recruited as the educators, gatekeepers, and manufacturers of "a more beautiful Turkey" in an attempt to create female citizens who are not only beautiful, but also gender norm conforming or, in the words of the ruling president quoted at the beginning of this book, "good, true, and beneficial." The aesthetic citizenship described in this book relies on the consumption of beauty products and services as an urban way of life that rhetorically downplays the role of invasive procedures while emphasizing the immense discipline and effort it takes to create proper feminine selves. In contrast to state-sponsored cosmetic surgery in Brazil, in Turkey such surgery for women is state-sponsored only in one instance, namely when a victim of violence against women undergoes surgery to protect herself from being recognized by abusive family members.[1] Accordingly, there is a moral economy underlying

---

1. According to a statement by the acting AKP Minister of Family and Social Policy, Fatma Şahin, just before the adoption of the Law to Protect Family and Prevent Violence against Women (Law 6284) on March 8, 2012. This policy has been criticized sharply by

the consumption of regular bodily practices as opposed to invasive cosmetic procedures: while the latter produces quick results and may result in ostentatious, artificial, and unnatural looks, the first relies on an ongoing commitment to gender norm conformity, beauty, and bodily discipline in everyday life. However, in order to achieve a highly cherished "natural" feminine look—not to be confused with an unprocessed look—both types of procedures may be necessary, especially at an advanced age. Within the current political climate, aesthetic body modification and more generally, beautification, is often linked to a broader project of "national progress."

Amid the aesthetic nationalism of the day and Istanbul's inclusion into the global beauty economy, this study shows that the urban sector of beauty services has become a viable career option and an entrepreneurial niche for women. In spite of the fact that beauty service work remains devalued, it is attractive to a growing number of women, not least because opening one's own salon allows them to combine work in an intimate social sphere with childcare, which, because of the neoconservative family-oriented welfare politics of the AKP, is hard to come by as a public service. Similar to other forms of intimate service work, beauty service work relies on the management of emotions. In contrast to what is implied in Hochschild's original concept, however, there is no generic script as to what kind of emotional labor is employed in the interaction between beauty service workers and their customers. Rather, beauty salons and clinics vary significantly in this regard, with some emphasizing female care and sharing as opposed to (medical) professionalism and authority. Whereas many beauty service workers pride themselves in making patients or customers feel (and look) beautiful, beauty service work may also include body shaming to provide an incentive for the ongoing consumption of services.

---

feminist organizations, including Mor Çatı (Purple Roof) Women's Shelter Foundation. Upon enquiry, a volunteer claimed that "[w]hile we are in touch with women who have changed their identity or are applying to have their identity changed, we do not know of anyone, who underwent cosmetic surgery in order to do so. . . . Women should not change their faces, but men and the state should change their behaviour" (personal communication, July 10, 2014).

Cosmetic surgeons, in turn, occupy a special niche in Istanbul's globalizing economy of travel and commerce. In the process, some have come to see themselves as agents of urban beautification within a rapidly changing urban environment. This has become especially clear from the analysis of female breast reduction and nose surgery procedures, commonly labeled "ethnic plastic surgery" by medical practitioners in Turkey. These are described as especially prevalent among women who are stigmatized as provincial newcomers or residents of the so-called *varoş*, a space seen as marginal within the urban beauty economy.

By choosing to engage in particular types of cosmetic surgery even when these raise concerns within their respective social milieus, those scrutinized as bodily Others often seek to "normalize" their features by investing in aesthetic capital for purposes of upward social mobility. From the perspective of cosmetic surgeons, invasive medicine is crucial to creating a more beautiful Turkey, as well as a more harmonious one, enhancing bodies through so-called ethnic plastic surgery and normalizing the bodies of the marginalized. Similar to what has been analyzed for Brazil (Jarrín 2017, 134), national ideals of mixedness function in paradoxical ways, on the one hand celebrating "one's own" beauty in a configuration of aesthetic nationalism, while on the other hand placing additional pressures on women to normalize their features and conform to the norms of hegemonic femininity. In line with what Shirley Tate (2016) argues for shade shifting alias skin bleaching in the Black Atlantic, female breast reduction and nose surgery, among other types of aesthetic body modification in urban Turkey, thus bring out and make visible ongoing social, gendered, and racialized inequalities.

Istanbul, this book has shown, is a conflictual space where women's consumption patterns and bodily self-fashioning are markers of their degree of belonging to the city, to the Republic and its current regime, as well as to the wider world. The attempts to achieve distinction and the resentment expressed by the anxious and belligerent voices of many of the women portrayed in this book have become characteristic of the state of affairs in Turkey. Narratives of distinction through bodily difference, Sara Ahmed (2000) contends, function not simply through hegemonic norms but through a "visual economy of recognition." Ahmed draws her insights from an analysis of the encounter with and the recognition of strangers in urban space, those who are "recognized [visibly] as not belonging, as being out of place" (Ahmed 2000, 21). The extraordinary body here becomes something that, when it appears in a particular spatial setting—a neighborhood, a community—must be expelled to protect the boundaries of the imagined community. Ahmed explains how technologies such as Neighborhood Watch recruit citizens to police the urban space, watching out for suspicious persons and strangers. This "visual economy of recognition" relies on the "eye" of the good citizen that "does not simply return to the body, as that which must be transformed and regulated as 'the seen,' but looks elsewhere, to and at others" (Ahmed 2000, 30). The good citizen, therefore, is "one who watches (out for) suspicious persons and strangers, and who in that very act, becomes aligned, not only with the police (and hence the Law), but with the imagined community itself whose boundaries are protected *in the very labor of his look*" (Ahmed 2000, 30, emphasis in the original).

The critical judges of beauty in present-day Istanbul, who claim as their own an upmarket city-center world of beauty against pious and supposedly lower-class female intruders, are good urban citizens in this sense. However, the secular middle-class femininity that they perform and scrutinize, genealogically linked to the emblematic secular Republican Woman, is no longer tied to ideals of female citizenship in a quasi-automatic way. Thus, in recent years, the often-quoted Republican Woman of Istanbul, who relies on a wide range of beauty services and who created a genealogy of urban belonging in beauty for many of my upper middle-class research participants, has been unsettled as the paradigmatic female citizen. Paternalistic protection, Deniz Kandiyoti (2016, 106) has shown, is now offered to those female individuals who visibly comply with the new religio-conservative gender order and dress and behave modestly, whereas it is withdrawn from those who "break the norms of modesty and protest in public." One of the more recent examples of this is the arrest and violent dispersal with tear gas and water cannons of the so-called Saturday Mothers (*Cumartesi Anneleri*), a group of mostly elderly women, who since the mid-1990s have held regular, silent sit-ins and vigils on İstiklal Boulevard's Galatasaray Square to demand justice for their forcefully "disappeared" or murdered relatives, in August 2018.[2] The picture of the detainment of eighty-two-year-old Emine Ocak, the white-haired and frail yet defiant cofounder of the Saturday Mothers, whose son disappeared in police custody in 1995, went viral and now forms part of an unofficial gallery of iconic female protesters that also includes the image of the so-called Woman in Red, a young woman in a red summer dress during the so-called Gezi Park protests in late May 2013, who is pepper-sprayed so forcefully by a police officer standing next to her that her hair blows upward. These protesters attest to the vitality and resilience of feminist and LGBTI+ movements in Turkey in spite of violent repression, the ongoing surveillance of women's bodies and sexuality and, since 2019, an alarming anti-gender mobilization (Özkazanç 2020).

Female bodies, this shows, have become a major site for the negotiation of citizenship, and norms of femininity have been shifting. As Michel Foucault famously described (1990, 1995), those subject to critical judgements of their compliance with dominant norms may resist, but most importantly, they typically reconfigure their subjectivities in the process. The Foucauldian notion of the "care of the self," which is so closely related to the notion of self-care repeatedly invoked by my research participants, helps us understand that persons comply with gendered appearance norms not because they are codified as a rule, but because they don't feel good about themselves if they violate them. Those who are unable to consume the services necessary to achieve the basic norms of urban femininity—or masculinity, for that matter—risk exclusion from belonging in the urban beauty economy on moral and affective terms, not as the poor, but as the unkempt, careless, and ugly. On this background, the recent boom in publicly visible tattoos and piercings on middle-class women's bodies clearly poses a challenge, if not outright resistance, toward shifting norms of femininity. Rather than being simply mundane, embodied acts of aesthetic self-fashioning must therefore be seen in the context of the political reproduction of class and gender in present-day Turkey. In an increasingly conservative and neoliberal gender climate, *all* female (as well

---

2. See, for example, the *New York Times* (2018).

as nonbinary, trans, or intersexual) persons are subject to public scrutiny and risk sanctions for violating gendered norms by the way they look or behave in public.

Rather than attribute the outlined shift in norms of femininity to an Islamist–secularist divide that some argue never truly existed in modern Turkey, I have pointed out the multiple contradictions implied in the labeling of others as "secular" or "religious," as well as of the unexpected coalitions and distinctions. These could be observed, for example, during moments such as the impressive mass *iftars*, the ceremonial meal breaking of the daily fast that took place during Ramadan against the background of the Gezi Park protests in 2013, as well as in the convivial encounters of rather diverse beauty therapists and their customers in beauty salons across the city described in this book. To repeat, in present-day Istanbul a feminine, well-groomed appearance is a social requirement for middle-class women across the rhetorical secular–Islamic divide. Moreover, the good female citizen and urban resident is someone who watches out for signs of aging, lower-class status, or simply carelessness not only on other people's bodies, but very significantly, on her own—in short, taking care of herself.

Finally, the popularization and normalization of aesthetic body modification and less invasive beauty treatments is also made possible by the opening up of more-than-local spaces of opportunity and imagination by global media, social media, and entertainment industries. This process is not particular to urban Turkey: social media influencers, global pop stars, and television beauties trigger processes of imagination that simultaneously fuel desires for aesthetic self-making and anxieties over the potentially resulting artificiality. Shifting ideals of feminine body images and looks are not simply regulated by patriarchal control of the female sexual body, but are fed by an emphasis on neoliberal self-making and affective desire. Global statistics of cosmetic procedures and products, just like the beauty industry's traveling notion that "there are no ugly women, just careless ones," point to a global rise in aesthetic standards and in the transnational circulation of body images and cosmetic products and services. Whereas earlier ideals of femininity may have been based predominantly on a desire for modernity and progress, not only in Turkey but also in many other emerging markets, more recent forms of femininity—whether rooted in neoconservative anti-gender ideologies or hyperfemininity—are always already embedded in a neoliberal consumer society that rests on beauty as one of its "spectral technologies" (Comaroff and Comaroff 2001).

This relates to what Michael Taussig (2012) has termed the "cosmic concern" with beauty, namely the "inseparability of the aesthetic and the magic of the [contemporary globalized] economy," in which "new worlds of aesthetic intensification and libidinal gratification . . . have taken center stage" (Taussig 2012, 6). Writing about Colombian cities like Cali and Medellín, which, like other urban spaces around the world, have become "notorious for their mix of poverty, violence, liposuction, breast enlargement, face-lifting, ass enlargement, and restoration of the hymen" (Taussig 2012, 9), Taussig coins the notion of cosmic, not cosmetic, surgery. In classical anthropological accounts of beauty, he reminds us, the close connection between beauty and magic has already been made. Thus, cosmic surgery "is nothing more than a gloss on a far more basic operation, the latest expression of ancient magical practices based on mimesis and physiognomy, practices such as masking, face painting, and body painting, carried out so as to greet the gods or become one" (Taussig 2012, 44). Rather than mere form, beauty is a force based on "emotional power and bodily excitement" (Taussig 2012, 2–3). Taussig sees this force at work in the form of a branded, immensely expensive sneaker displayed like a fetish in the lounge of Bogotà's domestic airport (Taussig 2012, 98–108), in the beauty salon of Nima, a "local goddess" with extensions in a small plantation town (Taussig 2012, 35–42), or in the bodily doings of Colombian paramilitaries and narcos, who change their identities and are "reborn" via cosmetic surgery (Taussig 2012, 109–26). While Istanbulite middle-class women's emphasis on beauty as cleanliness is certainly distinct from the aesthetics of the baroque described by Taussig for Colombia, both speak of beauty as a visceral form of desire.

To desire, Deleuze and Guattari (2000 [1972], pos. 127) have pointed out, "is to produce, to produce within the realm of the real." Desire as a productive force is based on passion rather than lack. Taking issue with

9. Advertisement on Başakşehir's main boulevard: in the early 2000s, young, upwardly mobile, pious fashionistas became increasingly visible in the urban public space . (Claudia Liebelt)

the psychoanalytical concept of sexual repression based on desire-as-lack, Deleuze and Guattari write that "[i]f desire is repressed, it is because every position of desire, no matter how small, is capable of calling into question the established order of a society" (pos. 388). In the libidinal economy outlined in Deleuze and Guattari's *Anti-Oedipus*, desiring is not an individual affair bolstered by individual needs, but makes connections as mutual care, which "always remains in close touch with the conditions of objective existence; it embraces them and follows them, shifts when they shift, and does not outlive them" (Deleuze and Guattari 2000, pos. 127).

From this perspective, Istanbulite middle-class women's transforming and transformative desires for beauty may be considered generative acts of healing from social suffering and tedious everyday routines, imaginative and relational in their world-making, a corporeal reaching out to the stars. Experiences of beauty and beauty work, this book has shown, are subjective and may be contradictory: they include the pain under drying hood machines or after surgery, the despair of finding time for supposedly obligatory beauty within a highly competitive work environment, *and* the immense comfort, self-satisfaction, and overbearing joy derived from nail polish, lipstick, or a new nose. There still is a dearth of anthropological analysis of gendered desire, beauty, and the actual workings of its growing market, despite the large body of literature on gendered agency in the Middle East. Much research is still needed to understand how the affective power of beauty is simultaneously able to support and challenge hegemonic norms of race, class, gender, age, and urbane belonging in modernity, especially in the global South.

The task of an anthropological approach to beauty, then, is to take beauty seriously as a cosmological concern, a widely shared desire and vital force in an increasingly virtual world filled with postindustrial debris and threatened by planetary destruction. In the realm of beauty everything becomes possible, and even by imagining oneself a part of it, things may change forever.

Glossary

References

Index

Glossary

abdest: ritual washing
abla: older sister
ağda: (sugar) waxing
annelik estetiği: mommy makeover (lit. motherhood aesthetics)
avret bölgesi: private parts
ayıp: shameful
bakımlı: well-groomed
çalışan kadın: working woman
çarşaf: chador (lit. sheet)
çirkin kadın yoktur, bakımsız kadın vardır: There are no ugly women, just careless ones
dinci: religious person
düğün: wedding
düzgün: straight, smooth, clean-cut
estetik merkezi: center for body aesthetics
estetik uzmanı: beauty expert
estetikçi: beautician
ev hanımı: housewife
ev kızı: unmarried daughter (lit. house-girl)
fetva: ruling (according to Islamic religious law)
fön: blow-dry
günah: sin
güzel/güzellik: beautiful/beauty
güzellik salonu: beauty salon
hacamat: cupping (treatment)
hadith: lit. traditions (source for Islamic religious law)
hanım/hanımefendi: lady
haram: forbidden (by religion)

hassas: sensitive
hoca: Muslim preacher, scholar, or clergy
hoş: nice
ikinci bahar: second spring
ırk: race
kadın: woman
kapalı: closed (used for veiled women)
kısmet: fate, destiny
kıl: body hair
kına gecesi: (pre-wedding) henna night
kız: girl, daughter
kokona: elderly (upper) middle-class lady
köylü kadın: village woman
laik/laiklik: secular/secularism (laicism)
mahalle: neighborhood
mahrem: intimate social sphere
mani: hindrance
menopoz: menopause
nikah: (civil) marriage
orta sınıf: middle class
pis: dirty
prezentabl: presentable
saç: head hair
samimi: intimate
saygı: respect
sosyete: elite, high society
süslü/süslenmek: adorned/to adorn oneself
temiz/temizlik: clean/cleanliness
tesettür/tesettürlü: form of modest veiling/veiled
türban tasarım: headscarf (lit. turban) styling
türban/türbanlı: form of modest veiling/turbaned
yaşlanmak: aging

References

Adal, Hikmet. 2020. "Cumhurbaşkanı Erdogan Evlilik Yaşı İddiası Ne Kadar Doğru?" [How Justified Is President Erdoğan's Marriage Age Claim?]. *BIA Haber Merkezi*. January 11. https://m.bianet.org/bianet/yasam/218421-cumhurbaskani -erdogan-in-evlilik-yasi-iddiasi-ne-kadar-dogru (accessed March 18, 2021).

Adanalı, Yasar Adnan. 2011. "De-spatialized Space as Neoliberal Utopia: Gentrified Istiklal Street and Commercialized Urban Spaces." *Red Thread* 3: 1–13.

Adrian, Bonnie. 2003. *Framing the Bride: Globalizing Beauty and Romance in Taiwan's Bridal Industry*. Berkeley, Los Angeles: Univ. of California Press.

Ahmed, Sara. 2000. *Strange Encounters. Embodied Others in Post-Coloniality*. London, New York: Routledge.

Akkir, Erol. 2009. "Laser Burns Genital Area" [Lazerle jenital bölgesi yandı]. *Hürriyet*. June 13.

Aktif Haber. 2005. "Cosmetic Surgery for Free for Bülent Ersoy!" [Bülent Ersoy'a bedava estetik!] *Aktif Haber*. December 23. http://www.aktifhaber.com/bulent -ersoya-bedava-estetik-57000h.htm (accessed March 4, 2015).

Alaimo, Stacy. 2010. *Bodily Natures: Science, Environment, and the Material Self*. Bloomington, Indianapolis: Indiana Univ. Press.

Amnesty International. 2013: *Gezi Park Protests: Brutal Denial of the Right to Peaceful Assembly in Turkey*. London: Amnesty International.

Appadurai, Arjun. 1990. "Disjuncture and Difference in the Global Cultural Economy." *Theory Culture Society* 7: 295–310.

Arman, Ayşe. 2004. "Only 5% of All Aesthetic Surgery Patients Belong to High Society" [Estetik yaptıranların sadece yüzde 5'i sosyetik]. *Hürriyet*. September 26.

Arman, Ayşe. 2009. "Headscarved Women Also Engage in Cosmetic Surgery" [Tesettürlüler de estetik yaptirir]. *Hürriyet*. July 18.

Armstrong, David. 1995. "The Rise of Surveillance Medicine." *Sociology of Health and Illness* 17: 393–404.

Arna, Sibel. 2009. "The Largest Breasts Are Those in Southeast Anatolia, and Marmara Residents' Biggest Mistake Is Wearing Brassieres While Sleeping" [En büyük göğüslüler Güney Doğu Anadolu'da Marmaralıların hatası uyurken sutyen takmak]. *Hürriyet*. June 14. http://www.hurriyet.com.tr/en-buyuk -gogusluler-guney-dogu-anadolu-da-marmaralilarin-hatasi-uyurken-sutyen -takmak-11857407 (accessed November 18, 2016).

Ataç, Ilker, Michael Fanizadeh, Volkan Ağar, and VIDC, eds. 2018. *After the Putsch: 16 Notes on the "New" Turkey [Nach dem Putsch: 16 Anmerkungen zur "neuen" Türkei]*. Wien: Mandelbaum.

Atkinson, Michael, and Kevin Young. 2001. "Flesh Journey: Neo-Primitives and the Contemporary Rediscovery of Radical Body Modification." *Deviant Behaviour* 22: 117–46.

Atkinson, Michael. 2002. "Pretty in Ink: Conformity, Resistance and Negotiation in Women's Tattooing." *Sex Roles* 47 (5–6): 219–35.

Aycan, Zeynep. 2004. "Key Success Factors for Women in Management in Turkey." *Applied Psychology: An International Review* 53 (3): 453–77.

Aycan, Zeynep. 2006. "Human Resource Management in Turkey." In *Managing Human Resources in the Middle East*, edited by Pawan Budhwar and Kamel Mellahi, 160–80. New Jersey: Routledge.

Aydin, Cemil. 2007. *The Politics of Anti-Westernism in Asia: Visions of World Order in Pan-Islamic and Pan-Asian Thought*. New York: Columbia Univ. Press.

Aydın, Ayşe. 2004. *The Secret of Beauty: Make-up Techniques Step by Step* [Güzelliğin Sırrı: adım adım makyaj teknikleri]. İstanbul: İnkılap Kitabevi.

Balkan, Erol, and Ahmet Öncü. 2015. "Reproduction of the Islamic Middle Class in Turkey." In *The Neoliberal Landscape and the Rise of Islamist Capital in Turkey*, edited by N. Balkan, E. Balkan, and A. Öncü, 166–200. New York, Oxford: Berghahn.

Balkan, Neşecan, Erol Balkan, and Ahmet Öncü, eds. 2015. *The Neoliberal Landscape and the Rise of Islamist Capital in Turkey*. New York, Oxford: Berghahn.

Barad, Karen. 2003. "Posthumanist Performativity: Toward an Understanding of How Matter Comes to Matter." *Signs: Journal of Women in Culture and Society* 28 (3): 801–31.

Bartky, Sandra Lee. 1988. "Foucault, Femininity, and the Modernization of Patriarchal Power." In *Feminism and Foucault*, edited by I. Diamond and L. Quinby, 61–86. Boston: Northeastern Univ. Press.

Bartky, Sandra Lee. 1990. *Femininity and Domination: Studies in the Phenomenology of Oppression*. New York: Routledge.

Beer, Bettina. 2014. "Boholano Olfaction: Odor Terms, Categories, and Discourses." *The Senses and Society* 9 (2): 151–73.

Behar, Cem. 2003. *A Neighborhood in Ottoman Istanbul: Fruit Vendors and Civil Servants in the Kasap Ilyas Mahalle*. Albany: State Univ. of New York Press.

Berkowitz, Dana. 2017. *Botox Nation: Changing the Face of America*. New York: New York Univ. Press.

Berlant, Lauren. 1997. *The Queen of America Goes to Washington City*. Durham, NC: Duke Univ. Press.

BIA Haber. 2017. "Tanrıkulu Wonders: 'Does Secular Propaganda Make You Guilty?'" [Tanrıkulu'ndan Soru Önergesi: 'Laikliği Propagandası suç mu?'] *BIA Haber*. January 2. https://bianet.org/bianet/hukuk/182279-tanrikulu -ndan-soru-onergesi-laiklik-propagandasi-suc-mu (accessed October 26, 2018).

Bildirici, Faruk 2009. "Aesthetic Surgery Is Not Like Heroin, It Does Not Lead to Addiction" [Estetik eroin değil bağımlılık yapmaz]. *Hürriyet*. October 11.

BirGün. 2017. "CHP's Tanrıkulu: 'Since When Is Defending Secularism an Offence?'" [CHP'li Tanrıkulu: "Laikliği savunmak ne zamandır suç?"]. *BirGün*. January 2. http://www.birgun.net/haber-detay/chp-li-tanrikulu-laikligi-sa vunmak-ne-zamandir-suc-141623.html (accessed October 26, 2018).

Black, Paula. 2004. *The Beauty Industry: Gender, Culture, Pleasure*. London, New York: Routledge.

Bora, Tanıl. 2010. "The White Turk Debate—A Dirty White" [Beyaz Türkler tartışması—kırlı beyaz]. *Birikim* 260: 25–37.

Bordo, Susan. 1993. *Unbearable Weight: Feminism, Western Culture, and the Body*. Berkeley and Los Angeles: Univ. of California Press.

Boris, Eileen, and Rhacel Salazar Parreñas. 2010. "Introduction." In *Intimate Labors: Cultures, Technologies, and the Politics of Care*, edited by E. Boris and R. Salazar Parreñas, 1–12. Stanford, CA: Stanford Univ. Press.

Bourdieu, Pierre. 1984. *Distinction: A Social Critique of the Judgement of Taste*. London: Routledge.

Bourdieu, Pierre. 1986. "The Forms of Capital." In *Handbook of Theory and Research for the Sociology of Education*, edited by John G. Richardson, 241–58. New York: Greenwood Press.

Brooks, Abigail T. 2017. *The Ways Women Age: Using and Refusing Cosmetic Intervention*. New York: New York Univ. Press.

Buğra, Ayşe, and Osman Savaşkan. 2014. *New Capitalism in Turkey: The Relationship between Politics, Religion and Business*. Cheltenham: Edward Elgar.

Butler, Judith. 1986. "Sex and Gender in Simone de Beauvoir's Second Sex." *Yale French Studies* 72: 35–49.

Butler, Judith. 1990. *Gender Trouble: Feminism and the Subversion of Identity.* New York, London: Routledge.

Butler, Judith. 1993. *Bodies That Matter: On the Discursive Limits of "Sex."* New York, London: Routledge.

Butler, Judith. 2004. *Undoing Gender.* New York: Routledge.

Butler, Judith. 2016. "Rethinking Vulnerability and Resistance." In *Vulnerability in Resistance,* edited by J. Butler, Z. Gambetti, and L. Sabsay, 12–27. Durham, London: Duke Univ. Press.

Cantek, Funda Şenol. 2017. *In Front of the Mirror, the Tweezer Flies [Aynanın Önünde Cımbızın Ucunda].* Istanbul: İletişim.

Çavdar, Ayşe. 2011. *Başakşehir: The Role of Religiosity in the Making of a New Town.* Paper presented at the International RC21 Conference, "The Struggle to Belong: Dealing with Diversity in 21st Century Urban Settings." Amsterdam. July 7–9.

Çınar, Alev. 2005. *Modernity, Islam and Secularism in Turkey: Bodies, Places and Time.* Minneapolis, MN: Univ. of Minnesota Press.

Clarke, Hester. 2016. "Shaping Eyebrows and Moral Selves: Considering Islamic Discourse, Gender, and Ethnicity within the Muslim Pakistani Community of Sheffield (UK)." *Sociologus* 66 (1): 53–72.

Clarke, Hester. 2018. "Moral Ambivalence and Veiling amongst British Pakistani Women in Sheffield." *Contemporary Levant* 3 (1): 10–19.

Cohen, Lawrence. 1994. "Old Age: Cultural and Critical Perspectives." *Annual Review of Anthropology* 23: 137–58.

Coleman, Rebecca, and Mónica Moreno Figueroa. 2010. "Past and Future Perfect? Beauty, Affect and Hope." *Journal for Cultural Research* 14 (4): 357–73.

Comaroff, Jean, and John L. Comaroff. 2001. "Millennial Capitalism: First Thoughts on a Second Coming." In *Millennial Capitalism and the Culture of Neoliberalism,* edited by J. Comaroff and J. L. Comaroff, 1–56. Durham, NC: Duke Univ. Press.

Coy, Michael William, ed. 1989. *Apprenticeship: From Theory to Method and Back Again.* New York: SUNY Press.

Craig, Maxine Leeds. 2006. "Race, Beauty, and the Tangled Knot of Guilty Pleasure." *Feminist Theory* 7 (2): 159–77.

Cumhuriyet. 2016. "Demand for Turkish Beauty Sector Grew by Six Percent" [Türkiye'de kozmetik sektörüne talep yüzde 6 arttı]. *Cumhuriyet Online Edition.*

December 14. http://www.cumhuriyet.com.tr/haber/ekonomi/645403/Turkiye
_de_kozmetik_sektorune_talep_yuzde_6 artti.html (accessed July 17, 2017).

Cumhuriyet. 2016a. "He Said: 'It's against Our Religion' and Opened Fire on the
Distributors of Depilation Brochures: 4 Injured" ['Dinimize aykırı' dedi,
epilasyon broşürü dağıtanlara ateş açtı: 4 yaralı]. Cumhuriyet. October 20.

Daily Sabah. 2020. "Health Tourism Earns above \$1B to Turkey in 2019, under Spot-
light with COVID-19." September 20. https://www.dailysabah.com/business
/tourism/health-tourism-earns-above-1b-to-turkey-in-2019-under-spotlight
-with-covid-19 (accessed February 18, 2021).

Davis, Kathy. 1991. "Re-Making the She Devil: A Critical Look at Feminist Approaches to Beauty." Hypatia 6 (2): 21–43.

Davis, Kathy. 2003. Dubious Equalities and Embodied Differences: Cultural Studies on Cosmetic Surgery. Lanham, MD: Rowman & Littlefield.

De Beauvoir, Simone. 1973. The Second Sex. New York: Vintage Books.

Delaney, Carol. 1991. The Seed and the Soil: Gender and Cosmology in Turkish
Village Society. Berkeley, Los Angeles, London: Univ. of California Press.

Delaney, Carol. 1994. "Untangling the Meanings of Hair in Turkish Society." Anthropological Quarterly 67 (4): 159–72.

Deleuze, Gilles, and Felix Guattari. 2000 (1972). Anti Oedipus: Capitalism and
Schizophrenia. Translated by Robert Hurley, Mark Seem, and Helen R. Lane.
Minneapolis: Univ. of Minnesota Press.

DeMello, Margo. 2000. Bodies of Inscription: A Cultural History of the Modern
Tattoo Community. Durham: Duke Univ. Press.

Demir, Sevim Atila. 2013. "Attitudes toward Concepts of Marriage and Divorce
in Turkey." American International Journal of Contemporary Research 3 (12):
83–88.

Demiralp, Seda. 2012. "White Turks, Black Turks? Faultlines beyond Islamism
versus Secularism." Third World Quarterly 33 (3): 511–24. doi:10.1080/01436
597.2012.657487.

Dilmener, Naim. 2007. I Was Born Free, I Will Live Free: The Ajda Pekkan Book
[Hür Doğdum hür yaşarım: Ajda Pekkan Kitabı]. İstanbul: Everest.

Dönmez-Colin, Gönül, ed. 2014. The Routledge Dictionary of Turkish Cinema.
London, New York: Routledge.

Douglas, Mary. 2002 [1966]. Purity and Danger: An Analysis of Concepts of Pollu-
tion and Taboo. London, New York: Routledge.

Duben, Alan, and Cem Behar. 2002. Istanbul Households: Marriage, Family, and
Fertility, 1880–1940. Cambridge: Cambridge Univ. Press.

Edmonds, Alexander, and Emilia Sanabria. 2014. "Medical Borderlands: Engineering the Body with Plastic Surgery and Hormonal Therapies in Brazil." *Anthropology & Medicine* 21 (2): 202–16.

Edmonds, Alexander. 2007. "The Poor Have the Right To Be Beautiful: Cosmetic Surgery in Neoliberal Brazil." *Journal of the Royal Anthropological Institute* 13 (2): 363–81.

Edmonds, Alexander. 2010. *Pretty Modern: Beauty, Sex, and Plastic Surgery in Brazil.* Durham, NC, London: Duke Univ. Press.

Edmonds, Alexander, and Sjaak van der Geest. 2009. "Introducing 'Beauty and Health'." *Medische Antropologie* 21 (1): 5–19.

Elias, Ana Sofia, Rosalind Gill, and Christina Scharff, eds. 2016. *Aesthetic Labour: Rethinking Beauty Politics in Neoliberalism.* London: Palgrave MacMillan.

Enis, Ayşe Zeren. 2013. *Everyday Lives of Ottoman Muslim Women: Hanımlara Mahsûs Gazete (Newspaper For Ladies) (1895–1908).* Istanbul: Libra.

Ergin, Murat. 2008. "'Is the Turk a White Man?': Towards a Theoretical Framework for Race in the Making of Turkishness." *Middle Eastern Studies* 44 (6): 827–50. doi:10.1080/00263200802425973.

Eriksen, Thomas Hylland. 2002. *Ethnicity and Nationalism: Anthropological Perspectives*, 2nd ed. London, Sterling: Pluto.

Erol, Maral. 2011. "Neoliberalism's Second Spring: the Social Construction of the Menopause in Turkey" [Neoliberalizmin İkinci Baharı: Türkiye'de Menopozun Toplumsal İnşası]. In *Neoliberalizm ve Mahremiyet: Türkiye'de Beden, Sağlık ve Cinsellik,* edited by C. Özbay, A. Terzioğlu, and Y. Yasın, 133–47. Istanbul: Metis.

Erol, Onur Ö. 2000. "The Turkish Delight: A Pliable Graft for Rhinoplasty." *Plastic & Reconstructive Surgery* 105 (6): 2229–41.

Errington, Shelly. 1990. "Recasting Sex, Gender, and Power: A Theoretical and Regional Overview." In *Power and Difference. Gender in Island Southeast Asia,* edited by J. M. Atkinson and S. Errington, 1–37. Stanford: Stanford Univ. Press.

Erşan, Mesude. 2003. "Plastic Surgery Surge, Prices Decrease, Cosmetic Surgery Explosion on the Urban Outskirts" [Plastik cerrah arttı fiyatlar düştü, varoşlarda estetik amaliyat patladı]. *Hürriyet.* December 13.

Erşan, Mesude. 2004. "No Upturned Noses for Men" ['Erkeklerde kalkık burun yapılmaz']. *Hürriyet.* May 5.

Erşan, Mesude. 2010. "Marriage of Twenty Years Rescued by Combined Cosmetic Surgery" [20 yıllık evlilik kombine estetikle kurtalardılar]. *Hürriyet.* February 14.

Erşan, Mesude. 2010a. "A New Fashion in Plastic Surgery: The Mommy Make-over" [Plastic cerrahide yeni moda: Annelik Estetiği]. *Hürriyet*. May 8.

Etcoff, Nancy 2000. *Survival of the Prettiest: The Science of Beauty*. London: Abacus Books.

Evin, Mehveş. 2013. "Red Lipstick." *Hürriyet Daily News*. May 3. Originally published in Turkish in *Milliyet*, May 2. http://www.hurriyetdailynews.com/red -lipstick-.aspx?pageID=238&nID=46120&NewsCatID=396 (accessed September 26, 2016).

Fadil, Nadia, and Mayanthi Fernando. 2015. "Rediscovering the 'Everyday' Muslim: Notes on an Anthropological Divide." *HAU: Journal of Ethnographic Theory* 5 (2): 59–88.

Faulconbridge, Guy. 2013. "Turkish Airlines Backs Down on Lipstick Ban." *Reuters*. May 9. http://www.reuters.com/article/us-turkey-airlines-lipstick-id USBRE9480HQ20130509 (accessed January 9, 2017).

Featherstone, Mike. 1991. *Consumer Culture and Postmodernism*. London: Sage.

Felski, Rita. 2006. "Because It Is Beautiful': New Feminist Perspectives on Beauty." *Feminist Theory* 7 (2): 273–82.

Ferah, Metin. 2005. "Our Religion Does Not Agree to Beauty through Surgery" [Ameliyatla güzelligi dinimiz tasvip etmez]. *Hürriyet*. September 10.

Foucault, Michel. 1979. *Discipline and Punish: The Birth of the Prison*. New York: Vintage Books.

Foucault, Michel. 1984. *The Care of the Self, History of Sexuality*, vol. 3. London: Penguin Books.

Foucault, Michel. 1990. *The History of Sexuality, Volume 1: An Introduction*. Translated by Robert Hurley. New York: Vintage Books.

Foucault, Michel. 1995. *Discipline and Punish: The Birth of the Prison*. 2nd ed. Translated by Alan Sheridan. New York: Vintage Books.

Fraser, Suzanne. 2003. *Cosmetic Surgery, Gender and Culture*. New York: Palgrave Macmillan.

Freedman, Rita Jackaway. 1984. "Reflections on Beauty as It Relates to Health in Adolescent Females." *Women & Health* 9 (2–3): 29–45.

Furman, Frida Kerner. 1997. *Facing the Mirror: Older Women and Beauty Shop Culture*. New York and London: Routledge.

Garfinkel, Harold. 1967. *Studies in Ethnomethodology*. Edgewood Cliffs, NJ: Prentice Hall.

Garland-Thomson, Rosemarie. 2009. *Staring: How We Look*. Oxford: Oxford Univ. Press.

Gauvain, Richard. 2005. "Ritual Rewards: A Consideration of Three Recent Approaches to Sunni Purity Law." *Islamic Law and Society* 12 (3): 333–93.

Gilman, Sander L. 1999. *Making the Body Beautiful: A Cultural History of Aesthetic Surgery.* Princeton and Oxford: Princeton Univ. Press.

Gimlin, Debra L. 2002. *Body Work: Beauty and Self-Image in American Culture.* Berkeley: Univ. of California Press.

Gökarıksel, Banu, and Anna J. Secor. 2009. "New Transnational Geographies of Islamism, Capitalism, and Subjectivity: The Veiling-Fashion Industry in Turkey." *Area* 41 (1): 6–18.

Gökarıksel, Banu, and Anna J. Secor. 2010. "Between Fashion and Tesettür: Marketing and Consuming Veiling-Fashion." *Journal of Middle East Women's Studies* 6 (3): 118–48.

Gökarıksel, Banu. 2009. "Beyond the Officially Sacred: Religion, Secularism and the Body in the Production of Subjectivity." *Social and Cultural Geography* 10 (6): 657–74.

Gökarıksel, Banu. 2012. "The Intimate Politics of Secularism and the Headscarf: The Mall, the Neighborhood, and the Public Square in Istanbul." *Gender, Place, and Culture: A Journal of Feminist Geography* 19 (1): 1–20.

Göktürk, Deniz, Levent Soysal, and Ipek Tureli, eds. 2010. *Orienting Istanbul: Cultural Capital of Europe?* Milton Park, New York: Routledge.

Grasseni, Cristina. 2004. "Skilled Vision. An Apprenticeship in Breeding Aesthetics." *Social Anthropology* 12 (1): 41–55.

Greenblatt, Stephen. 1980. *Renaissance Self-Fashioning.* Chicago: Univ. of Chicago Press.

Grosz, Elizabeth. 1987. "Notes towards a Corporeal Feminism." *Australian Feminist Studies* 5: 1–15.

Grosz, Elizabeth. 1994. *Volatile Bodies: Toward a Corporeal Feminism.* Bloomington, Indianapolis: Indiana Univ. Press.

Gül, Murat. 2012. *The Emergence of Modern Istanbul: Transformation and Modernisation of a City.* London, New York: I. B. Tauris.

Güncel Turizm. 2010. "Fat Air Hostess Polemics: Air Hostesses Shouldn't Have to Look like Baby Dolls" [Sisman hostes polemigi: hostesleri süs bebegi gibi görmek dogru degil]. August 10. https://www.turizmguncel.com/arsiv/ (accessed September 16, 2022).

Güneş-Ayata, Ayşe, and Gökten Doğangün. 2017. "Gender Politics of the AKP: Restoration of a Religio-conservative Gender Climate." *Journal of Balkan and Near Eastern Studies* 19 (6): 610–27.

Gürsoy-Naskali, Emine. 2009. "Temizlik" [Cleanliness]. In *Temizlik Kitabı*, edited by E. Gürsoy-Naskali and S. M. Arçın, 1–3. Istanbul: Kitabevi.

Haberler. 2013. "Seda Sayan Approaches Ajda's Cosmetic Surgery Record" [Seda Sayan, Ajda'nın Estetik Rekoruna Yaklaştı]. *Haberler.* August 23. http://www.haberler.com/seda-sayan-ajda-nin-estetik-rekoruna-yaklasti-4973116 -haberi/ (accessed March 3, 2015).

Habermas, Jürgen. 1989. *The Structural Transformation of the Public Sphere: An Inquiry into a Category of Bourgeois Society.* Translated by Thomas Burger and Frederick Lawrence. Cambridge: Polity.

Hainz, Tobias. 2014. *Radical Life Extension: an Ethical Analysis.* Münster: Mentis.

Hakim, Catherine. 2011. *Erotic Capital.* New York: Basic Books.

Hamermesh, Daniel S., and Jeff E. Biddle. 1994. "Beauty and the Labor Market." *American Economic Review* 84 (5): 1174–94.

Harris-Lacewell, Melissa Victoria. 2004. *Barbershops, Bibles, and BET: Everyday Talk and Black Political Thought.* Princeton, NJ: Princeton Univ. Press.

Harvey, David. 2005. *A Brief History of Neoliberalism.* Oxford, New York: Oxford Univ. Press.

Hedrick-Wong, Yuwa, and Desmond Choong. 2016. *MasterCard Global Destination Cities Index 2016.* https://newsroom.mastercard.com/wp-content /uploads/2016/09/FINAL-Global-Destination-Cities-Index-Report.pdf (accessed August 30, 2017).

Heiman, Rachel, Carla Freeman, and Mark Liechty, eds. 2012. *The Global Middle Classes: Theorizing through Ethnography.* Santa Fe, NM: SAR.

Hochschild, Arlie Russell. 2003 [1983]. *The Managed Heart: Commercialization of Human Feeling.* Berkeley, Los Angeles, London: Univ. of California Press.

Holliday, Ruth, David Bell, Olive Cheung, Meredith Jones, and Elspeth Probyn. 2015. "Brief Encounters: Assembling Cosmetic Surgery Tourism." *Social Science and Medicine* 124: 298–304.

Hua, Wen. 2013. *Buying Beauty: Cosmetic Surgery in China.* Hong Kong: Hong Kong Univ. Press.

Hürriyet. 1998. "Ministerial Audit for Beauty Salon" [Güzellik salonuna bakanlık denetimi]. *Hürriyet.* April 10.

Hürriyet. 1998a. "The Hopeless Cases Pose a Challenge For Me" [Salatadaki yaş bana bir ödül]. *Hürriyet.* June 30.

Hürriyet. 1999. "She Had Her Third Surgery" [Üçüncü kez ameliyat oldu]. *Hürriyet.* January 7.

Hürriyet. 2000. "Even If I was a Scientist I'd Engage in Cosmetic Surgery" [Fizikçi de olsam estetik yaptırırdım]. *Hürriyet Show*. January 30.

Hürriyet. 2000a. "Konya Religious Commission Committee: Aesthetic Surgery Is a Sin" [Konya müftülügü: estetik günah]. *Hürriyet*. December 19.

Hürriyet. 2002. "Women Now Prefer Small Breasts" [Kadınların tercihi artık küçük göğüs]. *Hürriyet*. March 17.

Hürriyet. 2003. "Medical Equipment Requirements of Beauty Salons" [Estetik merkezlerine tıbbi malzeme zorunluğu]. *Hürriyet*. May 12.

Hürriyet. 2003a. "In the Southeast, No Marriage without Cosmetic Surgery" [Güneydogu'da estetiksiz evelenilmiyor]. *Hürriyet*. July 18.

Hürriyet. 2005. "The Turbaned Have Tummy Tucks" [Türbanlı karın gerdiriyor]. *Hürriyet*. March 2.

Hürriyet. 2006. "Cosmetic Surgeon Durak's Indictment" [Estetik cerrah Durak hakkında iddianame]. *Hürriyet*. September 21.

Hürriyet. 2006a. "The Most Beautiful Women in the World Are Turkish" [Dünyanın en güzel kadınları Türkler]. *Hürriyet*. December 6.

Hürriyet. 2008. "S/he Burnt During Laser Epilation" [Lazerli epilasyonda yandı]. *Hürriyet*. December 6.

Hürriyet. 2009. "Ajda: I Had Several Cosmetic Operations" [Ajda: Bir kaç kez estetik yaptırdım]. *Hürriyet*. May 25.

Hürriyet. 2009a. "Cosmetic Surgery Map" [Estetiğin haritası]. *Hürriyet*. June 9.

Hürriyet. 2009b. "The Edirne Religious Commission Committee: To Undergo Aesthetic Surgery Is a Sin" [Edirne Müftüsü: Estetik yaptırmak günah]. *Hürriyet*. July 17.

Hürriyet. 2009c. "Their Noses Are Fashionable Now" [Simdi onların burunları moda]. *Hürriyet show*. December 14.

Hürriyet. 2010. "We Are among the Top Five in Cosmetic Surgery Tourism" [Estetik turizminde ilk 5'e oynuyoruz]. *Hürriyet*. July 27.

Hürriyet 2010a. "Beauty Salons That Do Not Turn into Policlinics until September 10 Will Be Shut Down" [Polikliniğe dönüşmeyen güzellik salonları 10 Eylül'den sonra kapanacak]. *Hürriyet*. August 31.

Hürriyet. 2010b. "Bu ameliyat için 6 ay sıra yok" [For this type of surgery the waiting list is 6 months]. *Hürriyet*. October 28.

Hürriyet. 2013. "A Penalty of 6,000 TRY for These Words" [O sözlere 6 bin TL ceza]. *Hürriyet*. July 18.

Hürriyet. 2014. "Turkey's First Women-Only Beach Hit by 'Topless' Crisis." *Hürriyet Daily News*. August 29. http://www.hurriyetdailynews.com/turkeys-first

-women-only-beach-hit-by-topless-crisis.aspx?pageID=238&nID=71103& NewsCatID=341 (accessed November 18, 2016).

Hürriyet Daily News. 2013. "Turkish Airlines Flight Attendants on Strike Join Gezi Park 'Marauders' with Parody." June 5. http://www.hurriyetdailynews .com/turkish-airlines-flight-attendants-on-strike-join-gezi-park-marauders -with-parody.aspx?pageID=238&nID=48307&NewsCatID=345 (accessed September 26, 2016).

Ipekeşen, Erdal. 2006. "Aesthetic Surgery's Clients and Famous Patients" [Esteti- ğin duayenleri ve ünlü hastaları]. *Hürriyet.* November 19.

ISAPS. 2017. *The International Study on Aesthetic/Cosmetic Procedures Performed in 2016.* Press Release on June 27. http://www.isaps.org/Media/Default/Current %20News/GlobalStatistics2016.pdf (accessed August 28, 2017).

ISAPS. 2019. *International Survey on Aesthetic/Cosmetic Procedures Performed in 2019.* Report released on Dec. 8, 2020. https://www.isaps.org/wp-content /uploads/2020/12/Global-Survey-2019.pdf (accessed March 15, 2021).

Ivanov, Paula. 2013. *Translokalität, Konsum und Ästhetik im islamischen Sansi- bar: Eine praxistheoretische Untersuchung.* Unpublished Habilitation Thesis. Bayreuth University.

Jafar, Afshan, and Erynn Masi de Casanova, eds. 2013. *Global Beauty, Local Bod- ies.* Basingstoke: Palgrave Macmillan.

Jarrín, Alvaro. 2017. *The Biopolitics of Beauty: Cosmetic Citizenship and Affective Capital in Brazil.* Berkeley, Los Angeles, London: Univ. of California Press.

Jeffreys, Sheila. 2005. *Beauty and Misogyny: Harmful Cultural Practices in the West.* London, New York: Routledge.

Jha, Meeta Rani. 2016. *The Global Beauty Industry: Colorism, Racism and the National Body.* New York and Abingdon: Routledge.

Jha, Sonora, and Mara Adelman. 2009. "Looking for Love in All the White Places: A Study of Skin Color Preferences on Indian Matrimonial and Mate-Seeking Websites." *Studies in South Asian Film and Media* 1 (1): 65–83. doi:10.1386 /safm.1.1.65/1.

Jones, Geoffrey. 2010. *Beauty Imagined: A History of the Global Beauty Industry.* Oxford: Oxford Univ. Press.

Jones, Meredith. 2013. "Media-bodies and Photoshop." In *Controversial Images,* edited by F. Attwood, V. Campbell, I. Q. Hunter, and S. Lockyer, 19–35. Lon- don: Palgrave Macmillan.

Jones, Meredith. 2017. "Expressive Surfaces: The Case of the Designer Vagina." *Theory, Culture & Society* 34 (7–8): 29–50.

Joseph, Suad. 1993. "Gender and Relationality among Arab Families in Lebanon." *Feminist Studies* 19(3): 465–86.

Kabasakal, Hayat, Zeynep Aycan, and Fahri Karakas. 2004. "Women in Management in Turkey." In *Women in Management Worldwide: Progress and Prospects*, edited by M. J. Davidson and R. Burke, 273–93. UK: Ashgate.

Kaivanara, Marzieh. 2016. "I Got Rid of Half of my Body: Bioethics, Aesthetics, and Bariatric Surgeries in Tehran." Paper presented at the EASA Medical Anthropology Network Meeting, July 16, 2017, University of Lisbon.

Kandiyoti, Deniz. 2002. "Introduction: Reading the Fragments." In *Fragments of Culture: The Everyday of Modern Turkey*, edited by D. Kandiyoti and A. Saktanber, 1–21. London: Tauris.

Kandiyoti, Deniz. 2011. "A Tangled Web: The Politics of Gender in Turkey." *Open Democracy.* January 5. https://www.opendemocracy.net/5050/deniz -kandiyoti/tangled-web-politics-of-gender-in-turkey (accessed March 7, 2018).

Kandiyoti, Deniz. 2012. "The Travails of the Secular: Puzzle and Paradox in Turkey." *Economy and Society* 41(4): 513–31.

Kandiyoti, Deniz. 2015. "The Gender Wars in Turkey: A Litmus Test of Democracy?" In *The State of Democracy in Turkey: Institutions, Society and Foreign Relations*, edited by K. Dalacoura and H. Seçkinelgin, 8–14. Vol. 4 of LSE Working Papers.

Kandiyoti, Deniz. 2016. "Locating the Politics of Gender: Patriarchy, Neo-Liberal Governance and Violence in Turkey." *Research and Policy on Turkey* 1 (2): 103–18.

Kang, Milliann. 2010. *The Managed Hand: Race, Gender, and the Body in Beauty Service Work.* Berkeley, Los Angeles, London: Univ. of California Press.

Karataş, Bahri. 2010. "Compensation for Silicon-Implanted Hanging Breasts" [Sarkan silikonlu göğüse tazminat]. *Hürriyet.* February 21.

Keyder, Çağlar. 1999. "The Setting." In *Istanbul: Between the Global and the Local*, edited by Ç. Keyder, 3–30. Oxford, Boulder: Rowman & Littlefield.

Keyder, Çağlar. 2005. "Globalization and Social Exclusion in Istanbul." *International Journal of Urban and Regional Research* 29 (1): 124–34.

Kroeker, Lena, David O'Kane, and Tabea Scharrer, eds. 2018. *Middle Classes in Africa: Changing Lives and Conceptual Challenges.* New York: Palgrave Macmillan.

Latour, Bruno. 2004. "How to Talk about the Body? The Normative Dimension of Science Studies." *Body & Society* 10 (2–3): 205–29.

Lazarus, Ellen S. 1988. "Theoretical Considerations for the Study of the Doctor-Patient Relationship: Implications of a Perinatal Study." *Medical Anthropology Quarterly*, New Series 2 (1): 34–58.

Lennon, Kathleen. 2014. "Feminist Perspectives on the Body." E. N. Zalta, ed. In *The Stanford Encyclopedia of Philosophy*, Fall ed. https://plato.stanford.edu /archives/fall2014/entries/feminist-body/ (accessed July 2, 2018).

Le Renard, Amélie. 2014. *A Society of Young Women: Opportunities of Place, Power, and Reform in Saudi Arabia*. Stanford, CA: Stanford Univ. Press.

Letsch, Constanze. 2011. "Turkey's Middle-Class Women Mix Fashion with Islamic Piety." *Guardian*. December 18.

Liebelt, Claudia. 2016. "Grooming Istanbul: Intimate Encounters and Concerns in Turkish Beauty Salons." *Journal of Middle East Women's Studies* 12 (2): 181–202.

Liebelt, Claudia. 2018. "Beauty and the Norm: An Introduction." In *Beauty and the Norm: Debating Standardization in Bodily Appearance*, edited by C. Liebelt, S. Böllinger, and U. Vierke, 1–19. New York: Palgrave Macmillan.

Liebelt, Claudia. 2019. "Aesthetic Citizenship in Istanbul: On Manufacturing Beauty and Negotiating Belonging through the Body in Urban Turkey." *Citizenship Studies* 23 (7): 686–702.

Lock, Margaret M. 1995. *Encounters with Aging: Mythologies of Menopause in Japan and North America*. Berkeley, Los Angeles, London: Univ. of California Press.

Lyon, David. 2007. *Surveillance Studies: An Overview*. Oxford: Polity Press.

M'charek, Amade. 2010. "Fragile Differences, Relational Effects: Stories about the Materiality of Race and Sex." *European Journal of Women's Studies* 17 (4): 307–22.

Mahmood, Saba. 2004. *Politics of Piety: The Islamic Revival and the Feminist Subject*. Princeton et al.: Princeton Univ. Press.

Maksudyan, Nazan. 2005. *Measuring Turkishness: Science Fiction Anthropology and the Racist Face of Turkish Nationalism [Türklüğü Ölçmek: Bilimkurgusal Antropoloji ve Türk Milliyetçiliğin Irkçı Çehresi]*. 1925–39. Istanbul: Metis.

Malmström, Maria Federika. 2015. "The Continuous Making of Pure Womanhood among Muslim Women in Cairo: Cooking, Depilating, and Circumcising." In *Gender and Sexuality in Muslim Cultures*, edited by G. Ozyegin, 139–62. Surrey, Burlington, VT: Ashgate.

Mann, Denise. 2014. "Ethnic Plastic Surgery: What's in a Name?" *Plastic Surgery Practice* 8 (6). http://www.plasticsurgerypractice.com/2014/08/editor-ethnic-plastic-surgery-whats-name/ (accessed October 5, 2016).

Martin, Emily. 1991. "Egg and the Sperm: How Science Has Constructed a Romance Based on Stereotypical Male-Female Roles." In *Beyond the Body Proper: Reading the Anthropology of Material Life*, edited by M. M. Lock and J. Farquhar, 417–27. Durham, London: Duke Univ. Press.

Massumi, Brian. 2014. *What Animals Teach Us about Politics*. Durham, London: Duke Univ. Press.

Miller, Laura. 2006. *Beauty Up: Exploring Contemporary Japanese Body Aesthetics*. Berkeley, Los Angeles, London: Univ. of California Press.

Mills, Amy. 2007. "Gender and *Mahalle* (Neighborhood) Space in Istanbul." *Gender, Place, and Culture: A Journal of Feminist Geography* 14 (3): 335–54.

Mills, Amy. 2010. *Streets of Memory: Landscape, Tolerance, and National Identity in Istanbul*. Athens: Univ. of Georgia Press.

Navaro-Yashin, Yael. 2002. *Faces of the State: Secularism and Public Life in Turkey*. Princeton et al.: Princeton Univ. Press.

New York Times. 2018. "Police in Turkey Break Up Mothers' Weekly Vigil." *New York Times*. August 26. https://www.nytimes.com/2018/08/26/world/europe/turkey-protest-saturday-mothers.html (accessed January 21, 2019).

Nişanyan, Sevan. 2009. *The Genealogy of Words: Etymological Dictionary of Contemporary Turkish [Sözlerin Soyağacı: Çağdaş Türkçenin Etimolojik Sözlüğü]*. İstanbul: Everest.

Ochoa, Marcia. 2014. *Queen for a Day: Transformistas, Beauty Queens, and the Performance of Femininity in Venezuela*. Durham, NC: Duke Univ. Press.

Ong, Aihwa. 1996. "Cultural Citizenship as Subject-Making: Immigrants Negotiate Racial and Cultural Boundaries in the United States." *Current Anthropology* 37 (5): 737–62.

Orbach, Susie. 1986. *Hunger Strike: The Anorectic's Struggle as a Metaphor for Our Age*. London: Faber and Faber.

Ossman, Susan. 2002. *Three Faces of Beauty: Casablanca, Paris, Cairo*. Durham, NC: Duke Univ. Press.

Özbay, Ferhunde. 1995. "Changes in Women's Activities both Inside and Outside the Home." In *Women in Modern Turkish Society: A Reader*, edited by Ş. Tekeli, 89–111. London, Atlantic Heights, NJ: Zed Books.

Özkazanç, Alev. 2020. "Gender and Authoritarian Populism in Turkey: the Two Phases of AKP Rule." *Open Democracy*. February 3. https://www.open

democracy.net/en/rethinking-populism/gender-and-authoritarian-populism
-turkey-two-phases-akp-rule/ (accessed March 18, 2021).

Özkoçak, Selma A. 2007. "Coffeehouses: Rethinking the Public and Private in Early Modern Istanbul." *Journal of Urban History* 33 (6): 965–86.

Ozyegin, Gul. 2001. *Untidy Gender: Domestic Service in Turkey*. Philadelphia: Temple Univ. Press.

Ozyegin, Gul. 2015. *New Desires, New Selves: Sex, Love and Piety among Turkish Youth*. New York and London: New York Univ. Press.

Özyürek, Esra. 2004. "Miniaturizing Atatürk: Privatization of the State Imagery and Ideology in Turkey." *American Ethnologist* 31 (3): 374–91.

Özyürek, Esra. 2006. *Nostalgia for the Modern: State Secularism and Everyday Politics in Turkey*. Durham and London: Duke Univ. Press.

Özyürek, Esra. 2008. "Miniaturizing Atatürk: Commodification of the State Iconography" [Die Miniaturisierung Atatürks. Kommodifizierung der Staatlichen Ikonographie]. In *Perspektiven auf die Türkei. Ökonomische und gesellschaftliche (Dis)Kontinuitäten im Kontext der Europäisierung*, edited by Ilker Ataç, Bülent Küçük, and Ulas Şener, 208–29. Münster: Westfälisches Dampfboot.

Plemons, Eric. 2017. *The Look of a Woman: Facial Feminization Surgery and the Aims of Trans-Medicine*. Durham, London: Duke Univ. Press.

Popenoe, Rebecca. 2004. *Feeding Desire: Fatness, Beauty, and Sexuality among a Saharan People*. London, New York: Routledge.

Radikal. 2013. "Cübbeli Ahmet: I Cannot Laugh about Cem Yılmaz" [Cübbeli Ahmet: Cem Yılmaz'a gülemiyorum]. *Radikal*. October 20.

Reinhart, A. Kevin. 1990. "Impurity/No Danger." *History of Religions* 30 (1): 1–24.

Rutz, Henry J., and Erol M. Balkan. 2009. *Reproducing Class: Education, Neoliberalism, and the Rise of the New Middle Class in Istanbul*. New York, Oxford: Berghahn.

Sabah. 2004. "The Turkish Delight Nose Is a Global Fashion" [Türk lokumu burun tüm dünyada moda]. *Sabah*. 16 March. http://arsiv.sabah.com.tr /2004/03/16/sag102-20040316.html (accessed January 15, 2014).

Sandıkçı, Özlem, and Güliz Ger. 2010. "Veiling in Style: How Does a Stigmatized Practice Become Fashionable?" *Journal of Consumer Research* 37 (June): 15–36.

Secor, Anne J. 2001. "Toward a Feminist Counter-geopolitics: Gender, Space and Islamist Politics in Istanbul." *Space and Polity* 5 (3): 191–211.

Sehlikoglu, Sertaç. 2018. "Revisited: Muslim Women's Agency and Feminist Anthropology of the Middle East." *Contemporary Islam* 12: 73–92.

Sehlikoglu, Sertaç. 2021. *Working Out Desire: Women, Sport, and Self-Making in Istanbul*. Syracuse, NY: Syracuse Univ. Press.

Selen, Eser. 2012. "The Stage: A Space for Queer Subjectification in Contemporary Turkey." *Gender, Place & Culture* 19 (6): 730–49.

Semercioğlu, Cengiz. 2010. "Don't Join the Game of the Cosmetic Surgery Lobby" [Estetik lobisinin oyununa alet olmayın]. *Hürriyet*. May 11.

Shissler, A. Holly. 2004. "Beauty Is Nothing to Be Ashamed of: Beauty Contests as Tools of Women's Liberation in Early Republican Turkey." *Comparative Studies of South Asia, Africa, and the Middle East* 24 (1): 107–22.

Sirman, Nükhet. 2005. "The Making of Familial Citizenship in Turkey." In *Challenges to Citizenship in a Globalizing World: European Questions and Turkish Experiences*, edited by F. Keyman and A. İçduygu, 147–72. London: Routledge.

Skeggs, Beverly. 1997. *Formations of Class and Gender: Becoming Respectable*. London: Sage.

Skeggs, Beverly. 2005. "The Making of Class and Gender through Visualizing Moral Subject Formation." *Sociology* 39 (5): 965–82.

Slupchynskyj, Oleh. 2005. "Ethnic Rhinoplasty." *Plastic Surgery Practice*. September 7. http://www.plasticsurgerypractice.com/2005/09/ethnic-rhinoplasty/ (accessed October 5, 2016).

Sontag, Susan. 2018 [1972]. "The Double Standard of Aging." In *The Other within Us: Feminist Explorations of Women and Aging*, edited by M. Pearsall, 19–24. New York, Milton Park: Routledge.

Spivak, Gayatri Chakravorty. 1993. *Outside in the Teaching Machine*. London: Routledge.

Stokes, Martin. 1992. *The Arabesk Debate: Music and Musicians in Modern Turkey*. Oxford: Clarendon Press.

Süsoy, Yener. 2000. "I Made Ajda Screen-Like" [Ajda'yı tablo gibi yaptım]. *Hürriyet Show*. July 16. http://hurarsiv.hurriyet.com.tr/goster/ShowNew.aspx?id=-168406 (accessed July 2, 2018).

Talbot, Alice-Mary. 2015. "Constantinople: City of Miraculous Healing." In *Life is Short, Art Long: The Art of Healing in Byzantium [Hayat Kısa, Sanat Uzun: Bizans'ta Şifa Sanatı]*, edited by B. Pitarakis, 78–88. Istanbul: Pera Museum Publication 73.

Tate, Shirley Anne. 2016. *Skin Bleaching in Black Atlantic Zones: Shade Shifters*. London: Palgrave Macmillan.

Taussig, Michael. 2012. *Beauty and the Beast*. Chicago, London: Chicago Univ. Press.

Terzi, Şermin. 2011. "I Accept Aging, but Rather than Confront it, I Console My-self with Aesthetic Surgery" [Yaşlılığı kabul ediyorum ama her an onunla yüzleşmektense kendimi estetikle avutuyorum]. *Hürriyet.* April 24. http://www.hurriyet.com.tr/pazar/17623069.asp (accessed March 4, 2015).

Tezel, Mevlüt. 2009. "I Can't Look at These Cosmetic Surgery Patients Anymore" [Estetiklere bakamıyorum]. *Hürriyet.* April 25.

Tokbaş, Yonca. 2013. "Let's Put on Red Lipstick" [Kırmızı ruj sürelım sürdürelim]. *Hürriyet News.* April 29. http://www.hurriyet.com.tr/kirmizi-ruj-surelim -surdurelim-23162286 (accessed January 9, 2017).

Tosun, Teslime, and Recep Aktepe. 2003. "Young Girl Died from Liposuction Surgery to Become Thin" [Zayıflamak için yağ aldıran genç kız ameliatta öldü]. *Hürriyet.* August 6.

Tremblay, Pinar. 2017. "Why Did Erdogan Sign Emergency Decree on Laser Hair Removal?" *Al-Monitor.* April 6. http://www.al-monitor.com/pulse/originals /2017/04/turkey-erdogan-signature-fatal-beauty-angers-islamists.html#ixzz 4n5DrAyXz (accessed July 17, 2017).

Tuduk, Mine. 2010. "Turkish Airline's Overweight Flight Attendants Go under the Knife" [THYnin kilolu hostesleri bıcak altına yatıyor]. *Referans Gaze-tesi,* quoted from *Airport Haber.* September 9. http://www.airporthaber.com /thy-haberleri/thynin-kilolu-hostesleri-bicak-altina-yatiyor-26923h.html (accessed September 26, 2016).

Tuna, Banu. 2001. "Most Complaints Come from Cosmetic Surgery Patients" [En çok estetikçiler şikayet ediliyor]. *Hürriyet Lifestyle.* October 13.

Turam, Berna. 2013. "The Primacy of Space in Politics: Bargaining Rights, Free-dom and Power in an İstanbul Neighborhood." *International Journal of Urban and Regional Research* 37 (2): 409–29.

Turam, Berna. 2015. *Gaining Freedoms Claiming Space in Istanbul and Berlin.* Stanford: Stanford Univ. Press.

TURKSTAT. 2021. *Marriage and Divorce Statistics 2020.* Ankara: Turkish Statisti-cal Institute. February 25. https://data.tuik.gov.tr/Bulten/Index?p=Marriage -and-Divorce-Statistics-2020-37211 (accessed March 18, 2021).

TURKSTAT. 2021. *The Results of Address Based Population Registration System, 2020.* Ankara: Turkish Statistical Institute. February 4. https://data.tuik.gov .tr/Bulten/Index?p=The-Results-of-Address-Based-Population-Registration -System-2020-37210 (accessed March 18, 2021).

Ünal, R. Arzu. 2018. "Fashioning the Female Muslim Face: From 'Hiding One's Beauty' to 'Managing One's Beauty'." In *Beauty and the Norm: Debating*

Standardization in Bodily Appearance, edited by C. Liebelt, S. Böllinger, and U. Vierke, 177–99. New York: Palgrave Macmillan.

Vartabedian, Julieta. 2016. "Beauty That Matters: Brazilian *Travesti* Sex Workers Feeling Beautiful." *Sociologus* 66 (1): 73–96.

Wacquant, Loic. 2012. "Three Steps to a Historical Anthropology of Actually Existing Neoliberalism." *Social Anthropology / Anthropologie Sociale* 20 (1): 66–79.

Wasti, S. Arzu, and Lilia M. Cortina. 2002. "Coping in Context. Socio-cultural Determinants of Responses to Sexual Harassment." *Journal of Personality and Social Psychology* 83 (2): 394–405.

Wharton, Amy. 2009. "The Sociology of Emotional Labor." *Annual Review of Sociology* 35: 147–67.

White, Jenny B. 2002. *Islamist Mobilization in Turkey: A Study in Vernacular Politics*. Seattle, London: Univ. of Washington Press.

White, Jenny B. 2004. *Money Makes Us Relatives: Women's Labor in Urban Turkey*. Austin: Univ. of Texas Press.

White, Jenny B. 2013. *Muslim Nationalism and the New Turks*. Princeton, Oxford: Princeton Univ. Press.

Williams, Christine L., and Catherine Connell 2010. "'Looking Good and Sounding Right': Aesthetic Labor and Social Inequality in the Retail Industry." *Work and Occupations* 37 (3): 349–77. doi:10.1177/0730888410373744.

Wohlrab, Silke, Jutta Stahl, and Peter M. Kappeler. 2007. "Modifying the Body: Motivations for Getting Tattooed and Pierced." *Body Image* 4: 87–95.

Wolf, Naomi. 2002 [1991]. *The Beauty Myth: How Images of Beauty Are Used against Women*. New York: William Morrow & Co.

Woodman, Josef. 2009. *Patients beyond Borders: Turkey Edition, Everybody's Guide to Affordable, World-Class Medical Tourism*. Chapel Hill NC: Healthy Travel Media.

World Economic Forum. 2019. "The Global Gender Gap Report 2020." Geneva: World Economic Forum. http://www3.weforum.org/docs/WEF_GGGR_2020.pdf (accessed February 26, 2021).

Yackley, Ayla Jean. 2013. "Secular Turks See Red over Airline's Lipstick Ban." *Reuters*. May 3. https://www.reuters.com/article/turkey-airlines-lipstick-idUS L6N0DK13220130503 (accessed September 17, 2022).

Yazıcı, Ayşenur. 2010. "Drawing Attention to One's Lips Is a Sexual Deficit" [Dudağa ilgi çekmek seksüel eksiklik]. *Hürriyet*. May 12.

Yenal, Merve. 2004. "My Beautiful Boss" [Benim Güzel Müdürüm]. *Hürriyet.* June 5. http://www.hurriyet.com.tr/kelebek/benim-guzel-mudurum-231334 (accessed December 20, 2018).

Yilmaz, Zafer. 2017. "The AKP and the Spirit of the 'New' Turkey: Imagined Victim, Reactionary Mood, and Resentful Sovereign." *Turkish Studies* 18:3: 482–513. doi:10.1080/14683849.2017.1314763.

Young, Iris Marion. 1980. "Throwing like a Girl: A Phenomenology of Feminine Body Comportment, Motility and Spatiality." *Human Studies* 3: 137–56.

Zaman. 2008. "Since Everyone Becomes a Cosmetic Surgeon, Things Are Going Out of Control" [Herkes estetikçi oldu, bu iş çığırından çıktı]. *Zaman.* January 30.

Zelizer, Viviana. 2005. *The Purchase of Intimacy.* Princeton, NJ: Princeton Univ. Press.

Zelizer, Viviana. 2010. "Caring Everywhere." In *Intimate Labors: Cultures, Technologies, and the Politics of Care,* edited by E. Boris and Rh. S. Parreñas, 267–79. Stanford, CA: Stanford Univ. Press.

Zola, Irving Kenneth. 1991. "The Medicalization of Aging and Disability." *Advances in Medical Sociology* 2: 299–315.

Index

CLAUDIA LIEBELT is professor of Social and Cultural Anthropology at the Free University of Berlin, Germany. She is the author of *Caring for the "Holy Land": Filipina Domestic Workers in Israel* and coeditor of *Beauty and the Norm: Debating Standardization in Bodily Appearance.*

www.ingramcontent.com/pod-product-compliance
Lightning Source LLC
Chambersburg PA
CBHW050807270326
41926CB00026B/4586